HIDDEN

Hidden Lives of Women in STEM

Lori Rodriguez

Daybreak Ventures Press

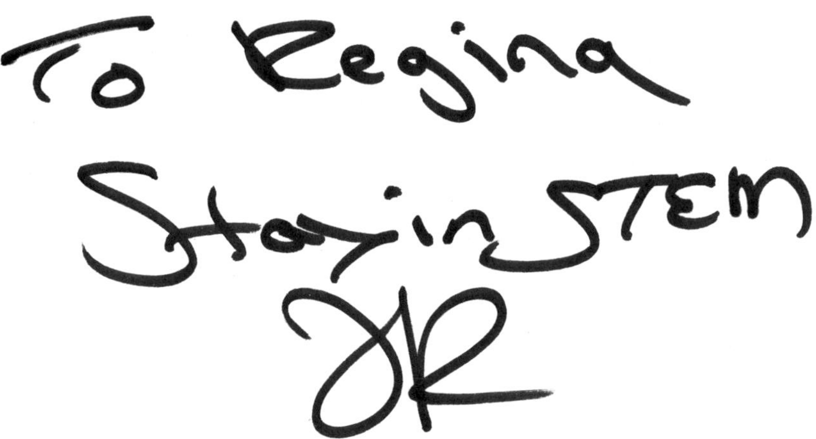

Published by
Daybreak Ventures Press
261 S. Main Street, Suite 158
Newtown, CT 06470

The stories in this book are true as remembered by the storyteller in live interviews with the author. The purpose of the telling is to share their lives with others so that those who follow after will be inspired to join and #STAYinSTEM.

ISBN: 978-1-970186-01-7

Cover design by: Lori Rodriguez

Dedication

To the women in this book who became the heroines of their own lives.
Your curiosity, grit, thoughtfulness, and ability
to create space for yourself and others lights the way for all of us.

To the women who paved the way and for all who follow after.

For anyone who's felt invisible or different.

To my children Andrew, Amanda, Samantha, Jessica, and Sarah.
And my husband John.

CONTENTS

Here's the thing

I love being a mom of five. And I love being a woman in tech.

Being both, though, was damn near impossible. I thought my frustration and exhaustion were just a me thing. The ever-moving goalposts. Having to continually prove my value at work despite being labeled a high-performer and the go-to for ideas. I knew my work was outstanding; the data proved it. So, why was my name not being drawn for roles I should have been a top candidate for? What was I doing wrong?

In my role as a VP at Gartner, the world's largest technology research and advisory company, I interviewed over a thousand C-Suite technology leaders. The lack of women in those key decision-making roles was stark, obvious, and unsettling. Still, when Gartner began hosting a Women CIO's cocktail hour at its leadership events, I was a bit conflicted.

Didn't segregating ourselves defeat our goal of equality?

But then the magic happened. I found myself in a room full of some of the most successful women on the planet. It was intoxicating! We geeked out over the cool technology sessions and business model workshops we had attended and were deep in the getting-to-know-you small talk when someone spoke out loud what we all felt – the loneliness of being one of the few in a crowd of ten thousand.

We piled on, joking that an IT conference was the only place with no line in the ladies' room.

While we all appreciated quick access to a mirror and a bathroom stall between conference sessions, we lamented the painful costs that the lack of women in technology imposed on women, businesses, and societies. We shared war stories about being an only in the workplace.

Turns out, it wasn't just me.

Intrigued, I started digging. I learned that more than half the women in STEM leave by mid-career. And those that stay hold less than a quarter of the C-Suite roles in tech and only one in ten of the Chief Information Officer roles. One tenth!

Yet the women at that cocktail hour had broken through. Why were they different? What was their secret? How could I follow their lead? Those questions haunted me.

Eventually, I left Gartner on a quest for those answers. I poured through the research, spoke with hundreds of women, and joined Women in Tech, a global non-profit, as their Chief Digital Advisor and US Chapter President.

This book is born from that quest for answers and a burning desire to help my sisters join, stay, and flourish in STEM.

With love, gratitude, and tenacious hope,

Lori

Real women. Real talk. Real life.

"You can't empower women without listening to their stories."
— Gloria Steinem

Hidden Lives is a collection of first-person biographies and reflections by twelve women leaders in science, technology, engineering, and math. Not only will you be moved by these thought-provoking and heartwarming stories, but you'll also have the opportunity for self-reflection and discussion through a set of questions and answers that delve into the secrets of these remarkable women.

This book is for women searching for relatable role models and fascinating career paths that read like a roadmap for their own lives. Wrapped in gripping stories of triumph, tragedy, and resilience, Hidden Lives is a love letter to our sisters, a chance for allies to walk a mile in our war-torn shoes, and a good read for people who love biographies.

Brutally honest and vulnerable, the women yearned to tell their sisters that we were not alone. That yes, we can thrive in STEM. And that they wanted us to stay. Indeed, the world needs us to stay.

In each story, a different woman shares her remarkable life with the raw intensity of an intimate conversation with a trusted friend. Infused with hard-won wisdom, you'll dive into crucial conversations at work, listen in on heart-to-hearts with partners, and witness true grit, courage, and resilience.

Along their unique journeys, you'll feel the rumble of lift-off to the International Space Station, workout on the fantail of a Navy destroyer, marvel at the contours of the ocean floor, choke on tear gas in Apartheid South Africa, and feel the heat of a Los Angeles sweatshop.

Profound and courageous. The women's lives remind us that a STEM career isn't really about the maths or sciences. It's about our shared experiences, the fullness of our life, and the lasting value we create for ourselves, our families, our communities, and the world we live in today and well into the future.

How to read this book. Read the stories in the way I ordered them or jump around. Binge in one sitting or grab a bite when you only have a few minutes of downtime. I've made each section snackable—a five-minute read—and most stories will take about half an hour to devour. A perfect way to transition from your busy day to a period of mindfulness and relaxation.

Self-care for your heart and soul!

The stories have two parts – a life journey and their reflections on that journey. It's tailor-made for contemplation and discussion. So, I encourage you to find a friend, read them in a book club, or bring the stories to your employee resource groups. I've even included a section with lots of discussion questions to get you started. Followed by observations on what made these women the exception, with tips for building your own set of success tools.

How to approach the stories. Before interviewing the women, I intentionally did little research prep beyond LinkedIn. I wanted our conversation to be like two friends getting to know each other over coffee or chai. That's how I want you to approach their stories, too — like a conversation with a new friend. Listen to what they are sharing. Be open and present with her story. Engage deeply with the content. Let it drain you; let it fill you up again. Reflect, get angry, be sad, laugh, cry, be energized.

Savor what moves you.

I ask, though, that you really see each woman. And in the process, begin to see the people around you, and perhaps yourself, in a new way. Tell these stories forward and add your own. Then, share them with someone who would likely never come across them on their own.

Why these women. While writing this book, I spoke with hundreds of women. Twenty-four of whom were kind enough to spend two to eight hours sharing their whole-life stories with me so that I could share them with you. You'll hear twelve in Volume One, with more to come in Volume Two. I met Renee Wynn, former NASA CIO and board member, through a mutual friend. At the time, she was deputy CIO at the Environmental Protection Agency (EPA) and, well... I'll let you find out the rest in her story. That chance meeting with Renee was the beginning of a long-distance friendship. She was the first person I reached out to when I began writing this book. She's been my champion and a key person on my personal board of advisors ever since.

This book would not have happened without Renee.

I discovered some of the women through my work as a Vice President at Gartner, the world's largest technology research and advisory company, others through my membership at Chief (a powerful and uplifting women's executive networking organization), and others through my current work at Women in Tech (a compassionate and action-oriented global non-profit on a mission to close the gender gap in technology). I also tapped people in my network to introduce me to women whose stories were not being told. I contacted people via industry organizations and associations and looked up alums from Historically Black Colleges and Universities (HBCUs). I DM'd interesting profiles on LinkedIn and pinged women I met during virtual events.

I wanted to show you, my dear reader, that you are not alone, whatever your life experiences and challenges you may face. Wherever you started from or are now, you DO belong.

Let me introduce you to the women you will meet during our time together. Yes, they have fancy titles at exciting workplaces. But, as you will come to know, what makes them truly remarkable is how they carry their scars.

- **Renee Wynn**. Retired NASA CIO and Board Member, Former Deputy CIO of EPA
- **Morẹ́nikẹ́ Ẹniọlá Ọláòṣebìkan.** Pharmaceutical Manufacturing Inventor and Founder, Licensed Clinical Pharmacist, and Multi-Pharmacy owner. Founder of The Ribbon Rouge Foundation
- **Janet Kavandi.** NASA Astronaut Hall of Fame Class of 2019. Veteran of three space flights. Former Center Director at NASA's Glenn Research Center, Currently President of Sierra Space
- **Melanie Chang Goldey.** COO & CFO, TMRW Life Sciences, Inc.
- **Daphne Lane.** Software Engineer Manager at Lockheed Martin Aeronautics
- **Andrea (Andi) Ruda.** Founder & CEO at Rainbow CFO. Former CFO at Alex and Ani and Geragos & Geragos
- **Francesca (Frani) Esquenazi.** CEO/Cofounder at Future Club
- **Melynda Barnes, MD.** Chief Medical Officer at Ro
- **Meghan Athavale.** CEO, LUMOplay
- **Juliana Vida.** GVP and Chief Strategy Advisor at Splunk
- **Caroline Belmont.** Head of US Global Innovation and US Regulatory Affairs, Boehringer Ingelheim Animal Health, Inc.
- **Lorraine Sefolo.** Gartner VP Executive Programs Africa, Former GM Information Technology South African Broadcasting Corporation

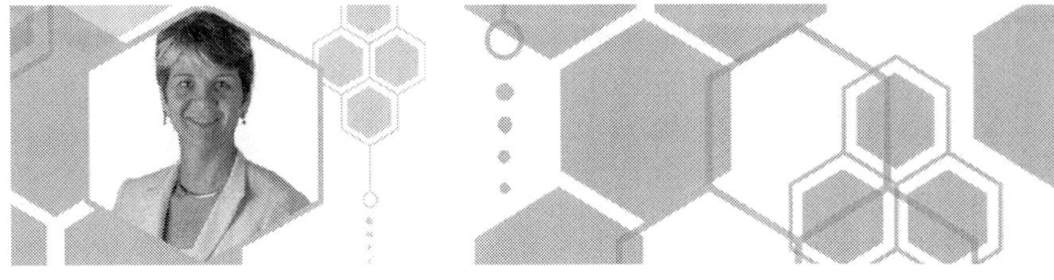

Renee Wynn

Retired NASA CIO and Board Member,
Former Deputy CIO of the EPA

I Keep Astronauts safe and deliver the highest integrity data from space for the benefit of humankind.

Belonging

Growing up, I loved playing sports and being part of a team. I played basketball, football, and softball. I also did gymnastics, cheerleading, swimming, and diving. The National Education Act of 1972 happened when I was in fourth grade, so I got to be part of that first generation of girls that would grow up being able to play sports in school. Title IX was a very positive development for me and other girls at that time. I remember this was back in the days when neighbors all still played together. Playing sports in my neighborhood of primarily boys helped me land in the upper echelon of the athletic girls.

You build camaraderie in sports. Even in cheerleading, we all helped each other and were very supportive. We were such a strong community. I never experienced the backbiting or the mean girls I read about or see in movies. I've always been very fortunate to have some really amazing women and men in my life.

My high school was a typical suburban school in Montgomery County, Maryland. It's since closed, but at the time, it was a highly regarded three-year school with around 1500 students, about 500 a class. I was in high-end math and science courses. I enjoyed the challenge, but I was always the only female in the class, especially in science, and I felt very self-conscious. I didn't feel like I fit in. It could be because girls are awkward in our high school years, and I was missing my friends. They were in different classes, doing different things. When we got together, and they'd be relating to each other about what they did in class, I'd be like, "Oh yeah, I was with the dorks. All of us dorks were hanging out together."

It really affected me because I didn't like being singled out that way as the only female.

My teachers were always very welcoming to me, but I am aware that some teachers were not supportive of girls in math and science and created what would now be termed a hostile environment towards females. It was all funny back in the lovely late seventies and eighties; it would not be tolerated now. Being the only girl in class did shape me.

On the academic side, I felt singled out, but in sports, I found a thriving and supportive environment for women athletes. It wasn't one-sided. Some changes, like Title IX, were embraced and happening rapidly; in other areas, like math and science, change wasn't happening that quickly.

After I took my SATs, I was recruited for engineering school. Having spent a lot of my high school and middle school years feeling alone in the higher math and science classes, I was not going to pursue engineering. I graduated with a Bachelor of Arts in Economics from a small liberal arts school. Fifty percent of that degree was financial; fifty percent was economics. That played to my strengths in mathematics.

After High School, I went to DePauw University, a small private school. I took the easier science and math classes because, again, I had this tape in my head that played, "If you take those courses, you're going to be the only girl in the class, and you don't like that." When you're younger, it's hard to manage your mindset because there's so much growth going on within you – hormonally, physically, and intellectually. So, I didn't take those higher-end classes, but I did spend a lot of time in mathematics because of my accounting and statistics classes. Statistics pretty much chewed me alive. I was lucky to get out of there with a C plus. Maybe engineering might've looked great for my SAT scores, but oh man, I probably would have struggled. Many engineers struggle in school, so I wouldn't have been alone.

Finding The Groove

When I left school, I wanted a big, important job that made good money. But it was hard to find a job in the mid-eighties. We were in a recession at that time. When I finally got a job, it was doing administrative and analytical stuff, reviewing bills, and helping get them lined up to be paid. I needed to get data out of the organization's computer system. I got tired of waiting for the programmers. So, I asked to take a SAS course, the language used in their computer system.

That's when things started to evolve in a different direction. Play the background music now. All I thought I was doing was learning just enough programming to get the data I needed to do the analytics I had to do. I'm really impatient. I understood the programmers had to prioritize, and I wasn't a boss; I was just administrative personnel. But I could go faster if I did it myself. So, I took the programming class with the guy that sat near me. It was just the two of us in the class, and we helped each other get very good at it. He was outstanding and went on to join the programming staff.

Learning programming became a change in career direction for both of us.

Now that I had learned this programming language, I started looking for and was hired for another job. The funny thing was that I got hired to do the SAS programming, but I would never actually program. I had excellent skills with the customer user interface. Because I understood the language and the database structure so well, I could work with the client and ask the right questions; then, I could translate what would happen with the data into requirements for the programmers. We could do the reports in fewer iterations for the client because I had been a programmer in that same language.

The company that hired me was a consulting firm working with EPA (Environmental Protection Agency). I fell in love with EPA's mission. I was now in my second job, about four years out of school, and I realized I needed to be intentional about what I wanted; then work with people on how to get it. I applied for and got a job with EPA as soon as possible.

I started with EPA in 1990 and finished my career thirty years later in 2020 at NASA.

At EPA, we were justifying budgets. Congress wanted to know what they buy with taxpayers' money. I had enough programming exposure to help me think about how to get the best output for our analytical needs. So, I joined the team to overhaul the whole system used for tracking contaminated sites (contaminated sites are polluted locations in the United States requiring a long-term response to clean up soil, groundwater, and surface water bodies). I was part of that team for several systems transformations. Until I became a supervisor overseeing several lines of business, I was always fairly close to programming and how IT can help justify budgets, how IT can help identify the best ways to spend limited taxes, and how to tell the story of the benefits of federal programs.

IT was about using the data and telling the stories.

I loved that work, and it was just so much fun. I was in a place doing something I loved, analytical work, surrounded by smart, successful women like Carol Browner, the administrator at that time. I told myself, "I can be successful at EPA, regardless of my gender. I just need to work hard and deliver on those results." And that's what I did. I then got to move into writing environmental policy. Moving from the analytical stage \to figuring out, "What does this mean for national environmental policy?" I was part of

EPA support for the Department of Defense (DoD) Base Realignment and Closure (BRAC) program, which accelerated environmental restoration and cleanup associated with closing select military bases to facilitate the reuse of the base property.

I participated in all five base closure programs spanning from 1988 through 2005.

All of this was built from my understanding of how data moves into and through the system and the importance of justifying budgets and being able to tell your story. This knowledge helped me move into environmental policy, where I got to negotiate a principles document on how the United States government would clean up unexploded ordnance in the base closure program.

When I think about it, I finally got back to what I was good at, mathematics and science, which, ironically, is what I tried to avoid in college.

I ended up using all of those skills, even though my degree was a Bachelor of Arts in Economics.

Seeing The Future

I remember distinctly when I started to step toward an IT career. I was driving back from a facility in the Norfolk Hampton Roads area. I was on I64 with a friend of mine. He and I had gone out to see some sites because we were writing some policies and wanted to talk to the groundwater engineers about how things were working at their site. We're out in the fields, and he and I were talking, "It's going to be great on that day when we're just there in the field, and we're working with our computers and all the data that we need to go to a site and record what's going on, it's all right there! Wouldn't that be so cool?!!"

Interestingly enough, he and I both ended up working using computers in the field.

This was before we had cellular phones and tablets like we have now. Still, we knew that at least if you could store it on your computer, even offline, and get your sample results and have them with you, it would be so much easier for a project manager in the field to be operating with a computer than it was with all of the physical paper diagrams that we usually had to take with us to the site. And we knew that the data would be cleaner because the sooner you get data in a system, the better it is. You're human. Even though you write things down, you might not recall the context or something. From then on, we always tried to make our business easier and more efficient. We were like, "Yeah, as soon as these computers come in, we've got to get them so we can go out to the field with them." We knew they would be part of how we should manage data at EPA.

I remember that day so clearly.

From then on, I made IT part of all my jobs. "No, you're not going to do Word Perfect documents and submit them to me." "We're going to put them into a system so we can all look back at them or add to the story." As IT advanced, it set me up for the career changes and strides I made.

A Fateful Lunch

Around the time of the Clean Air Act, EPA went on to establish, The Office of Environmental Information, which is effectively the office of the CIO [The Chief Information Officer (CIO) is the senior-most leader responsible for information technology (IT) in the organization.] While EPA went through that transition, I stayed in the program office doing policy and systems work. Ultimately, I became the Senior Information Official for the Solid Waste Emergency Response programs and worked closely with the CIO of EPA. We would implement the policies and start justifying our IT and systems expenditures.

That was all part of the evolution of IT in the federal government and the private sector at that time.

I held that job for so long that I worked with several different CIOs of the EPA. The CIO role at EPA is a political position, Senate confirmed. In 2010, the Senate-Confirmed CIO was looking for a deputy. I applied for the job and was selected for it. The intent was that I would be the civil servant to help him successfully navigate an agency he would be serving in for whatever his political term was going to be.

I'll back up just a little bit. The position hadn't been advertised, yet.

It was a fateful lunch. At the time, I was the executive in charge of nearly a billion dollars in funding for the area I worked on as part of the Recovery Act of 2009. My mentor and I worked very closely together as part of this program, and he and I went to lunch. So, I asked him, "Hey, you've got this Deputy Assistant Administrator job. I want to be competitive for that type of job someday. What do you think I need to do?"

The next day I met with the newly appointed CIO at EPA. I think I'm meeting with him because I will be working with him a lot. It was just a general thing that most people do when they're new on the job. You get to know your peers and the colleagues you will be working with. As it turned out, it was an informal interview. My mentor called me a week later and said, "Hey, they're going to be opening the advertising internally for the Deputy CIO job. You should apply." I was like, "We just went to lunch and went over things I needed to work on. I'm not going to apply; I will work on that for a year or so."

My mentor said, "No, I think you need to apply for the job." So, I updated my resume," which I hate doing, and dropped my name in the hat. I got selected, in part, because of the meeting with the newly nominated and selected CIO. My new boss, the new EPA CIO, laughed, "You had no idea I was doing a preliminary interview with you. Did you?" I'm like, "Nope. I thought we were just figuring out how to work together."

That's how I ended up ultimately in the Deputy CIO role. When the CIO left a few years later, I served as the Acting CIO for EPA until they could get a Senate-confirmed new one. However, for political reasons, not at all the individual's record or anything, the nomination wasn't going to happen. So, EPA split the role into the CIO and what was called an Assistant Administrator of Office Environmental Information (OEI). I ended up with three titles, Deputy CIO, Deputy Assistant Administrator, and Acting Assistant Administrator for OEI. Then the CIO position went to another individual.

When I served as the acting EPA CIO, I came to love the job even though I was shying away from it. It was a political position that I wasn't considering at the time. I was like, "No, I don't want the job. I'm not ready to go down that path yet." But of course, when you're in the job for nineteen months, you've got a choice: You can embrace it and go with it, or you can fight it the whole time.

I can tell you; your life is a lot better when you embrace it.

Mission Drive

When I rolled in to become the Deputy CIO of EPA, I was selected because I could help the newly politically appointed CIO, the "short-timer," navigate the organization, help him achieve his priorities, and succeed at EPA during his tenure. This is typical for a Deputy Assistant Administrator's role. I left doing the environmental policy, science-based, more technical work I had been doing, and now I was helping govern information management and IT's footprint.

In the environmental world, information about the environment–climate, water quality, soil samples, air samples, and all of that–is hugely important. The job of IT and information management is to preserve the quality and integrity associated with information.

I want to give you a little more context about how my job changed, what that really meant, and what I intended to do. I had to learn the IT piece because before, I had only been a consumer of IT. Now, I was going to be the provider of these IT services. This meant I was in a job where everything that was wrong with somebody's applications, like Workday (financial management and human resources management software), it's probably IT's problem. So that was a big adjustment from a mindset and an attitude perspective.

But I was thrilled to be there!

I was thrilled because I came from the mission. Now I got to serve the mission from a different perspective, which was important to me. First, in EPA IT, the data that we rely on to make decisions about the state of the environment is hugely important. So, it was critical that the network was moving the data fast and not being disrupted by a cyber incident. Secondly, we had to ensure the integrity and quality of that data. If the EPA should ever be challenged on information data quality by congress, the White House, or the public, we had to have set up the agency to be in a defensible position to support the decisions they made based on that data. I was responsible for ensuring those bits and bytes of data moved fast and were defensible on two fronts.

It was pretty cool to be working in this way serving in those two capacities. So that's how I ended up in the IT world, fully immersed in understanding network traffic and security operations. Learning about the bad guys through cyber security, understanding what a cyber incident is, how to protect ourselves, and participating in classified briefings. It was a different world and really a lot of fun. I loved working in IT.

I fell into something I hadn't realized how passionate I was about: IT and operations.

Landing at NASA

I had effectively three titles at EPA and was spending more time on "Who am I when I signed something" than advancing what I thought the organization needed to do. "Hmm," I thought, "I really liked the CIO role. Why don't I help someone be successful somewhere else and have less of a complicated administrative job?" So that's what I was leaving. It wasn't EPA; the job just wasn't for me anymore.

I was told that NASA was looking for a deputy. So, I chatted with the then NASA CIO, who would be doing the recruitment. "Thanks for taking my call. I need to be forthright with you. I will compete for this deputy job, but you need to know that I'm not from a technical field. I build teams to be successful and get people to play well together to achieve things. But I'm not the person who knows how to make the switches go on and off and move traffic through the network. I'm not that. So, if you want that, I'm not going to apply. But, if you want someone to help continue to build a strong team and have them deliver results together and play well together, then I'm happy to compete for the job."

The response from the then NASA CIO was, "Renee, this job's not technical. It's all about people."

Before our conversation, I thought, "It's NASA; it has to be all technical." My job as the deputy CIO at EPA and as the acting CIO at EPA was really about communicating well, bringing everybody together, and delivering results. Yes, we had to deal with technical projects, but that was more about asking a lot of good questions to understand what was going on. We had technical people to actually do the technical work.

I thought at NASA, I'd be doing like...well, I didn't know what I would do, but it's NASA; it's a very technical place filled with engineers, rocket scientists, and mathematicians. There are probably not a lot of economics majors floating around. The then CIO made it clear, "Renee, that's what I need. I need someone to bring everyone together to drive results." So, I applied for the Deputy CIO job. Unbeknownst to me, however, NASA was actually picking the person to be the next CIO. I didn't know that when I got the job.

Remember how earlier I talked about starting to poke at stuff, being intentional about your career and what you want? Well, that's how things began to happen.

A couple of weeks after I'd started, I was asked to be the CIO. I sat there dumbfounded. "Uh, um. What?" He replied, "I am going to retire," which I knew, but when he and I last spoke, it was at least a year out. I figured at the time, "Hey, I'll get a chance to figure out the job, and then I'll fill the gap while they recruit for a new CIO." He says, "No, we recruited you to be the CIO." I really had no clue, clueless. I said, "Well, one person in this room didn't know that." We chatted, and I said, "Let me think about it. And don't you think I should maybe meet who my bosses would be." At this point, I still hadn't met a bunch of people yet. NASA is big.

He replied, "That's a great idea."

So, I met with the people who would be my bosses, and it was a Deja Vu conversation. "Well, you were recruited to be the CIO." I looked at them and thought, "Okay, I'm still the only person that didn't know that." Meanwhile, I got a sense of the job and the people I had to rely on to be successful. There was no "I'll do it myself. I know what I'm doing, blah, blah, blah." I had no choice but to rely on their talent and my ability to pull the best of their talent out.

Two and a half months after starting at NASA, I was named the CIO. I knew enough about the talent that I had. And I knew I didn't know it all, only a tiny segment. In those early months, though, I had formed trust with enough talented people that I knew had it in me to exercise the right leadership muscles to build the team. I had a good core team, and I knew I could rely on them and have the kinds of conversations that bring the best out of people. And if I needed to move people around, just like any other federal agency, I would just have to navigate that issue. I needed to build my team. I got that, but I knew I could start my team with the core group I had already grown to trust.

People first. Then process. And then technology. That is how I always approached it. I came into this world with an economics degree and an environmental policy perspective. At EPA, we were negotiating with lawyers and engineers. At that level, soft skills are the first skills you have to have – it's about the people first. Then set up a decent process. Remove bureaucracy. Ask, "Wait a minute. Why are we doing that?!" And then it gets to the technology. For me, even technology is about drawing the best from your team.

The best technology selection is more about your ecosystem, including the people, than your favorite software.

Keeping Astronauts Safe

Being able to draw the best from your team and knowing you can rely on each other matters, especially when you're tested. So, when a mission network intrusion happened, we were ready.

Friday afternoons are notorious for bad news in IT. While I don't recall the exact day of the week, I distinctly remember sitting in my office listening to the NASA Chief Information Security Officer (CISO) and his Deputy outline the facts as they understood them then. An internet of things antenna, a sensor, was inadvertently put on the wrong network. At first, we thought the sensor had created a problem for a highly sensitive mission network that transports data to and from the spacecraft. When we dug into it, however, we found that there was actually a bigger problem on the mission network.

The bigger problem was, in fact, an intrusion.

They had already called the Department of Homeland Security (DHS) and initiated the process to get help from them and other agencies with world-class skills in investigating cyber incidents. However, given the system was a mission network used for space communication, we had to act quickly and transparently, and we had to get it right.

It may not have been a Friday, but it sure felt like one. In that moment of uncertainty, though, I knew my team was ready.

We sent a "first story" email to the Administrator's office and the head of Human Exploration. In addition, we shared information with our Johnson Space Center (JSC) contact, who understood their IT architecture of systems so that he could take immediate action to address any potential risk to the mission.

We then sorted through and analyzed a lot of data. We discovered that the intrusion was not created by a misplaced Internet of Things (IoT) sensor, as we first thought. But, in reality, it was an indicator of a cyber intrusion into the mission system. Intruders could be changing the data, stealing the data, or even just studying how the system works to create more problems in the future.

We resolved the intrusion and conducted thorough investigations with the assistance of other federal agencies. As a result, our recommendations strengthened security and improved coordination between agencies. Building trust and soft skills matter outside your team as well. For example, when my team found and solved the mission network intrusion, it was a turning point for the agency in two ways.

Better Partnership. First, it created a better relationship between the CIO and the human exploration mission. There's always tension between the CIO and the mission because IT are the ones that have to say "No," ...a lot. And nobody likes to hear, "No." Instead, we call it, "Yes, and." "Yes, and... here are the requirements needed to do that." We were able to demonstrate that a) we understood the complicated nature of their network, b) we were able to help them fix the problem and c) we were able to help them track this intrusion. We brought in the right expertise from outside of NASA to do a full assessment, and then we were able to hand them recommendations on how to run a better network in more modern and secure ways.

That was a turning point for the agency, too. From that day forward, we had a strong partnership between IT and the human exploration mission. They hired top-notch talent to run their mission and augment their mission network teams. And we created this amazing partnership of sharing capabilities and wanting to hear what the CIO team had to say.

When I left NASA, that partnership was still blossoming.

Even Better Reputation. Secondly, the CIO team was the one that discovered the intrusion on the mission network. We were the ones that brought the talent in for their benefit so that we could operate in a way that would preserve the integrity of scientific data coming down from space! That's a huge deal. People's entire careers are written off of scientific data and discoveries in outer space. Their reputation is on the line. If the data are not of the highest integrity. That's a direct impact on the mission.

I felt really good about my team. And I felt really good about the strong partnership we formed and how it would continue to grow stronger and better going forward. For example, the CIO office and the human exploration mission worked so well together that we would use them as a reference, "Go to talk to our friends in the human exploration office about how well we work with people." It got us an even better reputation across NASA.

It really is "better together." My team loves when they feel part of the mission and get to collaborate on projects. I saw the pride on their faces knowing they were helping the mission be better. As a leader, seeing that pride on their faces and seeing them rise to the challenge and be better, I couldn't ask for anything more for my job. When I look back and ask, what are the big impacts? It was this mission network intrusion issue that we dealt with for about a year plus. It was the head of the Human Exploration Office personally calling me on a different topic and saying, "I need your help." To go from, "No, let's do everything out of sight of IT" to being called and complimented and becoming a true collaborator with the mission, that's what it's all about.

It makes the hard or monotonous stuff easier when you're viewed with respect.

Renee's Reflections

On Intentional Careers

You don't stay in one career groove; at least, I didn't. All careers are intentional. I always have to take a deep breath when I hear people say to their supervisors and managers, "Well, you're not doing enough for me." My mindset is it's a partnership. You, as an individual, have ideas about your career and should invite your boss into what I'll call a "board of career advisors." People you talk to, trust, and can ask, "What do I need to do to be better?" Invite them to be part of your advisory board. It's not only what someone can do for you. It's also being intentional about what you are also striving for. I've seen bosses trying really hard to support their people, but it's not what their folks wanted. That also creates frustration: "Why is my boss asking me to do this?" "I don't want to do it."

Early career positions are for finding out what you want, volunteering for different challenges, and managing your reputation. You better deliver, though. I can tell you nobody likes to remind their people to do their timecards. You shouldn't need to be reminded to prove you should be paid. I'm not talking about when you're so busy you get home at night and go, "Oh, I forgot to do my timecard." I'm talking about the person that consistently doesn't do it. Don't make your boss have to remind you to do the little things. You want your boss to say, "Oh, you care enough about my success that I can invest in yours because I know you care." A lot of times, you're just looking for people to care. Care about the little things, and then people will be open to hearing about the gifts you may want to provide them.

On Seeing Women in Leadership

One reason it's essential to be around other women in the workplace is just the straight inspiration. You look up figuratively, and in my case, literally (there are a lot of people taller than me), and you see yourself. You say, "They did it. I can do it too." It's just that simple. "I'm like them. I can be like them." The stuff you think holds you back seems to fall away. You feel like you can talk to people like you and say, "Tell me about your career." I found women were always very open to that. Of course, you also saw behaviors you didn't want to emulate. But that's true of anybody, male or female, ethnicity or race. By seeing leaders like you, you begin to believe you can get there too. And you feel supported in your workplace because you're not the only one there. You can see your future.

On Transitioning to a Role in IT

Three things played a part in my ability to take on the Deputy CIO role and then the CIO role. One, having some experience in programming; two, being thoughtful about my own experience of being a customer of IT; and three, having a lot of experience translating customer requirements for the programmers.

One. As I mentioned earlier, having enough knowledge of programming and database structures helped me ask the right questions. Two, instead of coming up through technology as a network operator or something like that, I came to IT thinking, "Well, I used to be the one getting all these services, and here's what I would like to see from a customer experience." Having a customer mindset is thinking, how do you help people be successful? How do you understand how they think? Well, first, you have to understand the customer. Then from that understanding, you build trust so that you can have the conversations you need to translate their needs into technical requirements. After that, the third piece comes in. Once you have the technical requirements that support their needs, you have to figure out how to talk to the technical folks and bring them along so that they see the customer experience as well.

A fourth piece is the mindset. Leave your ego at home; you're there to serve. And serving isn't saying "Yes," to everything. Serving is understanding what needs to be done, translating it, and then double-checking that the translation is still aligned with what the customer wants. "Yes, and..."

A friend of mine, I think she was an English major, is one of the best technical people I've met in a long time. She took some classes to learn to program, but part of her ability is having both the right and the left brain engaged when trying to deliver a product. So you can come to IT from a different discipline and be successful, just like you can come from within a computer science or a programming background or be an electrical engineer and be successful.

On Staying in STEM

There were a couple of times when I was ready to quit.

It wasn't about the technology. It was about feeling that I had lost my boss's trust, compounded by the job's loneliness. I was fortunate to have two amazing deputies, sequentially, who were great partners. I don't know if they know this, but they helped me not be so lonely. I felt I had a trustworthy place to have an open conversation, including, "What is going on in these people's brains right now?" Just that full frustration conversation. That's not the language you would use publicly, but you would with someone you deeply trust. So I was able to share, not offload, but share with them that burden that had made me feel lonely when it came to some of the relationship hiccups you have at an agency when you didn't grow up there.

My last two deputies basically were at NASA for decades. Having that safe place for heartfelt, vulnerable conversations kept me in it during those times when I felt so different. I don't know if it's a female thing or not. At times, I did feel like, "Why am I even in this job when they are so much better than I am?" That little bit of the imposter syndrome. It's not like I wear it all the time, but it would sometimes hit, "You're right. I don't think I could stand up a server." When you can't do some of the things that fall within the span of your scope of your responsibilities, sometimes it can shake your ground. I didn't have many people that were like me, although I found that female friendship in other fellow CIOs in the government. I think some of the leaving we see happen with women in technology is the same reason I didn't pursue engineering.

You get tired of being the only girl in the room.

Those times when I did feel ready to quit were when I was tired of being lonely. Lonely that I couldn't have a conversation with some of my girlfriends about what it was like to be X, Y, and Z because they didn't know what it felt like. Denying my friends that conversation, however, was a decision I made. I've realized that I probably shouldn't have made that decision. I thought if I talked about IT problems or being the only woman in the room, I wouldn't get the camaraderie that I needed from my female friends. But I was wrong. I was wrong about not connecting with those who really cared for me and trusting the relationship enough to have those conversations, even if they didn't know what it was like to walk in my shoes.

Your network and your family get you through those times.

I'm a huge believer in having a mentor and a coach and the strength in oneself to feel so vulnerable. The best leaders I have seen are not the ones with all the answers. They're the ones that show you they are human. They inspire you to be better. Getting comfortable in the yuk is hard when you've spent so much time proving yourself and your technical chops, like at the entry level. Somewhere in there, you gotta be able to figure the network piece out, the coaching piece, the mentoring piece, and you certainly need an ally and an advocate. I advise finding a group of people with whom you can talk openly about what's troubling you and help you come up with solutions–after listening first. Then helping you work out how you stay in the game. Sometimes you move into a different place or organization.

But you need to stay in the field.

You stay in the game because women must have a voice in the solutions being built and in the decision-making that affects them. Look at the world around you. When we are not in the game, we end up with things like a lack of female crash dummies or not enough women representation in health decisions or dosage studies. I always ask, "Is this dose appropriate for someone of my weight?" Drink holders in a car. How grateful are all of us for those? Car design is a great example because we all get in a car and can relate to what's going on in a car. Even if you don't own a car, you've probably been in a taxi or something. Take the minivan, which I have, cause my bicycles all fit in the back. The way the minivan design is configured for me to reach the radio, adjust the temperature, turn on the defrost, turn the windshield wipers -- all of that is designed, I think, for a female body frame. For my husband, who is 6'1", everything's just a little off for him. It's just not as easy for him because his arm span and the way he sits in the seat are different. So that's why you stay in the game. If you look around this world and see something that you don't think fits for you, whether that is a diversity of race, ethnicity, male, female, or whatever gender you identify with, that is why you stay in technical fields.

The only way you change the world is to be there when decisions are made.

Women love to solve problems in general. Women love to serve, in general, and women love to be part of great teams. We love our communities of every kind. If you love these things, then science, technology, engineering, and mathematics are the way to go. You can solve problems, and you can focus on the areas that are of interest to you. For example, my niece is planning to study bio-robotics engineering. You look at prosthetics, arms, legs, and all that. Just think of how she would design them as female versus male athletes. We all don't look at the world through the same lens, and that's okay. That's a great thing. I think that's just a significant contribution to those that will be the receivers of prosthetics that she will have designed.

It will be that much better because it will be an integrated, diverse team.

On Public Service

Whenever I thought about leaving public service, there were a few reasons I intentionally decided to stay in the federal government, even when I had very lucrative opportunities to go into the private sector.

I looked around at the women in equivalent positions to me and felt that being in this community of women was important. We were breaking barriers. It was much easier to break barriers when you had colleagues in similar situations who shared commonality for conversations and challenges and could support each other for advancement or to be successful in our current jobs. I also got to meet a ton of great female engineers and mathematicians, and I felt I could make a bigger difference with a like-minded and similarly focused group of people than I could by going off and potentially being alone or with just a few female colleagues.

Being part of a strong community of women is one part of why I stayed in the federal government for my glorious thirty years.

Another thing that I really like about federal jobs is serving. I spent thirty years in public service, so service is obviously very important to me. In fact, I had a conversation just a few weeks ago when I was being screened for a private sector CIO position. The recruiter had commented, "I just don't know how come you work for so little." He didn't mean anything by it. He was acknowledging that there's a considerable price difference between a federal CIO and a private sector CIO in big firms. It hadn't dawned on me that money even really mattered. So when I answered him, I said, "Wow? Okay, yeah, I guess that kind of figure would be great to have. But where else do you get to meet astronauts regularly? I've held moon rocks. I was in a clean room holding moon rocks. I saw something called lunar trash. Made me laugh." There really was a bin labeled "Lunar Trash." At NASA, you meet curators of moon rocks. I didn't even know that was a job.

Where else do you get a front-row seat to see the making of technology that never existed before?!"

When I was describing that to him, I came back to, "Yeah, a few figures more would be nice. Life would be more comfortable, but I would never have had the experiences I got to have had I not been a federal employee." I've traveled the world. I've been to Russia. I've been to Baikonur, Kazakhstan to see a human launch, and it was really cool because, unlike the United States, you are close enough to feel the earth rumbling. You can REALLY feel it because you're inside a mile away. I stood there that close and got to see the screen of the astronauts in their capsule looong after they launched. And when the gravity situation changed, I got to see the little mascot that hangs in every capsule that tells the astronauts when they're in a no-gravity situation. It hangs like a rear-view mirror tchotchke. In no gravity, it floats everywhere. I got to see that mascot float firsthand. I got to talk to these guys. I met their families. I toured the history of the Russian rocket program in Russia with the Russians.

While working with the European Space Agency, I got to tour and have a cocktail party in the Vatican library. I met the Vatican librarian. Talk about a powerful position. He was a wonderful man.

After a presentation I made in a meeting about an upcoming launch, an astronaut pulled me aside and thanked me for the points I made and for how my team and I cared for the safety of the astronauts.

So, I got to serve all of these people.

Being so reliant on IT is great, but if anything goes wrong, it's a bad day! We have to ensure that we've got all sorts of backup plans for anything that could go wrong. We must ensure our astronauts' safety in everything that goes on at NASA. That's the kind of impact that you can have serving in the federal government. Those are the kinds of people that you get to hang out with. Your parents always said, "Be careful who you pick for friends because you want to hang out with the folks who are going to help you be better." I can't think of anything that helps you be better than really smart folks that have left the face of this earth and done things two hundred some miles off the planet in the International Space Station. When you meet them, you're like, "Yep, I will give you my best astronaut. I will." In addition, there's everybody else that you work for, but supporting astronauts that's the icing on the cake for your service. Knowing that this is what happens with your IT, the making of science fiction into fact, puts you into your "A" game.

Private sector CIOs made five or six times more than I ever did. But you can't put a price tag on shaking the hands of an astronaut. That's your impact.

On Balance

Let's say you're partnered up; however, you do that. It has to be a give-and-take relationship. Absolutely has to be, or one or both of you will suffer. You also have to leave behind the ideals of what you think a mother or a woman ought to do. Or what a father or man ought to do. Your home life should be designed based on the best capabilities or sometimes who has the best patience. Take a look at your paradigm, I'll call it a marriage, because that's what I have, in a marriage, you have to step back and not just repeat what your parents did just because they did it that way, what they did may have worked for them, but it may not be working for the two of you. You have to figure out what works for the marriage and managing the house because you have to manage a home and what works for raising children if you have them. You have to let some of it go. I didn't have a perfectly quaffed house when we raised our son. At some point, I just plain didn't have time. And if I had 15 minutes, did I want to run a vacuum, or did I want to sit and read a story? So yeah, the house was always a mess. In fact, I still need to put in a new carpet. It's been the same carpet since 1997. I had two dogs, a kid, and who knows what would come through the house back then. Well, now I have to pick the carpet, and I'm not very good at that stuff. All relationships are about consciously and subconsciously establishing a productive relationship where each person thrives. You have to have some conversations in there, and you have to check your habits.

You absolutely have to check your habits and rethink your ideals.

I had my heart broken. Even though I totally understood it intellectually, I had my mom-heart broken. We were in the car, and my son had hurt himself. I don't know how he hurt himself in the car, but he did. Steve was driving, and I was like, I got to help him. I said, "Hey buddy, blah, blah, blah," and I was just chatting with him. He said, "Not you. I want daddy!" Coming to terms with that was a) my husband quit work to stay at home, so he was the predominant person who cared for our son, and b) society told me that my son should always ask for mom when he cried. I had this crash of expectations, and it hurt...a lot. When I finally was able to move beyond being so hurt by it, it made sense because my husband was the one who was always there. I was working and making the money for the family; he was the one home all the time. It was vital for me to hear that and go through that growth. I knew that I had a different relationship with my son than maybe other moms would have with their sons. I had to work at the relationship I wanted, not the relationship that my paradigm, before that moment, was telling me I should have. You can't be the GoTo parent if you're not the one always there.

It's hard, and it doesn't always go well. But, if it didn't hurt sometimes, you probably wouldn't know when it was an amazing time.

On Intentionality in Recruiting

If we aren't intentional about creating a diverse and inclusive organization, we won't shine a light on our own biases that need to change. Sometimes too, you may feel like you are alone or frustrated.

You've got to persevere.

When I did my first recruiting at NASA. I intentionally changed the way I recruited. Human Resource's attitude was, "Oh, this is just too much work." When that got back to me, I went, "Oh, okay. Yeah, we're still going to do this differently." The federal government uses USAjobs.gov, which we're supposed to use. It's a good tool. But I also paid for additional postings on other job boards. I got push-back, "This costs money." My response was, "Yes. Okay. Thank you." I think it cost me a total of a thousand dollars for each recruitment I did. I used job advertising boards where women went or had a higher percentage of minorities. One of them was dice.com, and the other was women in technology. I advertised there.

I had statistical improvement in every executive recruitment that I did. The first piece of data was when I was recruiting for a Chief Information Security Officer. Recruiting had been started by my successor. Being new at NASA, I made the mistake of hitting the easy button. "However, it's written, let's just run with it, get it out the door. I need a Chief Information Security Officer." So, the recruiting process kicked off, and I focused on my new job at NASA, trying to swim and keep my head above water. We got the package of candidates back; there were only a few minorities and no women.

I thought, "Well, cyber certainly doesn't have a lot of women in it." So, we did the interviews. When I got done, two things struck me, and I know I hurt people in this process, but I couldn't, in good conscience, continue the path that I was on. First, I neglected to ask some questions about leadership capabilities. Secondly, I thought we could do better in having a more diverse slate for me to pull from. So, after many conversations, I used dice.com and WIT (women in technology). I went from about a hundred people applying to more than two hundred people applying. Instead of a couple of minorities in a slate of ten, I ended up having eleven interviews, three minorities, three women, and one of the minorities was a woman. That left six of the slots with white males. So, I went from two out of ten in the interview process to six out of eleven being female or minority.

Intentionality in recruitment is critical.

Also, when you're reading the resumes, you've got to be careful not to form biases. One thing you can do to protect against bias is to go through all the resumes and black out the name and school to gain greater anonymity.

Intentionality begins with recruitment and finding new ways to find the right people for the job.

On Allies and Advocates

I've learned that I have done better in job competitions when I've had allies and advocates than just straight putting in an application. That is key. I reflect on the makeup of the team or group of people I mentor, "Is this group diverse?" If they need me to be their ally, am I being an ally of men and women of minorities and non-minorities? When I was in the federal government, I advocated and asked for meaningful consideration of people who were competing for open positions. That makes a real difference from mid-career on up. It is all about people advocating for you and bringing you along. Hiring at the executive level is a costly proposition. The people recruiting for these positions learn a lot from your interview, but your advocates and allies are in an excellent place to tell your story. They know you. You become less of a risky, I'll call it, purchase.

It goes back to where we began, about being intentional. Every executive needs to be engaging, mentoring, and advocating a diverse group of individuals. If you go play golf, and somebody doesn't play golf (I don't), you have to ask yourself, "How am I supposed to meet the group of executives who don't play golf?" Who has access to me? Who am I giving my time to? Is it all people who are like me?

You've got to be intentional about finding other routes to bring that diverse pool of people within your line of sight, to nurture them, to let them learn from you, and for you to learn from them too.

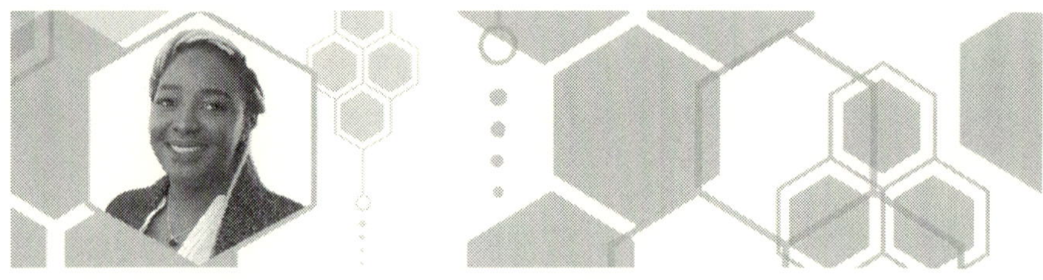

Morẹ́nikẹ́ Ẹniọlá Ọláòṣebìkan

Inventor and Founder, Licensed Clinical Pharmacist, multi-Pharmacy owner, and Academic Colleague at the University of Alberta

I'm a pharmacist. I own and operate a retail pharmacy and a standalone compounding lab. I'm a social innovator that founded and operated The Ribbon Rouge Foundation, a not-for-profit organization that uses arts for positive social impact. I founded a startup that provides turnkey, portable medications, and manufacturing solutions globally. I also teach and am a mentor at the Faculty of Pharmacy at the University of Alberta and am involved in a whole bunch of other community initiatives.

I have dedicated my life to contributing meaningful solutions to complex global health problems.

Lollapalooza Childhood

My parents had a tremendous influence on me and my siblings. We grew up in Lagos, Nigeria, in what felt like a normal household, but now I see that my childhood was not what everyone else was experiencing. My father is a physician, but he also published a monthly healthcare publication and the first peer-reviewed clinical magazine in West Africa. Then at the end of the year, he would throw this massive, wild, fun Healthcare Awards Night Gala–a sort of Lollapalooza artist meets political meets awards event.

My father paid his way through medical school by being a DJ. That's how he met my mother, so our household was also filled with music. My mom was honors chemistry, but she self-taught herself how to sew and opened a business making uniforms for all these companies. It's hard to think of a business that didn't go through that household. My mom had a bookbinding operation, a paper mill operated in our house. She had this sewing thing. At some point, there was cassava processing going on.

My siblings and I have this ongoing joke that if you came across my mom on the road and said to her, "Can you build us a spaceship?" My mom would not miss a beat in saying "Yes!" and then some way, somehow, we would be making spaceships on that plot of land. So that was the household I grew up in. Very eclectic, kaleidoscopic. Just all sorts of activities. Bustling.

There wasn't a division between science and arts or health and supporting communities. If my parents wanted to do something, they just did it. We all grew up to be very creative people who don't understand the concept of separate disciplines. We ended up gallivanting from one profession to the other, according to whatever passion or problem was fueling an urge at that moment.

That was a major influential thing in my childhood and one that I didn't notice was different until much later in my adulthood. The biggest strength that household gave me was this idea that you can figure anything out. That confidence to know that you don't have to feel boxed into any one way of looking at the world. That complexity is okay too. It is okay to see things from two opposite ends of the spectrum and see agreement–even when it looks very different at both ends.

From our childhood, we gained the confidence to imagine and invent and build whatever it is that is important to us.

Grandiose Ideas

I had an epiphany as a child. I remember where I was. It's really strange. It doesn't make any sense. I never say it out loud because it just sounds silly. I was on the balcony in Eric Moore Towers in Lagos, one of my childhood homes. I was maybe seven or eight. I had this thought. Now, I rephrase it to say, "I will be part of the HIV solution," but in reality, my exact thought was, "I will find a cure to HIV." It's a really strange thing for such a young child to think. I never said I wanted to cure HIV out loud, even to myself, because it just seemed like a really grandiose, wild thing to say.

The way I've been able to rationalize it later is that somewhere in the mix of my dad being a physician and my mom working for NAFDAC (the Nigerian Food and Drug Agency), there was probably a conversation about this sexually transmitted infection that was rolling through Africa and killing a lot of people. This was around 1990, and during that time, HIV was becoming a major issue in a lot of African countries. There was a high prevalence of people dying. It was beginning to make the news, and people were beginning to talk about this infection that is transmitted sexually. They hadn't really started the public health campaigns yet. We were beginning to see a generation of working people being taken out by this thing, and it was beginning to create a lot of fear. For Africans, it's not compartmentalized into sexuality or drug use like it was elsewhere.

HIV was just this thing that was taking out generations of people.

I knew I would find the cure for HIV. It's always just stuck with me. It's only recently that I've started telling people. It's just a weird thing to have experienced. To say that is just weird, right? People look at you like you're crazy. There are not many viral infections that have actual cures. That's why I generally don't say it out loud because you sound wild as a scientist when you say things like that.

I definitely have that personality that if I set my mind to something, I'm going to do that thing to the point of death. But there is something different about this thought though. It is an inner knowing that I'm going to do it. It wasn't something I committed my mind to; it is just a knowledge that that's what I'm supposed to do.

Path Dependency

In Nigeria, after junior high school, you must choose if you're going down the science or the arts path. Every major curriculum you build for yourself after that decision is determined by whether you are a science student or an art student. So, going into grade ten, I chose science. I dropped art my first year because they kept teaching us art history that wasn't African. It was a lot of rote memorizations of the Renaissance, Picasso, Leonardo da Vinci and all that stuff that later on I grew to really have an interest in. Still, as a nine-year-old Nigerian, these foreign people had no context to my life.

It just annoyed the hell out of me.

I'd been told that I was really good at biology, and somehow, I heard that people that are good at biology become doctors. So, got it into my mind that I was going to be a doctor. And the way to become a doctor was to be a science student.

When you think about path dependency, that might've changed my entire trajectory. My science path started with that decision to drop art because there was no bearing or reference whatsoever for me. Then it builds on, "Oh, you're good in biological sciences, and people who are good in biological sciences become doctors." This literally became the logic that then determined which branch I ended up in during secondary school, and that determined that I would be a science student.

Med School–Not

After High School, I studied in England, then quickly realized it was far too expensive. So, I applied to study in Canada, which had a much better standard of living at less cost.

I ended up at the University of Alberta. Then I discovered, like many of my fellow immigrants, that most Canadian universities don't accept international students into medical school. I was distraught. The only thing that helped me get through that disappointment was the realization that so many of my friends had done the same thing–they came to Canada to become doctors and had to change careers.

But I was tired of gallivanting around the world and concerned my parents were paying for all of this. I decided to get my initial degree in health sciences and then be able to pay my way through medical school. The Faculty of Pharmacy was the next logical place where I could still be a healthcare provider with patient interaction. So, I became a pharmacist.

Fun, Wild Social Enterprise

While I was in school, my eclectic childhood, with its mix of healthcare, arts, music, and community, wouldn't leave me. So, I started what is now my Ribbon Rouge Foundation to donate money to people living with HIV in African countries.

At some point in early adulthood, I contracted tuberculosis. The place where I received my treatment had a lot of people living with HIV. The nine months attending that facility opened my eyes to what it looks like to be really resource-constrained and fighting for your life. It changed my life, my worldview, and how I understood the patient experience. Like HIV, tuberculosis has a tremendous amount of baggage around it. I remember my illness wasn't something my family wanted me to tell people because there was an enormous perceived and internalized stigma around my having tuberculosis.

I can never quite know what it feels like to be a person living with HIV and the kind of stigma that still comes with that label in many places. But I was able to touch that, to actually feel a little bit of that experience of walking around this world, trying to masquerade something that is really painful and just trying to make do with that identity. Stigma and discrimination started to become this thing that I could relate with. And so, when I came here to Canada, I wanted to donate to Africans living with HIV.

Not only did I not have any money to donate, but also international students weren't allowed to work off campus. So, I had to figure out a way to hack the problem. I could sew. I could paint. I could draw. And I had a whole bunch of friends interested in helping me. So, I decided to put together a show on campus to raise money.

That's how my foundation started.

While I'm going through the Faculty of Pharmacy, it's this very fun, wild, stressful blur, and every year we put this fundraising show together that gets a little bit more intense every time. When it started, it was the most amateur show known to man. We charged $10 a head, and we were still profitable. I've now come to learn this is what people call a "social enterprise." I didn't know that at the time.

I was just trying to find money to send to people living with HIV in African countries.

With Distinction

I graduated with first-class honors, but it was one of my most miserable days on campus because I didn't get first-class honors with distinction. I missed it by 0.1 of a GPA. I missed it because I was busy plotting that year's Ribbon Rouge fundraiser, using the special occasion of my birthday for the event. On the day I graduated, I was trying so hard to pretend to be happy because my parents had traveled all the way from Nigeria. My siblings were there too. I remember putting on this mask. I'm smiling and looking happy in the pictures, but I was so miserable because I didn't have the "with distinction" attached to the first class.

On graduation day, I was beating myself up. "Did I really need this goddamn fundraiser? If I didn't do that stupid fundraiser, I would have graduated with distinction!!" I couldn't even joke about it for the longest time. It still pisses me the hell off. But, in the grand scheme of things, the fundraiser was important in the trajectory of my life, in the things that I am passionate about, and in the way that I will change the world; the fundraiser was the thing that really mattered.

I became a pharmacist, but there was always this yearning and longing to go back to Africa and do something that addresses the root causes of the health problems that we see. Over time that has transmuted from health problems, infections, and HIV into something bigger. It becomes more about the injustice of it.

The disparities in health outcomes are just completely unacceptable in my mind.

Leadership by Fire

In the initial place I worked, I did everything I could to stand out from other pharmacists. I started so many projects and pilots in that pharmacy, and I always made sure I did things that generated more revenue. I saw that I could improve the lives of my own pool of patients with the programs I created. For example, I created and implemented tobacco cessation and diabetes programs within my first two years of graduating. Because of that, the owner put a lot of support behind me when I decided I wanted to own my own store. The regional manager also already knew about me because I kept running programs that positively impacted their bottom line.

I acquired my own store within three years of graduating college while still on a work permit!

I was a 28-year-old immigrant with a staff of twenty-three. It was surreal, wild. I can't say wild enough. For many reasons, it was one of the most intense years of my life. I think of that childhood I'd had where nothing, just nothing, seemed impossible. Nothing felt like it was too much to ask. Nothing seemed like you couldn't figure it out.

I just didn't see what I was doing as something that significant until my friends started saying how different and significant it was. Mainly because I was not only young but also because I was an African immigrant.

So, I have this brutal one year of leadership learning by doing. What I thought was going to be difficult was making money; that was where my mind was. You know how to be profitable. No, it's the human beings that were the hard part. It's dealing with twenty-three humans as a twenty-eight-year-old African immigrant woman.

That experience was something.

My staff was a mishmash of people, but mainly whites initially. I had a whole bunch of my white staff quit within that first year. That's not uncommon for African immigrant entrepreneurs and business owners taking over an enterprise. In addition, in that first year, I had to learn how to fire people. I had to learn how to hire people. I had to learn how to influence, and how to negotiate.

It was trial by fire, that's for sure.

Authentic Leadership

There was an anecdote I kept close to my heart when I was acquiring my store. I kept saying my worst nightmare would be walking into the pharmacy I owned and my classmates would be there. Or someone I had worked with would be there. For whatever reason, I didn't want people who knew me to be in that pharmacy. And I kid you not, I walked into this pharmacy, and what did I see? One of my classmates and my former mentor.

They were pharmacists in my store.

My mentor, who had been a pharmacist for thirty-five-plus years, ended up working for me for a couple of years. My classmate still works for me. She's incredible. She's a pharmacy manager now. But when I walked into that store, I just wanted the ground to open up and swallow me. At the same time, in retrospect, I am thankful for that because, over the years, I've come to understand my leadership style. I'm what people might consider an authentic leader, and I'm very relational. You know what? I had no choice but to be an authentic and relational leader because these two people knew me.

I couldn't pretend to be someone else.

Interrogating Assumptions

By this time, Ribbon Rouge, my foundation and show, started to evolve. It stopped being this wild idea. I realized, "Yes, I can use the arts to make money." But I also realized I would never raise enough money to fix HIV with a fashion art music show.

Around this time, I started to learn more and more about how HIV disproportionately affects Black and indigenous people and men who have sex with men. I started to see that even in Canada, Black people, who for some reason are disproportionately affected, were six times more likely to have a new infection. And I do not understand why. It didn't seem like anyone had been asking why; it just seemed as if people just accepted that these are people from countries in which HIV is endemic, so that's just how things are.

My foundation started to become this place where I interrogated that assumption, where I used the arts to be an activist to talk about HIV, to put that into the public domain, "What are we doing about this?" And then over the years, it became the use of arts for research. And so, we had ideas like Photovoice, and theater for social change.

At some point, it occurred to me that this is an unusual thing that I'm doing–being a pharmacist, running the store, and operating the Ribbon Rouge foundation. So, I started to explore what this foundation actually meant to me, "Why is this something that I'm passionate about, and what is it about this particular problem that is driving me and keeping me engaged?"

It became obvious to me that it's all about the jarring health inequity. People with HIV in Canada can take a pill a day and live perfectly normal lives, while 60,000 children were born with HIV in Nigeria in 2012 because their moms didn't have access to drugs that prevent transmission. So, I knew I had to take it a step further.

By digging into what Ribbon Rouge Foundation meant to me, this thread unraveled more and more to show me why I'm passionate about the work I was doing. It became more about this unacceptable disparity, this inequity in health outcomes.

HIV becomes, in my mind, more of a symptom of deeper issues. So, I started to travel to African countries to understand the root causes of this health inequity, and because I am a pharmacist, the easiest access point for me was drugs. I didn't understand why we were not making our own drugs. I know it's a complicated and capital-intensive undertaking, but it's not rocket science. It's not so out of this world that we can't figure out how to direct-compress a few pills. And some Africans, too, have figured out even "rocket science," so why not drugs?

This was the motivator for my startup.

Mind-Boggling Stats

There are a lot of entangled complex issues that drive health inequity statistics. Up to 90% of meds are imported into Africa. In some regions, about 70% of what's imported is fake. Half the people living with HIV in a lot of countries still don't have access to medications.

However, the most mind-boggling statistic is how long it takes to order drugs. You order a drug in October. You will not get those medications until April next year. I just thought that was unacceptable. And yet, it's something that everyone has accepted. All the major philanthropists, all the major stakeholders involved in the supply chains have just accepted that it takes six months. By comparison, ordering medications centrally in Canada in the volumes that a central African country might order would take a day, 24 hours.

I was very curious about that. Why is that an acceptable situation in Africa, and why is that the case?

I learned, first of all, when you place your order is the day China is going to start making your drugs. It can take two months for them to make it, then it will take another two months to ship. Then it's another month for disembarking and customs at the ports in an African country. Then you have another month to get it to the point of sale. That just seems really inappropriate to me. I kept thinking and kept saying, if a life-threatening infection or virus comes through your country, you're trying to tell me everyone's dead between now and April next year, and that's okay.

That didn't make sense.

That's Wild

Even though I am not an engineer, I suddenly had to figure out an engineering solution to this problem. I just started reading a whole bunch of literature about manufacturing and began thinking about a solution. The first idea I came up with was to 3D print drugs. I went to one of my professors; he just kind of looked at me. "That's wild. You're not going to do that." But I had this example of an anti-seizure medication that the FDA approved that was 3D printed. It really didn't seem wild to me, "If they could do it, we can do it." He disagreed with me, and I couldn't get any engineer to bite on that idea.

I went, "Okay, we have to find at least a way to decentralize manufacturing because, in the current paradigm, there's no way it can work in Africa. We need a portable, small footprint, decentralized medication manufacturing. That's what we need."

This is how my startup, Kemet Advanced Manufacturing LTD., came about. I was looking for a solution for medication access in African countries, and the idea I conceived is a turnkey portable drug manufacturing facility–a pharmaceutical factory in a box.

Trade Delegation

Over lunch, I told one of the former board members that I wanted to find a cure for HIV, thinking he might be the only person that wouldn't think this was the wildest thing. We got into this conversation of what I really wanted to be doing–that I wanted to find a cure for HIV, and I wanted that cure to come from Africans. I told him I wanted it to come from Africans because if it comes from somewhere else, they'll put a patent on it, and it will be twenty more years before we get our hands on it. So, it had to come from the continent.

So, I'm having this conversation with him, and he's like, "You should do a trade delegation to Botswana." And I'm like, "Huh?" And he's like, "Yeah, I'm the Honorary Consul for Botswana to Canada. We can organize a trade delegation for us to go to Botswana."

At first, I thought, "Okay, that's funny. Sure. We're going to do a trade delegation to Botswana." Well, he wasn't kidding. Within six months, he had contacted the ambassadors. He had emailed all the correspondence that organized trade delegations. Three other people signed up, and next thing I knew, I was on a trade delegation to Botswana.

I had been trying to get into Nigeria. I'm Nigerian; my father was connected through his healthcare work; it's the most logical place for me to have started something like this. I'd done a bunch of insight interviews; reached out to people in ministries and some companies, but I wasn't taken seriously. I'd been trying for about a year before my lunch conversation with this board member. The delegation to Botswana would be the first time I intentionally went to an African country to understand medication and access.

It was an incredible opportunity because I met with the heads of all these ministries and permanent secretaries in trade, economic development, and health.

Any ministry I wanted to talk to, they organized it. They organized the travel from the main city into an economic region where they struggled for foreign direct investment.

Botswana became the first country of many.

I did end up going back to Nigeria and doing interviews there. I traveled to Chad. I went to Zanzibar around my wedding and interviewed people there too. I went to Uganda. I went to Kenya. I went back to Botswana maybe four times to deepen my relationships. I went again with another organized tour through the Canada Africa Business Forum. They had invited me to speak at their conference.

The Most Feminist Man

When I traveled to Africa, my husband was my fiancée for part of that time, and there was never any resistance to me going. Even this year, before COVID, he suggested we go back to Chad, "You have to talk to the head of the central medical stores there." If anything, his influence has been making sure I see the results of what I've started. He's very supportive that way.

My husband might be the most feminist man that I know. He really does talk the talk and walk the walk in a way that is super comfortable to me.

We have a very non-traditional setup because we have two houses, one in Edmonton, where my pharmacy is, and one in Calgary. He stays here with me in Edmonton for half the month. Then I stay with him, in Calgary, for about half the month. The idea of actually having a single household where you are splitting chores is far from applicable to us because there are two houses. And then I don't cook. I know how to cook; I just don't have the time for it. I have someone that cooks my food for 14 days. My husband loves to cook; that's how he unwinds and decompresses. For cleaning, we kind of just go with the flow. Some weeks it's him; some weeks it's me. It's basically what needs to be done, and then we just share it and do it together.

For me, that works amazingly. It's never a thought that crosses my mind that I should cook and clean because I'm a woman. It just doesn't apply in our marriage.

What took getting used to, though, is when we're traveling. Somewhere in my mind, I'm thinking my husband is going to get my box (suitcase). I would find out that he doesn't even consider it as something he would do. So initially, when we first started dating, it would bubble up. Then I realized, "Oh, he just doesn't see you as a person that he has to help out in that way at all." In his mind, we really are partners. We're living together, and we're in love with each other, and we want each other to survive and succeed and thrive, and we're just...for each other.

So, every now and again, when I'm like, "Oh, there are all these men carrying their wives' boxes," I let it go because I know how much I hate cooking. I'm not going to make him carry this box because the last thing I want to be doing is cooking every week. Nope.

My husband is Kenyan. He makes fun of how entitled Kenyan men feel around these sorts of situations. I'm Nigerian. So, very often when he meets Nigerian people, one of the first questions they ask him is if I cook and how good my food is. When we look at all the other couples around us who are our age and from similar life experiences, we really are different in the patterns we've fallen into. We are able to see how couples treat each other and then how we treat each other. We know what's important to us and what's not important to us, and we know that's different than most couples, but it's comfortable for us.

So, we keep at it.

I am blessed because I married someone who wants me to reach my full potential as much as I want him to reach his. We're both very supportive of each other's careers. Sometimes, I think I'm spoiled because I really do a lot that I don't think other married people get away with doing.

A Resilient Bunch

A lot is going on right now in Nigeria; it's an interesting place. This is an oversimplification. When you look at most of the economic activity, it's women driving a lot of those businesses, a lot of the markets, a lot of those small to medium enterprises. I don't know the percentage, but it feels like over 90% of it is women. And then you have a lot of the political and public service positions held by men. So, the people making decisions on how the country will run are men. The people making money for the country are women.

It's still pretty patriarchal, as is Canada.

Nigerians are one of the most educated immigrant communities in the world. Nigerians are the highest population of grad school degree holders in the UK and the US, higher than whites or Asians. So we are a very educated bunch. At the same time, if you look at how much we spend on education in Nigeria, last time I checked, it's like 0.02% of GDP. It's abysmal.

Nigeria is this place of just weird juxtapositions of things.

I don't know what kind of struggles women in STEM in Nigeria face in their lived experience of it. But I can't imagine it's easy because we're socialized to ascribe to wealth and beauty. To figure out hair, makeup, beauty, and fashion, that's how we're socialized. So, I can't imagine that it's the easiest thing to be a woman in STEM. But at the same time, I have a lot of female Nigerian engineers, mathematicians, and scientists as friends.

I guess we are just a very resilient bunch. I can say that much.

Pharmacist Turned Engineer

My initial plan for my startup was very much me thinking I was building something that truly has legs. It was me wanting to learn, design, and build my startup as a direct response to what I heard and saw firsthand.

And now I've formed relationships in a way that there's buy-in. I'm not just building something for Botswana out of nowhere. I'm building something that directly responds to problems I've heard from people in Botswana. These relationships also allow me to get feedback. Every time I do something, I call, text, and WhatsApp. I send messages back, "Okay, what do you think about this part? And this part?" I make sure different players are involved with me in understanding and creating a potential solution to the problem. So, there's buy-in at all the levels, with the ministers, people on the ground, people in the economic development unit, the chief pharmacist, the central medical store—all the critical leverage points in the system are involved in creating what I'm building.

It takes a lot for me not to cry anytime I talk about it. It does have this emotional impact.

When I traveled to these African countries and saw what the problem was, I came up with four core things that my solution has to involve.

- It had to be a small footprint-facility.
- It has to be scalable. It has to be small enough to serve a tiny country like Botswana but scalable so that I could serve all the sixteen countries in the SADC (the South African Development Community, which includes sixteen countries in a trading block) if it needs to. A tiny country like Botswana struggles because it's rich enough to pay for its own drugs but isn't big enough to attract drug companies. As a drug company, you don't hit economies of scale to build a facility for its tiny population. It's only like 2 million people. You have to be able to think of how you can capture enough market size in that whole region even though you're in a tiny little country like Botswana.
- Within the facility, you have to have agile processes. You want to be able to switch from making one drug to another drug very comfortably because you don't necessarily have a guaranteed market for huge volumes, like what is currently manufactured.
- It has to be just in time. I could not get over the six-month thing. So, the idea of just-in-time manufacturing became super important. If someone needs drugs today, they have to be able to order their drugs today. There has to be some kind of manufacturing solution that enables that. It's not okay that it takes six months to get them their drugs.

These four things became the constraints I was working with. But I'm not an engineer. So, the next problem became, "How the hell is a pharmacist supposed to build?!"

I talked to my professors from college. I connected with my former colleagues and fellow students who were engineers. I started to read a lot of engineering textbooks. I signed up for manufacturing training. I had to study about this world that I had now found myself in.

In my travels and conversations, I came up with the idea of modular manufacturing, where I would retrofit shipping containers. If you're looking for something that's small footprint, scalable, and portable, you have shipping containers everywhere. So, how do I retrofit a shipping container to make it meet ISO and regulatory standards and be able to make drugs? So, I came up with this idea of a containerized drug manufacturing module and then started looking for engineers, architects, technologists, and quality management specialists–all the core people you would need to pull this off.

Next was how to reach economies of scale.

You have to have communications between all these modules so that a container in Botswana knows what you're making in South Africa. You can regulate what you make, depending on what is needed just in time. I started to piece together all the tech I was going to need and how I might build this distributed network of manufacturing. I got referred to an incubator in Boston which connected me to a bunch of researchers I hadn't known about. I found out that there was another startup that had this same idea of decentralized manufacturing that's modular. They call themselves On Demand Pharmaceuticals, which affirmed for me that this thing I'd come up with as a pharmacist is not wild.

Turns out, there's technology out there with studies and research behind it.

When COVID-19 Hit

In Canada, we've already had drug shortage problems that have progressively worsened over the past five years. We've had issues where we import medications, and the active pharmaceutical ingredients are polluted. For example, we've had to recall all the angiotensin receptor blockers for blood pressure. We had to recall all the ranitidine (Zantac) drugs because they had NDMA carcinogens in them.

When COVID hit this year, drug shortages that were already bad became critical. You now had these tier three drug shortages, which were important medications that were now shorted. So all of a sudden, the Canadian government starts to pay way more attention to the fact that we've been having drug shortages.

What COVID did in the most bizarre twist of circumstances is it opened an opportunity for me. It turned out that the top reasons for drug shortages accounting for >80% of the shortages, even in North America, were problems with manufacturing facilities, problems with manufacturing processes, and manufacturer discontinuations. In addition, polluted or toxic active pharmaceutical ingredients account for about 8% of these shortages. This meant that my solution targeting innovation in the facilities and processes was even insightful in Canada! Because our turnkey drug manufacturing facility is something that could also be used as an emergency response solution in Canada and contribute a solution to the Canadian drug shortage problem, I pitched it to the Canadian government. Then the National Research Council Industrial Research Assistance Program partnered with us.

Now we're looking to build the first minimum viable product in Alberta.

After we have tested it and used it here, the intention is to start shipping from Canada to the African countries I've developed relationships with. The intention is to register it here; we build it here. When it has a Health Canada stamp of approval, we can start to ship these solutions to different African countries. Then they will be able to manufacture their own meds just in time, in a very small footprint facility, locally, in a scalable fashion. My goal is that by 2023, we'll develop the first facilities, and we can start the tech transfer at some point in 2022/2023.

That's the story, and that's where I am now.

Morẹ́nikẹ́'s Reflections

On Belonging

I always make jokes that I feel interstitial in many ways; I'm not quite any one thing.

In Canada, I am a so-called visible minority. People always ask where I'm from. When I start to get comfortable as a Canadian, someone inevitably reminds me that I'm not either by a racist event or just an off-hand comment. I never quite feel 100% Canadian. When I go back to Nigeria, I'm not Nigerian anymore either. As much as I can talk the talk and speak my language, they can just smell me from afar that I haven't been in Nigeria for a while. So, I'm not quite Nigerian; I'm not quite Canadian. I'm a pharmacist, but am I really a pharmacist when I run this not-for-profit, and I'm building this startup?

When I think about my childhood, my mom's Christian, and my dad's Muslim. Am I Christian; am I Muslim? What does that even mean? People say they are introvert or extrovert. I did a personality test, and I showed up 49/51. So, I've always sort of just thought of myself as this interstitial character that just never quite picks a side. In almost every debate, I can make a very good argument for either direction on nearly any topic. (Although once it starts becoming about discrimination and racism, I can pick a side very quickly.)

Yet, I don't feel like someone without a home.

I think I have a home everywhere that I identify with. I think of home more in the feelings of home. When I think about my siblings, they feel like home. When I visit my sister in the States, that feels like home; my cousins in the UK that feels like home too. It's more in the feeling of belonging that's home for me. It's a feeling more than a place.

I don't feel like I am a person without a home. I feel like I have many homes.

On the Suffering of Racialized People

I can never be able to say why the white people in my pharmacy quit really. A common experience of racialized people and Black people is when you are experiencing something that is potentially racist, part of the reason it causes so much stress and turmoil is you're not actually able to put your finger on it. To say for sure that it is racism.

There's the suffering you're experiencing—my staff have left me—there's also the suffering you experience in trying to figure out if it was racism or not, or if there were cultural differences or if it was age differences or if it was a different way of leading. That uncertainty in itself is another layer of suffering. I can assure you that both sufferings are very real and very painful.

As the immigrant, as the racialized person, you experience two levels of suffering. And it's almost worse, that second layer, than if someone were to just say it to your face. It's easier for you to just know that that's what it was than the covert way we usually experience racism.

You never have that closure.

That experience is not unique to me. Several other store owners had that white flight experience too. What gives me comfort is even though I don't really quite know if it was stuff that was in my control or stuff that wasn't in my control, it's actually worked out so well for me that people who didn't want to work for me left. That is a good thing. Years later, I look back at the people that left, and I'm like, "Yes, I give thanks that you left."

When people who don't want to work stay with you in any discipline or field, it makes life so much harder for everybody.

On Seeing People As More than Units of Productivity

I've learned along the way that a lot of the things corporations do that they say would make them profitable are just lies. We keep lying to ourselves about things like the balanced scorecard and productivity trackers, and we make everything about human beings as units of productivity. I don't buy into that. It took me a while to make peace with the difference between how

I see people and how corporations see people.

Because, in reality, if you lead well and trust people, you're more profitable.

My natural inclination as a leader has always been to trust that my people in this pharmacy actually want what's best for my patients and that they are smart enough to self-govern. We all have our strengths, and it works well for all of us if we play into our strengths, gifts, and talents instead of spending all of our time performance-managing everybody to metrics, trying to make everyone fit into all these labor-unit boxes.

Thinking this way has been a lifesaver for me because when people can bring their whole self to work, and we function from a place of trust and strengths-based self-governing, what starts to happen is you OVER DELIVER on all these key performance indicators like profitability, patient care, and customer service. So I don't have to be at my pharmacy as often as you would imagine in a traditional corporatized structure. This strengths-based, trust-based leadership style has allowed me to maintain my Foundation and build my startup while overperforming at my pharmacy.

As a leader, I imagine myself as a gardener, which is ironic because I really suck at gardening. My husband says I have a thumb of death. But a gardener is the best analogy in this particular realm of building organizations and bringing people together to do things.

A gardener doesn't go plant a seed and then pull the plant out of the seed and then pull the fruit out of the plant. A gardener plants a seed, fertilizes it, waters it, figures out how much sunlight, figures out the environments in which there will be production, and focuses their energy there. Morning, noon, night, come rain, come shine, the Gardner helps the plants grow.

In my mind, this is what happens in my store.

People have come to know that I trust them. It took a while to get there! And some weeds had to be taken out. Together we set up our commitments to which we will be held to account. There is maintenance that has to be done. There is nurturing, thinking, speaking, and praying life into the organization. There is indeed holding people accountable to commitments; accountability is a secret sauce in building a high-trust environment. There is connecting with people, developing and nurturing those relationships—all that goes into it.

And yet I feel no obligation and no need to spend the whole of my days watching the seeds grow. When you take that approach to leadership, what happens is people show up as their best selves. People make far superior decisions often than what I, as the leader, would have done in that situation. Their decisions are better because they are closer to the problem.

Even though it's a tiny store in the grand scheme of things, I feel that this way of leadership is more life-affirming. It allows people to be themselves.

The way that feels good to me to lead allows me more freedom and allows the people working in my pharmacy more freedom. At the same time, we are more profitable. We consistently overachieve on the targets set for the store by the head office.

Some people are uncomfortable with this way of leading because they can't quantify or figure out the risk bubble that something fits into or what liability bubble it fits into.

There have been a lot of books that have changed the trajectory of my thinking or even my life. But this one, Reinventing Organizations: A Guide to Creating Organizations Inspired by the Next Stage of Human Consciousness by Frédéric Laloux, just validated the whole of me. I had been leading this way for years before reading Reinventing Organizations. So, when I read it, I'm like, "Oh, that's what I thought!"

It's this idea of a Teal Organization where organizations evolve towards self-management, wholeness, and a deeper sense of purpose. It borrows from a developmental lens of leadership around long-term growth and progression and looks at some of Ken Wilber's theories about consciousness. I like reading about other leaders who have similar ideas. In my position, it's easy for me to think I'm wild and that what I've been doing is nonsense, so learning from like-minded thinkers like this validates me.

On Living Your True Life

My husband and I have these red-flag conversations. About once a month or so, we sit down and talk about how we've each changed. I read a book or listened to a podcast about how couples wake up one day and don't recognize each other. Over the years, they changed little by little. I didn't want that. I thought, "What if we actually named it?" What if we sat down and actually said to each other how we've changed? Maybe we can track and trace how we've evolved over the years. In that conversation, we also talk about any "red flags" in our relationship. What things can we identify that look like risk in our relationship? We have actual conversations about this. We laugh off things that we can recognize as us making mountains out of molehills. We joke about things that are not real problems.

But for me, it makes me feel like I'm living my real life, that I'm being true to what makes me happy.

I really love the way we engage with each other, I love our relationship, the way we live with each other, the way we celebrate with each other–that brings me joy. Unfortunately, I find too many of us spend so much of our life wanting to fit in. My life experiences have brought me to a point where I just don't care much about fitting in.

I care more about being joyful from the depth of my heart.

The expectations society puts on relationships on couples and what families should look like, as with most things, are completely ungrounded and unrelated to my life and my reality. So, I just picked joy. In everything, I just pick what actually brings me joy, and I do that. I try to keep out the noise because nobody knows what it feels like to be him or me or you. And yet everyone feels like they have the right or the space to judge and have an opinion, which is so weird.

In this world, being true to what makes you happy and what brings you joy can be an act of courage.

On Creating Space for Children

My husband works as a manager for Amazon, and I do a hundred things. But, for my well-being, I want to scale back on how much I've taken on. So, I think I will leave my foundation; I will hand in my resignation to the board at the end of this year, which will leave more time for my startup.

Over the years, I've always been the person that does a lot at the same time. Now that I'm married and planning to have children, I don't want to have children and never be there. When we have children, I definitely want to be the kind of mom that is around a lot. I want to be a mom that my kids can talk to. That's going to influence how I build my startup and how I staff it. I want my colleagues to bring children to work with spaces built to accommodate families, not just workers. I've spent a lot of time thinking about how to build my company in ways that build our families too.

When you have children or babies around and spaces for family at work, people are kinder to each other. I think it's hard for you to be, forgive my language, a dickhead when your children are there.

I'm so early in this path of family life that I don't have advice yet; it's more like a wish. I wish that as we raise our sons, we raise men who can see themselves in, empathize with, and be fair about people who identify in a diversity of identities, including gender. A key point of change in society comes from family life in how we raise people, especially those who identify as men, so they can embrace their wholeness and the wholeness of others.

It's still a pretty patriarchal society. But if men can embrace their masculinity and their femininity and their ability to be vulnerable and their ability to be fair, that will enable society to be better overall.

So that's my wish, that we raise people to be fair and empathetic.

On "Leaving Space for God"

Remember that personality I described earlier where I said that if I decide to do something, I will die on that hill doing that thing? I used to be a really religious person. I'm not so much anymore; I guess I'm more spiritual now. And what I've recognized is that I can either force myself into a whole bunch of work and a whole bunch of accomplishments and really kill myself doing it, or I can live my life in my strengths, gifts, and talents. It's not that these things are easy and comfortable; there are challenges in living that life too. But there has to be a balance. I've come to describe it as "leaving space for God," where somewhere deep down, intuitively, I know the things that I should struggle for and the things I shouldn't.

My advice to my younger self is to live in your strengths, skills, gifts, and talents to the best of your ability but to leave space for God. To actually acknowledge that some things are beyond your reach. This is something that you can only know intuitively. It's not something that's completely rational. It's a different way of knowing that I think we all have.

But, over years of western education and knowledge systems, we've lost that intuitive, deeper knowing.

I would tell my younger self to make peace with what you have and do the most with it. But also to trust that there are things beyond your control in life. The best will happen when you do what's within your control, within your gifts, strengths, and power. Trust in yourself. But then also trust in life. You have to trust in a force beyond you, trust the process, trust the journey, trust that you're doing all that you can in your space and that there is something beyond you that also enables what you're doing.

You've put your best foot forward, and the rest will happen in a way that is not in your control.

COVID came fraught with a lot of guilt with the knowledge that this thing that is hurting so many people is actually the thing that is enabling my startup. This idea of creative destruction, where a forest goes on fire, but that forest fire is essential for new growth. This year has been creative destruction for me in a lot of ways. There's also the Black Lives Matter movement that has resurged. My Foundation work is more or less likely going to be funded now because of that, even though we've been saying the same thing for years about Black health inequity, Black injustices, and health disparity for Black people as a public health issue. This hasn't been something that any funder cared about listening to for a while. And then this year, when George Floyd dies, all this pandemonium ensues, and now we're getting the ears of funders.

The Jungian way of saying what I'm saying is called synchronicity, which holds that events are meaningful coincidences. Some things happen that are entirely beyond me. And now that I know this, it's still a practice for me of trusting I'm going to do what is within my power, and then there is a process to life that is beyond me–whatever we call it, nature, God, life, process–that also enables me once I have done my part. It's not all within my control.

Making peace with that over the years has been crucial.

On Final Thoughts

I don't want to come off as someone who's got it all figured out because I'm pretty far from feeling that way. Life is a giant school, and I'm always hungry to learn more.

I hope for any young African girl reading the book to know that all the things that make you unique and stand out are very important. In all the education and in all the learning you will go through, don't lose that. I want you to embrace yourself in the fullness of your identity, even when it doesn't conform or doesn't belong in these spaces where you find yourself. It is not conforming, not fitting in, and not belonging that will attract your calling, purpose, and tribe you belong with. That's pretty important. Ironically, the things that are now celebrated about me were not the things that made me feel like I fit in or belonged anywhere.

If you feel like that, I want you to know that you are valid, and your tribe, they'll come. And it's also important to know that if you don't feel like you belong in the spaces you're finding yourself in, you can create your own space.

You can create what makes sense to you, and you belong there. That's my message.

Janet Kavandi, PhD

Astronaut Hall of Fame Class of 2019. Former Center Director at NASA's Glenn Research Center, President of Sierra Space, an aerospace company.

Sierra Space is building a new commercial spacecraft for NASA. We're working on a new space plane, space stations, lunar habitats, and lunar landers. Ultimately, we want to push habitats to Mars.

Prior to this job, I was the center director for the Glenn Research Center, one of NASA's ten centers. We did everything from low-speed wind tunnel tests to hypersonic testing. We worked on components for the service module for Orion's spacecraft, which contains the propulsion and power for NASA's next crew module. The Orion capsule will return to the moon as part of the Artemis program. In Greek mythology, Artemis was the sister of Apollo. NASA named its new lunar program the Artemis program because NASA plans to put the first woman on the surface of the moon in this decade.

I am a veteran of three space flights.

Tragedy Strikes Early

My childhood is a bit of a sad story. I was born in Missouri in a very small town of about 1,100 people. I had two working parents. My dad worked for the county, and my mom was a secretary at the county courthouse. It was a really great childhood at that point. I was pretty much a tomboy and loved being out in the country. I was the type of kid who was climbing trees, fishing, digging in the garden, riding horses, and raising baby chicks—a very hands-on, outdoorsy, adventurous kind of kid. I didn't like to go into the kitchen to bake cakes and things like that. That wasn't me.

My dad was a private pilot, and unfortunately, my mom and dad perished in an airplane accident when another plane collided with their plane in midair.

I was eight years old. That was a huge disruption to my early childhood.

My dad had been a really nurturing father. I remember being with him in his hangar while he worked on his airplane. He would ask me to hand him the wrench and let me think I helped him fix things. He was very encouraging and involved with us. For Christmas, I got Barbie dolls, but I also got a toy medical kit because my dad always encouraged me to dream big and think about all the things I could do.

Even though this was in the 1960s, he was not the stereotypical "your job is to be a good housewife" kind of father. It was also unusual that my mother was a working mom because most mothers at that time stayed at home. So I saw early in life that both parents could work, and they encouraged me to do what I liked.

One of my favorite memories from my time with my dad was before my parents died. We would lie outside on our patio at night in the summer and look at all the stars. Since we lived in the country, you could see the Milky Way under the brilliant, beautiful night sky. We could also see the early satellites passing over our heads. My dad would ask me, "Gosh, what do you think it would be like to be on that satellite right now? Or to be able to look back at the earth from there? Wouldn't that be amazing?!" Right then was probably the moment that inspired me to really think big. To think about what it would look like to be able to look back at the earth. Would you see our house? Would you see a city? I had no idea what you could actually be able to see, but I liked to imagine what it would be like to go into space. At this time, it was still the beginning of the US space program. We had received President Kennedy's challenge to go to the moon, and we were in the space race with the Russians. So, it was a period of intense focus on getting to the moon first.

I remember those nighttime conversations with my dad, and I guess they stuck with me.

After my parents died, my sister and I went to live with our aunt and uncle. They did a wonderful thing by taking us in. It was very generous of them, but we missed that nurturing atmosphere that we had experienced with our parents. At our new home, we had to get our homework done, go to our rooms, and stay there. My aunt and uncle weren't very social people. We really weren't allowed to have friends over.

So, it was a very isolating time for the next ten years.

Education Meant Freedom

After moving in with my aunt and uncle, I just focused on doing well in school, working hard, and being the best student I could be.

I really loved my math classes and was more comfortable talking about the science and engineering side of things. I even tutored my friends in math; I was not in the cool clique; I was in the nerdy kid clique. I was not the prom queen. I was not a cheerleader. I was voted most studious in high school.

You just accept that you're going to be the nerdy kid and maybe the smart kid.

Although I had an aptitude for math, I studied really hard. It gave me pride to understand topics like math and science when I worked hard at them. I wasn't a prodigy or anything close to that; it didn't come naturally. I didn't think about whether math and science were geared toward girls or boys.

I just did math and science because I really liked them.

I was typically only one of two or three females in most of my classes. While taking chemistry, maybe a quarter of the class was female. When I went on to advanced classes for my master's and, ultimately my Ph.D., there were significantly more men than women. I never really thought about it until somebody pointed out, "You're the only girl in the class." I'm like, "Really? I guess I am." But it didn't matter to me.

As I got older, I knew we didn't have money for me to go to college, but I also knew I didn't want to be dependent on a husband to give me things in life. I just wanted to be able to take care of myself, which meant I needed an education. Education meant freedom to me. Freedom and the ability to choose my own path in life.

But I knew I needed a scholarship, so my focus in high school was to get a scholarship so that I could afford to go to college.

I graduated high school in 1977. I ended up being valedictorian of my class and getting a full scholarship to the local University, including tuition and books. All I had to pay for was my room and board, which I did with a little bit of income from my parents' social security until I turned twenty-two.

I chose chemistry as my major because I had a very inspirational high school chemistry teacher. Most people didn't like her because she was so tough. She didn't coddle people. But I really appreciated that she was demanding. She challenged me.

I wasn't advised to be an engineer because I don't think my advisors knew a lot about it, or maybe they just didn't think girls did engineering. Had I known what engineering was, I probably would have majored in engineering. Instead, I studied chemistry and ultimately achieved a Ph.D.

Chemistry came in very handy throughout my career because it allowed me to provide a diversity of thought in a field where I worked mostly with engineers. It's essential in any kind of job to have diversity of gender, of education, of background, etc. Scientists are trained to approach problems differently than engineers. When you have a scientist challenging some of the engineering approaches, it can be frustrating to the engineers, but it makes people stop and consider a different perspective.

Ultimately, I was lucky that I ended up training as a scientist versus an engineer. It's always served me well to provide that additional insight that a traditionally trained engineer might not have. I provided the scientific perspective to a lot of problems that we faced, and in turn, I also learned a lot about engineering from my fellow engineers.

Reaching for the Stars

I became interested in becoming an astronaut after President Kennedy's space race speech during those long talks with my dad. The United States had already started flying the Mercury and Gemini programs and was just beginning the Apollo program.

You've heard of the Mercury Seven—it was the John Glenn's and Allen Shepherd's and all those guys who were flying when I was starting to think about being an astronaut. All were military test pilots, and there were no women. When I was in high school and thinking seriously about the possibility of being an astronaut, they had just started selecting women, scientists, and engineers in addition to military test pilots.

My dream became possible right about the time I was getting out of high school, which gave me the added incentive to say, "It's my time! I could actually possibly qualify for this if I work hard enough."

From then on, it was all about, "How do I get there? How do I qualify myself? How would I compete with all these brilliant people who would share this honor?"

I rushed through my undergrad studies in three years to get a whole year of my master's program while I was still eligible for my parents' social security to pay for my room and board. I also had a teaching assistant job and a research assistantship to cover my tuition. I was almost done with my master's degree at the University of Missouri, Rolla, now called Missouri University of Science and Technology, before I ran out of money.

Just before I turned twenty-three, I got married and got a job at a company that made batteries for aerospace and defense applications.

After a couple of years, I applied for and was accepted into the Ph.D. program at the University of Texas. I chose Texas to be close to Houston and the Johnson Space Center, where I ultimately wanted to apply to the space program. I would have had to quit working and be a poor student again. But before I decided to move, I was offered a job in Seattle at the Boeing Aerospace company. I told them I would like to return to school to finish my Ph.D. They said, "Okay, we'll pay for your college education if you come to work for us." I was like, "Ooh, problem solved!"

So, my husband and I moved to Seattle. I worked at the Boeing Aerospace company. The University of Washington would not allow a part-time Ph.D. candidate, and Boeing needed me to work full-time. Therefore, I went in at 7 a.m. and worked till 10 a.m. Then, I'd drive to the University to take classes until midday, and in the evening, I would go back to work until seven at night. I still got my Ph.D. in four years.

I wanted my Ph.D. thesis to be space related. I came close. It was aeronautics related, having to deal with a new pressure-sensitive paint that you could apply to an aerodynamic surface, like an aircraft model. It would do pressure mapping over that model in real-time. We got patents for that invention, and it's still used in aeronautics research today, which is pretty cool.

Ironically, when I went to the Glenn Research Center many years later, I learned that NASA used much of the technology from that research when designing NASA and other commercial aircraft.

Getting Close to Houston

Everything I did in my education and work was to intentionally get close enough to Houston to visit the Space Center and figure out how to be more competitive for the space program. I looked at the astronauts' biographies at the time; about thirty to fifty percent of the people in the space program were military test pilots. I was not qualifying through that route. About half of the folks in the office were scientists and engineers.

I started applying while I was still in my Ph.D. program. In my application, I would say, "I'm working on a Ph.D. at the University of Washington. I'm working in the aerospace field at Boeing. My title is aerospace engineer." I would tell them, "I am designing power systems for spacecraft, although my doctoral research is on a different topic." I didn't want to be "typecast;" I wanted to show my diversity of skill sets as a scientist and as an engineer. As soon as I graduated with my Ph.D., I was asked to come and interview at NASA.

That was a wonderful day!

They cycle the interviews every two to four years, depending on the need. I graduated with my Ph.D. in 1990. My son was born in 1991, almost exactly nine months after I graduated. My daughter was born two and a half years after that. The selection process was in 1994. There was a four-year gap from when I graduated to the first opportunity to interview. I'd had my two kids in between while I was still working at Boeing aerospace. The timing was just perfect.

I was selected in that first interview process, which was lucky. Usually, people go through two or three interview processes. So I was really, really fortunate. I started in March of 1995 at NASA in the fifteenth class of astronauts.

The Right Stuff

I had all those wonderful things happen within five years–I got my Ph.D., we had our two kids, and I was selected to be an astronaut. So it was a really cool time.

And then it got better.

During the two years of basic training as an astronaut, we went through all the technical and simulator training, we got to travel to all the different NASA centers to see what they did, and we got exposure to the media and politics and Washington. So it was a very exciting time.

For my first space mission, I got to visit and train in Russia and go to Mir, the Russian Space Station, which has now deorbited.

It was a dream come true.

"When I was sitting on the launch pad looking around the spaceship, I thought, "I can't believe I'm here." Then the engines lit. I felt the vibrations and then lift off. I was like, "I'm actually going to space; this is what I've been waiting for my whole life!" I remember the tears coming down and going right into my ears. I couldn't believe it was actually happening.

When I returned, I was immediately reassigned to a second space flight, a Shuttle Radar Topography Mission. The point of that mission was to map the entire earth at a very high resolution. It was an eleven-day mission sponsored by the National Geospatial Agency, where we mapped 95 percent of the earth's mass surface.

My last mission was in 2001, which was to help build the International Space Station. We added the airlock onto the space station—the piece where we astronauts go outside to do spacewalks. It was a really, really fun and fast-paced time.

During the time I was flying, the trickiest part was trying to balance family life with two young children in preschool and elementary school. My husband, an airline pilot, was flying a lot too. As a mom, I was always trying to manage time, maintaining family unity while still being able to do my job. I credit my husband a huge amount for bidding his flights around my schedule so that he could be home with the kids when I wasn't there, and I could be there when he was traveling. If we both had to travel at the same time, his parents would come and stay with our kids. I really owe a lot to him, his family, and some of our neighbors who would pick the kids up after school and babysit for an hour or two.

Disaster in the Skies

In 2003, shortly after my third space flight, the Space Shuttle Columbia disaster happened. All seven crew members were killed. Three of my classmates were on Columbia; my best friend was on there. It was just devastating and the beginning of a very sad time.

For my best friend's family, I became the Casualty Assistance and Calls Officer (CACO), a military term that NASA adopted for the person who helps the family after a traumatic accident. After a period of time, I was asked to be the CACO for all seven families. I represented their needs to the NASA Administrator for consideration. I arranged all the memorials and the Arlington cemetery burial.

The crew recovery was a very difficult time for me. It was a traumatic time for my kids, too. They saw what I was going through, what I was doing. Of course, their first response was, "Mom, we don't want you to fly anymore." They knew. Ironically, my daughter was eight years old at the time, the same age I was when my parents died in the plane crash.

She and my son were both very protective at that point, especially my daughter. Whenever we ever talked about me returning to space, it became a very emotional event. She would have nightmares and run crying and crawling into bed with me. Eventually, it became clear that I wouldn't fly again. I was offered several more flight opportunities, but it was so traumatic for my kids that I told the Chief of the Astronaut Office that I just couldn't do that to them.

I loved flying, but I had asked my family to sacrifice too much for me at this point. I now wanted to dedicate my time to helping them become successful and reach their own goals in life.

My son is now an engineer, and my daughter has a master's degree in biology. They both did really well in school. I'm so proud of them. But it was hard to get there, trying to balance essentially four careers. Each child's career and our careers happened because we helped each other out and sacrificed for each other at different points in our lives. That's what a family does. You love each other, you sacrifice for each other, you help each other out, and you help each other succeed.

Return to Flight

I took a management role in the Astronaut Office, where I was the astronaut representative for the International Space Station and the experiments onboard. As part of the CACO process, I became deputy chief of the Astronaut Office.

During my time there, we successfully brought the Shuttle back and returned to flight.

When we started flying again, I became deputy director of Flight Crew Operations, the director just above the Astronaut Office. It encompassed the Astronaut Office and the Aircraft Operations of all the T38, the high-altitude WB 57, and the Guppy, the large-capacity airplane that carried International Space Station modules inside of it.

After a couple of years, I became director of Flight Crew Operations and was in that position as we flew out the remaining shuttle flights. I helped assign the crews and participated in selection boards. The Astronaut selection board I chaired was the first time we ever selected an equal number of men and women. That was a proud moment, but it wasn't as intentional as some people thought: "Well, there's a female chair, so of course they had to pick women to make up half of the crew." That wasn't the case at all. We just had women in really remarkable positions. We were able to select an F18 Marine fighter pilot. We had an army helicopter pilot with two hundred plus combat missions under her belt. We had our researcher who had done biological research in Antarctica and all over the world. And we had an engineer who ran an NOAA station pretty much all by herself in the South Pacific—she fixed everything that broke, everything. She had to.

It wasn't an intentional "Look for females." They were just so accomplished that they came out to be in the top eight contenders, every bit as deserving as the men.

It was cool to see that transition during my lifetime and during the period when I was in the office.

Getting the Call

After my time as Flight Crew Operations director, I got to do some of the medical stuff that I really liked.

I became deputy director of Health and Human Performance at NASA's Johnson Space Center, where they monitored much of the medical experimentation work. The Johnson Center decides what kind of research we can allow to be conducted on humans in space to help NASA prepare for long-duration missions to the moon and eventually to Mars. For instance, you receive more radiation when you're in space than on Earth, so you need to know how that affects the human body: Is it affecting women differently than men? Which organs are targeted? How about the bone loss issue—how do we study that, and how do we supplement bone loss? We studied muscle loss in space, too, due to atrophy of muscles, as well as intracranial pressure increases and the effects on vision.

Then I got this phone call out of the blue from the Center director at the Glenn Research Center. He said, "Hey, I'm looking for a deputy for the Center in Cleveland." At first, I thought there was no way I would move to

Cleveland. Then I thought about it; I'd worked with them before and knew it was an amazing workforce. I thought this would be a really cool opportunity, so I visited the Center.

Since I went into management, I have grown in my leadership skills, going from being a scientist to an astronaut, running some of the small directorates within the Astronaut Office to becoming chief and then finally director. I learned a leadership style that worked for me. This was an opportunity to test it on a much larger scale, to run a whole center.

My husband and I talked about the opportunity, and ultimately, I took the position. I would commute up to Cleveland during the week and be back in Houston on the weekends. We made that work for five years. It was wonderful. I really loved it.

After my first year there, the Center director took another position at NASA headquarters, and the administrator asked me to take over as director. I got to set up a really great team, establish a new culture, and lead us to become a really well-oiled machine that worked exceptionally well together.

During this time, we generated "Glenn's 7 Expected Behaviors" for my leadership team, and I put that in their performance evaluations. We decided on "Seven" because of the Friendship Seven spacecraft that John Glenn flew. In turn, he named it Friendship Seven after the original seven astronauts; he was taking all of his friends with him to space. So, of course, the Center was also named after him, and so were these guidelines. John Glenn was a wonderful human being. We then flowed the expected behaviors down to the entire population in the Center. They're not unusual expectations and are common for most organizations.

NASA Glenn 7 Expected Behaviors

1. **Helping All to Succeed.** Embracing diversity and innovation and being inclusive of others in the execution of our goals and objectives. Identifying opportunities and assisting others to succeed.
2. **Excellence.** Being the best technically; producing results that exceed objectives and deliverables and continually learning and improving personally and professionally.
3. **Respect.** Demonstrating esteem, admiration, and appreciation toward others and ourselves. Suggestions are respectfully acknowledged and considered for incorporation.
4. **Openness.** Providing access to knowledge and information about our mission, organizations, facilities, workforce, and programs and projects.
5. **Integrity.** Knowing the right thing to do and committing to do the right thing.

6. **Cooperation.** Seeking first to understand; proactively partnering and supporting our peers for the benefit of the Agency and the Center.
7. **Safety.** Demonstrating a vigilant commitment to a safe work environment through good situational awareness and communication.

Going Beyond

Then I came to the point when I could retire from NASA, though I wanted to work for about five more years. So after being a civil servant for a long time, twenty-five years, I had one more chance to try something different.

I decided to work with the commercial side of space.

NASA will continue doing deep-space exploration with the lunar and the Mars programs, and commercial companies will take over some of the low earth orbit (LEO) transportation, The Dream Chaser spaceplane at Sierra Space—the company I now work for, is an example. The Dream Chaser will visit a space station and bring payloads and people back to a runway like the Space Shuttle did.

That brings me to where I am today. I am president at Sierra Space, a commercial aerospace company. I'm kind of doing what I did at NASA's Glenn Research Center. I'm helping the CEO build a cohesive team that works well together, is very efficient, and has a singular goal in mind of launching this vehicle, bringing it back safely and becoming a successful player in the commercial space field.

I've been very fortunate in life.

Janet's Reflections

On the Power of Encouragement

If you think there's a possibility you can achieve something, don't overthink it. For me, I never considered I couldn't do something. Maybe that came from my dad giving me that doctor's kit for Christmas. "You mean I can be the doctor, not the nurse?" My dad was like, "Oh yeah, sure you can! Why wouldn't you be able to? You are as smart as anybody else." Coincidentally, I had a female pediatrician too, which was rare during the sixties. I did consider being a cardiac surgeon for a while, which was my fallback if I didn't get into the astronaut corps. I was really fascinated with medicine, especially surgery.

If I ever had any doubts, I would hear my dad's voice: "You can do anything." I must admit a lot of what I did was because I really wanted to make him proud. Unfortunately, I lost him too early. He was my champion. He was the guy who really motivated me, who gave me hope. He was the guy who said that I could do it. He was the one who let me hold the wrenches and showed me how to do technical things that you didn't normally get to do as a young girl. I just wanted to show him that all his efforts and love would not go to waste.

When I speak to middle and high school students and parents, I tell the parents, "You have no idea how significant your words can be, even if they're sometimes expressed in challenging times," like, "No, you will turn in that assignment. You're not going to give up. You ARE going to take this test tomorrow. You're not going to stay home and pretend to be sick. You are going to persevere. You're gonna make it." And they're mad at you, right? They're like, "No, I'm not; this is impossible. I hate this. I don't want to do it!"

I tell parents what's important is to give your children guidance and enforce your words, to be rigid about schoolwork, to help kids learn to set up goals for themselves, to encourage them to find something that works for them, to follow their intuitions, and to never give up. I tell the kids we all have to do things we don't want to do, but if we persevere and keep on pushing ourselves if we don't quit and don't give up, we will be so much happier in ten years because we'll have so many more choices ahead of us, which will lead to a better life.

On Two-Career Families

My husband had always wanted to be a pilot, and I had always wanted to be an astronaut. We both got to do what we wanted in our careers and have a family as well. We have had such fortunate lives in that respect.

But making it work as a two-career family can be every bit as challenging as the leadership and technical skills you must acquire for your job. First, if you're married, you and your spouse must support each other's careers. At times, I sacrificed for my husband, and at times, he sacrificed for me.

For example, I sacrificed for him when our kids were born, and he was based out of New Mexico. He would have to commute back and forth between two states. When I was pregnant and raising our little ones as an engineer at Boeing, I did that myself most of the time. It wasn't entirely a single-mom situation because he would come home and help on the weekends but getting up for the 2 a.m. feedings and all that other stuff was mostly on me, as well as taking them to the doctor and daycare and then going to work and being sleep deprived. I supported him when he needed to build his career, and then he supported me when I needed to build mine. He moved from our really nice home in Seattle, a place we loved, to Houston for my astronaut career. He was also supportive when I moved to Cleveland, and we were living apart. So, that sacrifice for each other was essential.

To raise your kids to succeed, you need to be a mom or dad when you are home. For example, even though I was really busy at work, when I came home, I had to become a mom. I had to make dinner. I had to wash the clothes. I had to help with the homework. I had to give them baths and read bedtime stories every night. Then after we had said our "I love you's" and they fell asleep, I was back to being the professional working again on my computer until ridiculous hours in the morning just to keep up.

Later, when the kids were going to college in the Houston area, where we still had a house, I was commuting to Cleveland and running the Center while my husband was flying all over the world internationally. So it was a very weird time when our family was scattered to the winds.

But we made it work. We're still together, and the kids are doing great.

Oh, there were stresses for sure, especially in high school and the early college years, that phase all parents and teens go through, but in the end, we ended up great. When you have a life like mine, there isn't a lot of "me time" for things like manicures and massages. I don't want to discourage people, but the family-career thing does take a lot of sacrifices and hard work. It's very fulfilling, though. I got to do it all, and I don't regret any of it!

On Naysayers and Allies

My advice to young women is to follow what feels natural for them. For me, it was a natural path toward wanting to do science, math, and engineering. I knew that if I studied hard enough, I could compete with anyone, and I proved that I could. I never thought that I couldn't do it. I told myself, "You can do this. Never give up. If you don't try it, you can never become it."

You just can't worry about what other people think is the right thing for you to do. I did experience discouragement from others. If I didn't have my dad's encouragement at the beginning of my life, telling me to never give up and giving me that shove in the back to "go do it, you can do it," I might've had more self-doubt. But because he had given me all of that, I just learned not to worry about what others thought.

I learned, though, that I couldn't tell most people I wanted to be an astronaut. I would get made fun of: "You're going to be an astronaut? Janet, women aren't astronauts; besides, you must be a military test pilot." My husband was the first guy who didn't laugh at me when I said it. Instead, he said, "Okay. Cool. Let's make it happen. I know you can do it!" So again, I had another important guy in my life who acknowledged that I could do it if I wanted to. I never had to fight him about that, and he supported me with encouragement and by making his own sacrifices. That was so helpful.

On Living a No Regrets Life

The main theme of my story is to never give up trying to make things happen.

It got really hard in college while I was doing my bachelor's degree in three years and had twenty-one hours per semester versus the normal seventeen. One semester I had organic chemistry, physics, computer science, and calculus, all at the same time, not trivial classes. So, over my desk, I put in big block letters, underlined with exclamation marks, the Winston Churchill quote, "NEVER GIVE UP!!". At two in the morning, when I was studying for my exams, I looked up to see those words: "NEVER GIVE UP!!". And I had a picture of an astronaut floating in space underneath those words. I knew that if I gave up and was tempted to go to sleep at two in the morning, I would fail that physics class, and everything would go down the drain. I just could not quit. At that time, I did not have enough money to make my time in college stretch any longer. I was between that rock and that hard place. But I had to do it. And so, I did it, and it paid off. You must be disciplined enough that you're willing to make sacrifices to make it happen.

Among the other quotes I liked and wrote out for myself, there's also the John Kennedy quote, "We do these things not because they are easy, but because they are hard." That's also very inspirational. Just pick one quote or make up your own.

If you have the fortitude and stick to it, you can persevere and accomplish great things. Half of it is just a battle with yourself to get there and not quit.

At the end of my life, I want to look back, smile, and think, "There wasn't anything I wanted to do that I didn't try. I tried it all. Even if I didn't succeed, at least I tried to make it happen." I don't want to have any regrets at that point in my life— that I should have treated somebody better or that I should have done something in a different way.

I want to say, "I tried it and did the best I could!"

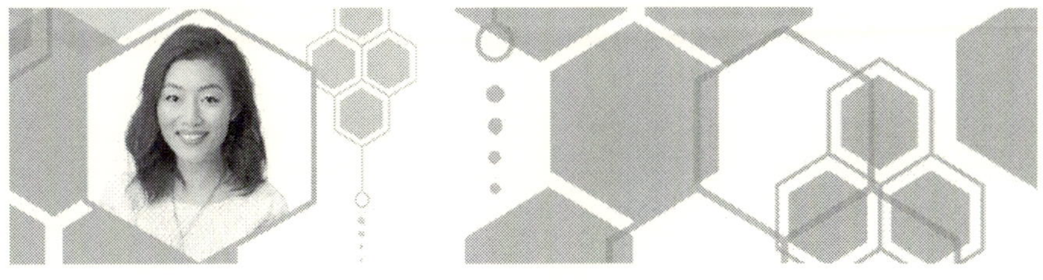

Melanie Chang Goldey

COO & CFO, TMRW Life Sciences, Inc.

I'm Chief Operating Officer & Chief Financial Officer of a life sciences technology company, TMRW Life Sciences. We have developed the world's first and only software-guided specimen management system for the frozen eggs and embryos used in in vitro fertilization (IVF).

A Father's Gift

I was born in the suburbs outside of Portland, Oregon, in a town called Beaverton. When I was young, nobody knew where that was, but most people know of it today as the hometown and headquarters of Nike, the sports company. It was also the headquarters for several semiconductor companies and burgeoning tech companies, like Intel, Tektronix, and lots more. As a child, I didn't realize the impact that growing up near these tech companies would have on me.

My brother and I were born in the United States, but both of my parents immigrated to the US when they were fairly young. My father was from Taiwan, and my mother was from Hong Kong. So, we were first generation. They came here with their families and immediately started to work. My mother was a seamstress at Jantzen Swimwear, also based in the Portland area. After saving up some money, she took some English classes at a community college. She didn't see herself working in a factory at an early age, so she moved on with better English and worked at a bank. My father created light boxes for photographers to look at film and sold the marketing rights to a large drafting equipment manufacturer. After that, he started an import/export business for drafting equipment, office supplies, and desk lights.

My father was a big figure in shaping who I am and where I am today. He never liked doing the import/export business. It was fine; it paid the bills. But he didn't really have any passion for it. There was a lot of travel, and it was pretty hard. So, in his spare time, he taught himself how to code. He ended up creating a point-of-sale (POS) solution for small retail businesses, mom-and-pop stores on the West Coast. It was a sales program that they could use to sell their products.

He went up and down the West Coast selling this point-of-sale solution. It was so entrepreneurial and risky, but it was something he was truly passionate about. Over the years, that started to evolve, and he eventually became an information technology (IT) consultant, which was how he spent the rest of his career before he retired. He was helping companies with their network infrastructure, IT departments, etc. He would go in and help set it up and then help them hire a team before moving on to the next one. So my father's career evolved over nearly two decades.

I remember sitting in my father's den in our house. It wasn't very big; it was modest. But we had this room that he would use as his office, and I would sit in it with him, and he'd be taking apart motherboards and putting other things together while I would be playing with the same motherboards or playing with the chips like a kid would play with blocks. I have old photographs of me sitting there just playing with computer chips and other equipment. Again, I had no idea at the time the impact it would have on me. What it did for me was drive this innate understanding of technology, where I learned to have a natural comfort with it and an understanding of how quickly technology changes. When you're, a month seems like a really long time, and it seemed like he was always coming home with all these new "toys," I'd be like, "Oh, it's so different." The pace with which I understood technology could change was apparent to me then and in a way that I would recognize later in my life.

When I was in high school, the online chat program ICQ came out, which was a competitor to AOL's Instant Messenger. My friends in high school and I would be like, "Oh my god!" We'd do our dial-up modem, we'd get on late at night, and we'd sit there talking over ICQ. I remember exactly what it looked like. It was so bulky, a terrible interface, but it was the cool, latest, new thing, and we were absorbed. I've always believed that technology can really change people's lives because I was always at the forefront.

A Mother's Gift

My mother stopped working after she gave birth to my brother. She threw herself into her family and raised her kids. I'm very fortunate that she was able to spend so much time with us. She's the one who really helped shape my values of resiliency, grit, and honesty. She always said, "You must be honest with everyone and yourself." She was a big champion of whatever I did. I realized later in life that, coming from a traditional Asian background, she was expected to be "the mom." I don't think she ever wanted to be a seamstress, but I do think she, in the back of her mind, had always felt, "Well, what would it have been like if I could have had a career?"

When she looks at me now, she always says how proud she is that I was able to have one. So today, whenever the company I work for announces something or if I have any news, the first people I send them to are my parents. They are ultimately my biggest champions. My successes have all been because of them.

Dabbling in a Lot of Things

I didn't know what I wanted to be when I grew up. I kind of just dabbled in a lot of different things. I played the piano for ten years. I also attended modeling school when I was four. When I was three, my older brother would go to school every day, and I would cry and cry, "I want to go to school." My mom would say, "Well, you can't go yet." So, she put me in modeling school, a little odd perhaps, but it was recommended by a friend of hers. I guess that was a thing in the eighties, or perhaps just an interesting social experiment. I started to do print ads for local companies, including Hannah Anderson, headquartered in Portland, and one of my longest gigs.

Modeling back then wasn't what it is stereotypically thought of today. It wasn't pageantry. I was young, and it was just fun to me. "We're going to take some fun pictures, and then you get to see them in a magazine." But I had to show up. I had to be poised. I had to interact. My mom wasn't a stage mom, so there was no pressure. Sometimes I didn't get jobs, and I had to understand the failure around that. I say failure broadly; I had to understand that I wasn't going to get everything I wanted. I had to deal with the disappointment. So I was able to learn social development concepts in a constructive way.

That whole experience taught me self-confidence and an understanding of social engagement. It gave me the chance to explore that playful side of me. It was an exciting and formative experience for my ability to assert myself in STEM and finance — both heavily male-dominated environments.

Joy Luck and Curiosity

Over time, I pivoted and started acting. I learned how to express myself, take on different roles and characters, and reflect on who I am and how I can become a certain role. When I was ten, I landed a pretty meaningful role in a major motion picture. The character I played was a firstborn Chinese American girl with a set of traditional parents and customs to whom I could genuinely relate. It was a pivotal moment because it was another opportunity for me to have the self-esteem and confidence to get up in front of the camera and, because of the nature of the role, to hold up a mirror to my identity as a first-generation Asian American woman.

The film was *The Joy Luck Club*, based on the book by Amy Tan.

In hindsight, it was such an important thing to have happened to me because it helped to affirm my identity and my heritage and empower me as a woman and a child of immigrants. It brought so much of my heritage to light, even my relationship with my mother. My mother is very traditional in her practice of Asian culture, kind of a tiger mom in some ways, with a focus on academics and career success. But she was also pulled toward Western culture where children here are taught to pursue and explore their passions. "Oh, it's okay if you major in art history. Go for it." That is not a traditional Chinese thing to say. So, there was all this stuff going on in my childhood that I was only able to make real sense of later in life.

What stuck with me from my childhood was the deep love of learning and curiosity my parents instilled in me. The very little money that my parents had, they spent on buying me books and taking my brother and me on trips to places where we would learn something. Washington, DC, New York, and France were big trips for us, especially coming from Portland. When I found technology later in life, it was that natural affinity I had for it, coupled with the curiosity that had been nurtured in me as a child, that made me really want to understand how things work and how we can use technology to make things better.

Cancer and College

My mother was diagnosed with cancer in my junior year of high school. I had applied to colleges and had gotten into a few schools. I was making all the normal plans kids do, and then we found out this terrible news. I really didn't know what to do with it.

Luckily, it was caught early on and wasn't late stage. But it was a very big question mark. I decided to stay home and go to the state school, which was a two-hour drive from my house, so that, God forbid, if anything happened, I could be there. And so that my father could pay for her medical treatments. I got a scholarship to the state university, which helped my family financially.

We were very fortunate; she got through it. When she went into remission and after we knew she was going to be okay, she sat me down, and she said, "You didn't really want to stay here. You wanted to go and try something new. You applied to all these different schools." She urged me to transfer. I was like, "Huh. That's an interesting idea." It was an incredible sacrifice for her to say that to me. Her own experiences had shifted her perspective because the more logical and traditional thing for her to have said was, "Stay home. Be near me; family stays together," that kind of thing. She was an incredible beacon of strength and incredibly intentional.

I did end up transferring. It's crazy, but that was a critical turning point for me. I ended up moving across the country, but not on purpose. I applied to a bunch of schools again as a transfer, and the one I found really special was Wellesley, an all-women's liberal arts college outside of Boston. I didn't know anybody there. I only knew people in Oregon, and I had some cousins in California and a couple of relatives in Washington. Most of my friends from high school stayed close to home. So, I just took a leap and said, "Look, this will be really good for me. It'll be a chance to figure myself out and what I want to do." So, that was another really good decision, again, pushed and supported by my mom.

During my time in college, even though it was liberal arts, I learned I had a knack for quantitative analytics, logic, and data. A part of my father came through in me. I took a few computer science classes and loved it, that way of thinking — how to think logically about something, how to think ahead, if/then statements, nesting, and all of that. It was just so interesting to me because I was like, "Oh my gosh, this is so linear and logical." I liked that it all fit together. It forced me to think ahead about the objective I was trying to achieve and how to create a program or whatever it was to accomplish that objective. That's strategic, right? It's not just putting in a bunch of code and seeing if it works. The best software comes from people who are thinking about the end game and working backward to make the code seamless and nice, and not bulky. That was interesting to me.

Wafers, Semiconductors, and Dad

When I graduated, I said, "Okay, well, what am I good at? I'm good with numbers. I feel good with logic and reasoning and computer science modeling, that type of thing." Then, the investment banks came on campus to recruit. And I thought, "Well, everyone else is going through this recruiting thing. Maybe I should do this, too." And so, I did. I ended up finding my way to a bulge bracket investment bank. They said, "Which group do you want to work in? We're organized by industry. So, you can work in oil and gas and . . ." I'm like, "Hmm. No, thanks." They said, "You can work in financial sponsors..." I replied, "Hmm, that's maybe not for me." Then I asked, "Do you have a technology team?" And they said, "Yes, we do. It's out in San Francisco." I jumped at the chance, "Please put me there!" Luckily, they did. I moved out to San Francisco and started covering software and semiconductor companies — some of the same ones down the street from the house where I had grown up. I thought, well, isn't this cool! My parents were very proud that I had gone into banking, working in financial services and at a big brand name company.

This was also one of the most special times in my life when I felt like I could have an adult conversation with my dad. Ordinarily, he was always very fatherly, asking me, "Are you okay? How's it going?" But that would be the extent of the conversation. However, this was the first time in my life when my dad and I could talk about things like radio frequency identification. We could talk about wafers. During the time I lived in San Francisco, my parents moved to Los Angeles. I would fly down to see them every Thanksgiving and Christmas. When my parents picked me up from LAX, we would have an hour-long drive to where they lived, in the desert outside of LA. When I told my dad that I was covering semiconductor companies and asked if he knew their names, he said, "Of course, I know those names. Those were all those chips in all the computers I used to put together." So we started chatting about wafer manufacturing and the like. Our conversation went from there.

Meanwhile, my poor mother is sitting in the passenger side, completely bored out of her mind. During dinner, my mother would prepare my favorite childhood dishes, we'd sit around the table, and the conversation with my dad would just keep going. And it was just very weird and strange in such a good way. I remember thinking, "I don't think I've ever sat down and talked to my dad for this long in one continuous conversation." It's so silly, but it was a connection back to him. And in a way, he felt like I was honoring his past and his experience. It's very personal and a big reason I continued to lean into that.

Digitally Powered

After five long years in banking, which I loved, I came to the realization that I wanted to switch. I've always viewed myself as more of a principal than an agent. I wanted to be part of a company and help grow it. With client-based projects, I found myself asking, "Oh, we did that deal for that software company. Whatever happened to them?" Yet, inside I knew my personality was calling, "I want to be part of something for the long haul and help grow it and contribute in that way."

I still remember Wellesley's mission statement, "Non Ministrari sed Ministrare," Latin for "Not to be ministered unto, but to minister." That's always stuck with me and impacted me even years later when I was looking for job opportunities and how I could build a career. I decided I wanted to work for mission-oriented companies that hopefully, were based in innovation and science. Ideally, I wanted to work in a technology-based healthcare company.

I left banking and found my way to a digital health startup using the internet's power to bring health and wellness information online to consumers, patients, and caregivers. I joined them because I wanted to help build a company. There were about forty people when I joined, and it was super scrappy, growing very quickly. I really lucked out because the people were amazing. I was one of the first finance hires and worked side-by-side with my boss, the CFO, who is still a very close friend and mentor. I stayed for nine years, helping grow the business. Time flew by because every year was different.

It was a really interesting time; there were all these digitally powered companies using the power of the internet to find people or to change their lives. For example, Priceline and Kayak completely changed how people travel. There was TripAdvisor, where you could write reviews and put them online for anybody to find. Suddenly, somebody could sit at their desk in their home and share how they felt about a hotel, and someone else could benefit from it. Our company happened to be the healthcare-focused version of such digitally powered companies. We were bringing health and wellness information online and helping aggregate data from patient communities suffering from chronic conditions. Our mission was to help people live healthier lives by being able to access this information.

While I was there, we also worked with healthcare professionals to create a digital platform for doctors, nurses, and healthcare practitioners to find those patient communities and connect with them. At the very end of my tenure, we also plugged in a hospital element and then a payor element so that there was one whole healthcare ecosystem. Through our marketing and advertising business model, we leveraged data and analytics to show healthcare marketers that the work they did with us made a real difference in prescription usage or lift, and that even in some cases, health outcomes were better.

I just found this whole thing incredibly fascinating and a mission I could get behind. It further developed my thesis that technology, the internet, and data would eventually disrupt and change every industry, even like healthcare, where people still had paper records in folders.

I believe in hard work and expertise, but I also believe there's an element of luck and timing to life too. I got lucky because the world of digital information and analytics was growing so rapidly around the time I began working in it. At the same time, there were a lot of shifts happening in the traditional healthcare world, which was kind of like a parallel universe. But they started to collide. Take Obamacare, and all this talk about outcomes-based reimbursement, compliance, whether people are actually taking their medicine, how they can be rewarded by their insurance company for doing so, and how the doctor can be involved in a communication loop back to the patient. Well, guess what helps you do all that —technology and data! That's how we were building a business and helping people live healthier lives by connecting the moving parts and using data and analytics to make that experience more powerful and helpful for everyone involved.

Shift Happens

You have these moments in your life where something shifts. Well, a shift happened to me in 2016. I had just given birth to my son, and here I am, this person who has always believed in working hard and furthering my career, with parents who had always cared about my academics and career, not really knowing what to do.

Taking my maternity leave was already hard for me. I said, "How am I just shutting it off? I'm just gonna shut it off, just like that?" My husband was successful in his own career, coming up on almost ten years at a non-profit organization in the education space. He was at a turning point in his career too. He said, "I've done what I've done. I liked it a lot, but I want to move on and do something else." This happened right when I was about to take my maternity leave, so I said, "Well, why don't we just take parental leave together? We'll just be a family for a few months." That worked out really well. In fact, my husband ended up becoming a stay-at-home dad, which is the primary reason I've been able to continue doing what I've done in my career. It's not for everybody, but that's what worked for us.

When I was going to go back to work after my maternity leave, I had a panic attack. I said, "I don't know how I'm supposed to do this. How do I go back? Do I ask to go back three days a week? Do I do some sort of transitional schedule?" I had kept in touch with my manager during my leave both because I wanted to but also to satisfy my FOMO (fear of missing out). I told him and the CEO, "I'm really anxious about coming back. I don't really know my role." Before I left, I had elevated some of my team members who were doing a great job running the day-to-day, but now I was coming back to a different situation, and I didn't know what it would be like.

I told my manager and CEO, two men who were fathers themselves, "Look, I have to pump. Where am I going to do that? In the bathroom or in the closet?" I was still nursing and had no idea how or where I would do that. At that time, there weren't company requirements to have a nursing room, mother's room, or wellness room – that's obviously changed today. We also didn't have any sort of transition plan. Our maternity leave policy was about insurance, very kind of black and white. I said, "I think we should have some sort of program for people returning to the office from leave. Why don't we do some thinking ahead of time, so people aren't feeling like I am right now? We need a plan." Meanwhile, as much as I loved my career and was excited about returning to work, I also had this little baby I loved. I felt a push-pull that was very new to me.

At the end of my conversations with my manager and CEO, my CEO said to me, "You're very passionate about this, and you have some good ideas.

So, when you come back, why don't I give you the team and the authority to change things. You can run the People Operations team." I was like, "Okay, thank you, but I'm a finance person." And he replied, "Sure, you're going to have to learn what you need to learn about HR. You'll pick it up." We already had an existing HR team, so he said, "Look, that's going to be your team. You have to rely on them, and you're going to learn from them, but you can bring in a different, strategic, modern perspective." I said, "Okay, I'll do it." That's how I fell into running HR, which I soon discovered is a huge passion area for me and has helped me to get to where I am now, in more operational roles.

I say this and make a big deal about it because there's no way to separate work life and home life, with a big wall in the middle, especially for women. We can't do that. We're not wired to think that way. If something's not going right at work, you bring that home with you. If something's not right at home, you bring that with you to work. You're not your best self if you have to separate those two things. They can't be separated. Trying can be exhausting, and it's narrow. So, I started thinking more about people and working, and I wondered, "Why does the workday need to be linear? What does it mean to be "nine to five"? What if I want to go home early so I can feed my baby and eat dinner with my husband, and then I'll get back online?" I shifted my perspective on work-life balance because it's really about balancing your whole life. This also places the focus on responsibility and accountability and impact, not on what time it is when you send an email — that's a philosophical difference.

If more companies embrace this idea, more women will not need to take that step back. At the time, if somebody had said I could work in the office four days a week and work from home on the fifth, oh my goodness, it would've made an enormous difference. I had never known that to be an option, and many people just assume it's not on the table and don't think to ask. This was a shifting moment for me and my career, and I started to look at things differently. Companies are now approaching these topics better and better, and certainly, with COVID-19, everybody's perspective has changed.

My main takeaway was to ask for what you need. What do you need to feel balanced? Or what do you just need? Don't be afraid to have that conversation. The worst thing anyone can say is, "No." And if so, then think about whether that works for you. I would also mention the importance of having allies, including men, who support you. Whenever I talk to younger women who are seeking mentorship, many automatically think it has to be a woman. Well, you can have male mentors too, and perhaps they won't mentor you in the same way, but that is a great way to include diversity of thought. It is huge to have a man as a mentor and to have them advocate for you openly to other men in executive positions. That will help you forge your path. I was given the opportunity to lead and change things through my relationship with these two men and having a conversation where I was vulnerable and said, "I don't know what I'm going to do. Help."

Time for Something Else

I was happily running HR, finance, and corporate development at my company, and then, opportunistically, somebody came along and wanted to acquire the company. I worked on that deal, and we sold it to a big media company. After that, it was time for me to do something else. I had helped achieve a positive outcome, which was a nice way to move on.

I found my way to another startup, not a STEM company, but a media company focused on empowering women and uplifting the voices of marginalized communities through content and experiences. It was, again, centered around a mission. It was also my first CFO role. I want to tell you this story because I was a Senior Vice President when I left my previous company. My husband had suggested I look for a CFO job, but I was very nervous because I didn't think I was qualified. For example, I don't have a CPA and a lot of employers want their CFO to be a CPA and to have previously worked in an accounting firm. I took a different route through banking and didn't have that. I'm also relatively young, a woman, and a person of color. I told my husband, "It's going to be an uphill battle." He said, "Well, I don't know why you wouldn't just try, and maybe they'll say no. But why not try?"

So, I tried. I got shot down a lot, for the reasons that I mentioned. Recruiters would come back and say, "Well, the company is really looking for somebody with a bit more experience," or, "We're really looking for a chartered accountant." It was upsetting and disappointing. I thought, maybe I'm not cut out for this, and it hurt my confidence. Nobody would say it, but I did think, "Is it because I'm a woman? Is it because the traditional CFO is an older man?"

But I kept pushing. Finally, through my network, I met the founders of what became the next company I worked for. I readied myself. I knew the referral had gotten me to the door, and now I just had to shine. I had to sell and assert myself. I had to get over feeling bad for myself. If they don't want me, this isn't right. As soon as I was in that negotiation, my confidence went back up. I was like, you know what? I will only get the job if I stand up straight, lean in, and go for it. I got the job. They gave me a chance, and I ended up loving it.

I stayed there for almost three years. As CFO, I helped to reignite growth in the business. We opened three international offices and started new businesses, which did very well. I met the most fantastic people. I grew in a different way. I came into myself a bit. Interestingly enough, we ended up being acquired as well. I have a pattern, and that's a fantastic thing. I joke about it, but it was a great deal and outcome. The unfortunate thing about CFOs in an acquisition situation is that they're usually the first ones to be out of a job. I knew that, and I said, "Hey, look, this was a great opportunity for me because it had allowed me to take that C-level position and grow personally and professionally. But what do I do next? And how can I meld all of these things together—my love of technology and my desire to help people—can I return to healthcare? And how do I do all this while honoring my role as a mother?"

A friend of mine, who is also a successful woman, career person, and mother, called me and said, "Hey, I know a couple of people starting something in the fertility space, and it's really cool. You should totally talk to them." It took me about a month to get the call scheduled. During the call, they said, "You're a mom. Well, we're bringing technology to fertility clinics. And we're helping people to build and expand their families through the safe and secure storage of their eggs and embryos. "I said, "Wow, tell me more."

It just went from there. I was so riveted by the fertility space, and the power technology can have to improve the process. I was excited because this was an opportunity to make a real impact.

I joined the company when there were only about 25 employees, and the product was still in development and testing, the earliest stage company I'd ever worked for. So there was an inherent risk in that. But I couldn't believe the amount of opportunity to help grow the company and to bring all of my previous interests into one place. The disruptive, innovative technology used to help people, a brilliant team with whom I knew I would love working, and a mission that could make a tremendous impact in the world.

The current processes fertility clinics use to store the frozen eggs and embryos used in in vitro fertilization (IVF) are analog and manual, with risk and potential for error. Think handwritten labels, paper logs, and no cloud-based data or monitoring capabilities. Error is bound to happen using an outdated manual storage system, with millions of eggs and embryos that need to be kept in cryogenic temperatures for extended periods of time until these patients are ready to have their children. The concept is easy for people to understand. But the technology and the development of the solution had to come from outside the industry.

Innovation doesn't necessarily come from an incumbent. Instead, it comes from bringing together people with diverse backgrounds, perspectives, and experiences from different industries, with the ability to ask different questions and push boundaries. That's how we were able to innovate and develop a solution that helps bring an analog, manual process into the modern era through technology, automation, and data.

Decision Frameworks

As I looked at new opportunities, I created a framework to think through what was next for me. I had kept notes in a notebook, but it needed to be more structured. Then I noticed I used similar words to describe specific opportunities, like culture, great team, sound business model, and mission I believed in. So, to create more structure and pull-out common themes, I put it into a grid to help me think through the criteria and assign a point system.

I created two sides to the grid—the left side described the company's characteristics (e.g., the business model), while the right side described my skills and traits. Then I further divided the lists into specific criteria. For example, under the business model, I asked myself: What do I want from the company? Was it a mission I could get behind and a team I wanted to work with? Did I feel comfortable with the leadership? Do they have a values-based approach? Was there enough open-mindedness and trust to work it out if we disagreed on things? Could I imagine a healthy working relationship with these people?

Another criterion I had for the business model was risk— both business risk and financial risk for myself. Even if it's the right company and the right mission, and you see the opportunity for growth, you need to calculate risk. While an opportunity can be risky, it can also have tremendous reward, and you need to find a balance. I am personally quite risk averse, though I've gotten better at taking risks. You shouldn't feel paralyzed in making a decision about your life to the point where you never take a risk. As much as I want to say that money doesn't matter, it does, particularly because my husband and I have one income. So, it is an important factor and another criterion on the list. The last one was learning opportunities. What's exciting about STEM fields is that the constant innovation and the pace with which those fields are growing means there's always some cool new thing to learn, whether it's a small, fun fact or a whole new science. I feel very fulfilled if I'm in an environment where I can say, "Oh, I didn't know that. That's interesting."

The list on the right of the grid included things I am personally good at, my hard skills, and strengths, such as quantitative and analytical thinking, organizational infrastructure, finance, and strategic thinking. I also realized that I love operations and am pretty good at working with founders who are visionaries to take their vision and turn it into a plan and execute it. This is what led me to pursue more than just a CFO role, but a CFO and COO role.

When I checked for all those criteria, the fertility startup came out on top. So, I was very fortunate to have the opportunity to not just stay in the finance lane but also do a lot more than that, especially in the earlier days when it was still feasible to wear a lot hats at all levels of the organization.

Isn't the ultimate job the one that someone can feel happy and fulfilled by, the one where they feel like they can they're going to do well? That is the Holy Grail. In short, this is the grid: What do I want? What do I desire? And then, what am I actually good at? And finally, putting it all together. Nothing's ever going to be a hundred percent perfect. Understanding that and taking a step back, and seeing the big picture were helpful for me.

The grid also helps you to think outside the box. You may be in one type of functional role now, but you may discover that you could be even better or even happier in a slightly different role. The grid can help you think these through: What kinds of jobs should I apply for? What kinds of jobs should I seek out? What skills am I missing that I may need to acquire for the jobs I want?

One day I went to my husband and proudly said, "Look at my grid. I checked all these points and ended up with a decision." He said, "I could have told you that one was the right opportunity." I responded, "Well, okay, that just burst my bubble. How did you know?" He smiled, "I could tell from how you talk about it. It's the one you get the most excited about." He was right.

Revolutionizing IVF

It is a great fortune to weave my deeply personal interests into my current role. We have a technology solution for facility clinics, specifically around the storage of the eggs and embryos that will be used in IVF.

It's projected that three hundred million people will owe their lives to IVF in the remainder of this century. Just wrap your head around that. Three hundred million. It's a hockey stick in terms of the exponential activity of IVF. One in eight people is infertile, meaning that a relatively large percentage of people need assistance from a doctor to have a child. The prevalence of infertility and miscarriages are extremely high.

That being said, talking about infertility is still somewhat taboo. It's only been recently, the last five years, that people are having more conversations about it. Somehow there's always been shame involved in that, but more and more stories are being shared now. And the facts are that many people need assistance.

Many of these stories turn out to be success stories—but it can be a struggle. It's a long journey, and it's very emotional. In the US, particularly, it's extremely expensive. IVF was always carved out as an elective procedure, which is a bit shocking to me because it's not the same as getting cosmetic surgery. Because of this, fertility clinics were never really regulated, and their services are very expensive, often cash transactions, which makes gaining access to fertility services economically divisive.

There are a lot of interesting macro things going on in IVF right now. These trends are significant. Not only is the number of people relying on IVF to build their families significantly increasing, but there are also social things going on, for example, people having children later in life, which can lead to challenges that require assistance. The definition of a family is also changing. In some clinics we work with, twenty-five percent of their patients come from the LGBTQ+ community. Single individuals want to have children now with donor specimens. Millennial women are saying, "Well, I want to take control of my fertility years and freeze my eggs so that ten or fifteen years from now, I can go back and have a healthy pregnancy." All these things are happening right now, and people are researching in preparation for the future. Still, they are not necessarily thinking, "How are my embryos stored and kept for however many years that they need to be in a safe environment?" Right now, even the IVF clinics that have been super innovative in the science behind what they're doing are not prepared to handle the skyrocketing number of specimens that will be in their care.

In addition, unfortunately, there have been real catastrophic events resulting from the old manual way of operations where the wrong embryo goes into the wrong patient. There have been tragic events where thousands of embryos were lost because of an error in a manual process or a faulty alarm system. Let me give you an illustration. You've probably had a snowflake land on your arm and watched it completely melt within milliseconds, right? That's basically the same delicacy an embryo has, except it's much smaller than a snowflake. Until now, the old processes to identify embryos and keep them safe were largely manual and full of risk.

My current company is trying to partner with fertility clinics to address these problems. We are bringing a fully automated, technology-based platform that includes unique radio frequency identification for patients, a digital chain of custody and audit trail, and 24/7 remote monitoring to ensure that these precious specimens are cared for with the most sophisticated technology available.

We've been able to do all this because of innovation and how it sometimes takes outsiders to come into an industry to push things forward. We're leveraging technology to solve problems. Being part of a company that brings technology, automation, data, sciences, and analytics to help patients have smoother fertility journeys and healthier pregnancies is what I'm excited to do every day. Seeing something come to life and the impact it can have on the world is very rewarding.

Melanie's Reflections

On Stay-at-Home Dads

My husband is a stay-at-home dad. If he wasn't, I don't know that I would have been able to take some of the career opportunities or risks that I've taken. Not just changing jobs, but in my day to day, feeling very committed to both sides of my world. Being able to be successful in my career, which fulfills me, but also feeling successful when I come home. My son is four, and he's going through incredible developmental changes every day. I don't want to miss any of that.

Our setup was a very intentional decision between my husband and me. I am extremely grateful. Other people have their own ways of raising a family. For us, that was the way that I could do both. We can't just put our work life on one side and our personal life on the other. They blend together. How you show up in one or the other does affect the other piece. We are human beings at the end of the day. You can't just box different parts of our life separately into different compartments. We all seek fulfillment, and however, we each get there could be a totally different path for everybody. It is about melding your personal desires and wants and needs with your professional desires and wants and needs and making it work for you and your family.

On Working Through Conflict

Women are very hard on themselves. We are our own biggest, harshest critics. We're multitasking all the time, even while we have other things going on in our heads, like our kids. So, when you're in a situation where you don't feel supported on top of all that, and you feel you don't have the ability to make an impact the way you want to, it can be very hard.

There was a point a few years ago when a bunch of things was going on, and I felt a lot of burden on my shoulders. I was working closely with a colleague who I felt didn't have the same values I did. It was not about all those things in my grid. It was about how I was working with this one person. I felt like I wasn't being heard and didn't have a partner who had my back. It ended up being very hard, to the point where I said, "You know what? I'm not happy. I just want to stop. I want to quit." I was surprised that this one relationship could get me to that point.

The way I ended up working through that was with the help of an executive coach. My coach pointed out, "If you want to leave, leave. But don't leave because you're feeling sorry for yourself, don't know what to do, or feel helpless. It's okay to feel bad; you should get all that out. But now we should turn that into action." She spent time with me, pushing me, asking me a lot of questions, "Well, why do you feel this way? Do you really think that's the issue, or do you think it might be this or that?" We talked about what I could control on my end, what I brought to the relationship, and how I could make it better versus how it made me feel. I ended up staying and having a series of heart-to-hearts with this particular person. We said, "Let's just reset. This is how I feel . . ." It was almost like couple's therapy. Just facing it, head-on is the punchline. We just got it all on the table, which was very healthy.

On Generating Opportunities

You could do equally well at a small company or a large company. Small companies have the benefit of fewer people and less structure. You may have more ability to be nimble and fluid around your role. Your exposure to other roles is greater and easier in any sort of startup-type company. Before COVID, we were all in one office at my current job. I can look over there and see what somebody else is doing and ask to learn or help. Sometimes that can turn into an interesting conversation around roles, job movement, and mobility.

Meanwhile, at larger companies, you benefit from real structures and programs that encourage internal mobility to move people around. The point is – to get up from your desk, talk to people, be curious, lean in, and learn. That's what generates opportunities.

On Advocating for Others

I didn't realize how much I would enjoy advocating for women. When I was a teenager deciding to go to an all-women's college, the thought did cross my mind that I was making a big mistake. But after two or three months on campus, I knew I could not have made a better decision. I walked away from my college experience with a strong urge to support women, whether in a job or with my friends, in every little thing. "How do I give back? How do I help someone else?"

I'm happy that I've been able to do this throughout my career. I started a women's leadership program at one job. Then, I worked for a company whose whole mission was elevating underrepresented voices. Now, I help people struggling with fertility or anyone else on their path to being a parent and building a family. I've also worked with my fantastic finance team to start a high school women's STEM program.

It's heartwarming whenever I see women using their platforms to raise other women up. You could be changing someone's life, even in the smallest way. If a ship is sailing and it navigates five degrees to the left, they're going to end up at a whole different destination. These small shifts and acts of helping one another have real, tangible outcomes, and it's so wonderful to see and be part of them.

On Advice to My Younger Self

Life throws you curveballs and surprises. Things don't necessarily work out the way you plan them. Be open-minded about that. Be curious; lean into it.

It could be the smallest little thing. The reason why I even looked at Wellesley College was because a high school teacher had submitted one of my essays to the Wellesley Book Award contest without me knowing it... and I won. He presented me with a gift, the Oxford Guide to Literature, and inside the front cover was a Wellesley brochure. That small gesture changed the course of my perspective and, ultimately, my college experience.

Sometimes things happen when you least expect it, and what may seem like a confusing turn of events could actually turn out to be a pathway to the most phenomenal, amazing next opportunity. My advice would be to always be open-minded. Sometimes things are disguised as bad things, but they could become great opportunities. It's about leaning in, being curious and proactive, and being open to forging a new path that may not be what you planned.

What has always guided me was just being true to myself and my passion. I want all women to feel that way. If you're true to yourself, hopefully, that leads to what's right for you. Wherever you go, your success is defined by how true to yourself you can be, not by your accolades or your title, or someone else's measure of success.

Epilog

I am still leaning in and learning as much as I can in my work. My husband and I also welcomed our second child, a son, to our family and are happily enjoying being a family of four.

Daphne Lane

Software Engineer Manager, Lockheed Martin Aeronautics

I am a software engineer manager for Lockheed Martin, a government defense contractor. I manage a team of thirty Skunks Works engineers in the Aeronautics business unit. My team is very fast-paced and focuses on innovative solutions through research, prototyping, and forward-thinking to solve and provide for our customer's needs.

Video Games

In elementary school, I had a passion for math. I loved numbers and problem-solving. I also really enjoyed calculus and tough equations. My teachers saw that in me and put me in higher math courses more tailored toward technology, like a computer elective dealing with problem-solving in math.

This is where it all started for me.

I loved computers and was fascinated with them. Back then, we had floppy disks and much larger computers. When we started using computers in school, I was intrigued by how you could get everything on this one machine. This led me to want to learn and do more with math and computers. I knew technology was becoming a big thing, and I realized I wanted to get into that field and learn as much as I could.

Back in the day, I had a Nintendo, and as my younger brother got older, he started playing the Xbox. The graphics for those games were so advanced to me, much more advanced than whatever I played growing up. This intrigued me because I saw what they can do with video games and wanted to know, "How does all this work?" I knew that game developers had to create a lot of graphics, and this was the technology I was interested in. It was also the only part I knew.

I had not been exposed yet to all the other things you could do with computer science or computer engineering.

Falling Into Computer Science

Everyone thought I would be a nurse because that's what my mom was. I knew I wanted to go to the same college, Tuskegee University, which is an HBCU, (Historically Black Colleges and Universities) that my mom went to in order to continue the legacy. I got accepted and also received a scholarship. I was very excited to be going to the school I wanted to go to. But I quickly realized when it was time to pick my major, they didn't have the one I was looking for.

I wanted to do computer graphics at the time.

At first, I was bummed when I found out they did not offer any computer graphics courses. I almost didn't go to Tuskegee because I had my mind set on computer graphics as my major. But after talking to people and telling them what I wanted to do, one of the counselors in the registrars gave me a packet and told me about the computer science department and the classes and degrees they offered.

One of the majors was computer science.

I took time to look into it because I had never thought about programming software before. After reading more about it and learning more about software, I ended up choosing Computer Science as my major. It was still based on computers and technology, and I realized it had a lot of problem-solving.

Interestingly enough, in my freshman year, I did very well in the entry-level classes. I think that was because of my passion and love for math and problem-solving. I was very good at it, to the point that as a freshman, I went on a programming trip competition with the juniors and seniors in the department. We went to Daytona, Florida, and competed with different teams from other universities. They gave us various problems, and whoever solved them first advanced in the contest. There were about twenty or twenty-five teams, and our team made it to the top ten.

This opportunity opened my eyes because now I've been exposed to others at different universities doing the same thing and being in the software field. I could talk to other individuals, meet other women who were into computer science, and see what their schools were teaching. It was a very good networking experience.

Freshman year gave me exposure and allowed me to see that I actually enjoyed computer science as my major.

Almost A Drop Out

I did pretty well in school and became a teaching assistant (TA) for my department. I would give quizzes, collect tests, grade them, and help my professors out. It also afforded me an opportunity to get scholarships within my department. Having access to scholarships was a very big reason why I was able to stay at Tuskegee.

Twice in my college career, I thought about changing my major.

It was never because I didn't like it or didn't want to do it. It was more of the extenuating circumstances. During my sophomore year, I took a calculus III course that was required for my major and that was heavily weighted. I got a passing grade, a C, but I needed to keep a 3.0 for the scholarship I got when I was accepted. That C dropped me below the minimum I needed, so I lost my scholarship. At that time, I didn't know what I was going to do. This was one of the reasons I almost didn't finish school. My university is a private school and is very expensive. I didn't get much federal assistance, so I thought about taking out a loan.

I had to go back to the drawing board to figure things out.

A lot of people come up against things like this in college, especially if you don't have a full scholarship or your parents don't pay for school. That was one of the first reasons I almost didn't stay in STEM. Luckily, like I said, I was the TA for the dean of the department. So when I talked to him about it, he helped me find other scholarships that worked for me since I still had the grades everywhere else.

Still, it was crushing for me because I've always been an A or B student. I won't say school came easy, but with high school and everything, I didn't have to do a lot of studying. In college, I had to learn how to study, so it was a wake-up call when I got the C. It was a passing grade, but it could have changed my trajectory in school. Looking back now,

I almost changed my major because of one course, but it was that course that prepared me for the future.

The best part about college for me was learning how to help and develop other people. Once I understood and got better at programming and problem-solving, I became a tutor helping other people who were taking the classes I had already taken. My university had a summer program, Pre-Freshman in Computer Science (PREFICS), for incoming freshmen to start their computer science courses early. I ended up staying on campus during my last two summers to tutor the incoming freshmen who came into this program. That allowed me to help others grow while also sharpening my skills. As I got older, I would always go back to volunteer.

I realized that college is where helping others started for me.

I noticed during my summer volunteering that there was and still is a lack of women in the engineering field. At Tuskegee, we had a small incoming group of about twelve or thirteen, and there was always just one female among all the guys. That's how it was with me as well. There might have been only two or three women at most out of probably twenty or twenty-five in each class.

There were just not a lot of women in this field, and that always puzzled me.

It didn't bother me at first because everybody was friendly, and we all helped each other. We all had the same goals. But, as time went on, I noticed it more and began to have that lonely feeling as the only female. Sometimes I felt like I had to work harder to fit in and be heard. If you have at least one other person, that helps. I noticed this was also the case for people coming up behind me, and I wanted to help them stay. That made me gravitate to the younger women I tutored because I knew they needed somebody else. It's good to see somebody who looks like you or somebody you can relate to. "Oh, she did it", "She looks like me", or "She's in this field with all the guys, and she's holding her own as well."

I wanted to help make them comfortable and make sure they had what they needed to stay.

Prepared for Life

It's funny because a lot of people know that computer science has a reputation, even those outside of the field. There was one professor in the computer science program, Dr. Chen. He was crazy smart. He pushed you a lot, but it was for your own good. He tried to make you think outside of the box. When you were in his class, he was hard on you, and most people hated it. A lot of people dreaded his class and were just trying to pass or get out of there. There are a lot of people who changed their major or didn't stay in STEM because of Dr. Chen's classes. But once you went through it and understood what he was doing, you appreciated it. He gave you the harder questions and the harder tests. He thought outside the box and required you to think in the same way. The lessons you learned always stuck with you and took you the extra mile.

He's one of those professors you will never forget because he prepared you for life.

In the computer science program, we had labs that would be like weekly homework assignments. We would sometimes be working in the lab until two or three in the morning. It was a little lonely, and I think that's what drove the friendships and the sense of community within the computer science department. I'm still close to a lot of the people in my class. We still talk and keep in touch on Facebook. I've built strong friendships with the other females in the program. There were four of us—two in my cohort, one the year before, and another two years before us. We always stuck together and helped each other out. We really bonded because there weren't many of us.

Today, we still check on each other, talk about the companies we're at, what we want to do next, and various other things.

Wanting Something Bigger

In the latter half of college, I started to focus on getting a job. In my senior year, we did career fairs and mock interviews to start preparing. I did two major interviews: one was with Morgan Stanley in New York, and the other was with my current company Lockheed Martin.

The first was with Morgan Stanley, my first time going to Manhattan. I loved the trip. The interview was in January or February, so it was freezing. I'm originally from Alabama, and it was a shock for it to be that cold. I really enjoyed the interview, but I knew I would have been bored doing that type of software— financial websites and data. I wanted to be able to develop something I could see and wanted to be more hands-on. Morgan Stanley was a great company, but once I interviewed with Lockheed, it opened up the possibilities.

I knew a lot of people from my university who went to Northrop Grumman, Boeing, Lockheed Martin, or Raytheon—the four competitors. They would do different career fairs at our university, showing their different technologies and the things they worked on. Once I got to see those things, I knew it was something I wanted to work on and be a part of. A lot of stuff now you can't see it. Like the cloud or website—you just write code to save things in a memory or a space. Don't get me wrong, I love apps and the cloud. I love my phone.

But I just wanted something bigger.

I appreciate the route I took because it has afforded me so much. I tell people all the time: some of this stuff I've gotten to work on, some people will never see in their lifetime. One of the coolest things was when I was working on displays for a Navy submarine. One of the displays allowed us to look at the contours of the ocean floor. We all know what it looks like to see the sky, the clouds, the buildings—the top part of the world. But we never get to see the ocean floor, the bottom. And that was just the coolest thing to me. I like knowing that the things that I've worked on are going on a fighter jet, submarine, etc.

That's the reason I went the way I did.

Interviews with Lockheed Martin were in DC, in Crystal City. In one day, I interviewed with three different people who were looking for three different positions at three different locations around the DC area. I accepted an offer in March.

The position I took was a classified position.

I would need a security clearance to start work, so I did all my security paperwork ahead of time. When I graduated in May, I expected to start work in June. However, I was still waiting for my security clearance to be granted. It was a little frustrating because all my friends who had graduated with me were already working in their new jobs by June, while I was back home with my mom, working at Macy's.

I worked at Macy's my entire college career. I began my freshman year. Then I started doing seasonal, weekends, and holidays when I went home. Around my junior year, they made me part-time. So, I started coming home every weekend since school was only about two hours away. Being a starving college student, if you're going to give me hours, I'll come home and work!

I continued working at Macy's while waiting on everything to work out with Lockheed. It got so frustrating. I started thinking things like, I went to school all those years, only to come home and work at Macy's. Don't get me wrong, there's nothing wrong with that, but I was excited to get out into the world and start my new journey. I didn't know clearance could take a while to come through, so I even thought that maybe it was denied and wouldn't come through. I had peers whose jobs needed security clearances that had already come, so I couldn't understand it. That was another time in my life when I started to think about not staying in this field, "Do I need to go back to school? What's going on?" I was about to start going to career fairs and looking for other companies when I was cleared that September.

When I finally got to work, everybody else I graduated with had already started and already had their living situation sorted out with roommates. I couldn't afford to move to DC and live by myself, but things worked out. That's when I knew the company was for me. When I told HR that I was looking for a roommate, they connected me with an older woman who was an electrical engineer. She had just bought a townhouse and was looking to rent out a room. She could also show me around and introduce me to the company. She was like a live-in mentor. This was exactly what I needed, and timing is everything.

I was mad about how it happened, but everything worked out so perfectly.

Creating Advanced Technologies

At my company, we work on a lot of very innovative technology on the government side. We have five different business units. For example, our space business unit helped make what we know now as GPS, the Global Positioning System. When I started, I worked in RMS, Rotary and Mission Systems, whose focus is underground and undersea systems and whose primary customer is the Navy. This was where I got to work on submarines.

The business unit that I work for right now is Aeronautics. In my career with Aeronautics, I worked on the F-22, a US fighter jet that no other country has. I have also worked on the F-16, an international fighter jet. We sell these jets to our allies. We also have the F-35, which is our newest international jet. A lot of the jets build off each other's configuration and how we modernize and sustain.

I currently manage about thirty software engineers. The majority of programs that my engineers support are the advanced development programs. These are the programs where we're coming up with innovative solutions by doing research and prototyping, looking at where we are now—the software and hardware we use on a jet—and then looking into the future, thinking about what we will need in the next fifteen or twenty years. We are a very fast-paced team. We go out, research things, get ideas, make quick prototypes, and then send those prototypes to the government to get bids on. If we win a bid, it becomes a production program, and we now have more work to implement.

Software refers to computer language. My team uses C, C++, Python, Lua, and Java to write their code. This code tells the hardware in the jets what to do. There are many types of software. Let's say, for instance, in our line of work, that we have displays in the cockpit. We write the software that lines up with the displays and makes them come to life. We do the colors and the touch-screen software. So, if you hit a touch screen and want it to turn off some lights, we write the software behind the scenes to make it do that.

We also have a group that does weapons software. Early in my career, when I wrote software, I worked in a group that wrote the software that loaded weapons on the jets. It took inventory and kept the weight of the weapons. Since it's a fighter jet and it's up in the air, you have to make sure that both sides of the wings are balanced, so we wrote the software to do those checks and balances. We also worked on the software where if the pilot presses a button, they can make the missile shoot out.

Closer to Mom

Let me back up. I had been in Alabama all my life, and even when I went to college, I was just two hours away from home. My job at Lockheed Martin was my first time moving away, which was big for me. It was very different and fast-paced. I was nervous, but the good thing was that I had some friends from college there, including one of my close friends—one of the few women from my program. She had been there since June and had already figured things out.

Having somebody else there that I knew helped a lot.

A little about my family. On my mom's side, I'm the oldest. On my dad's side, I'm the youngest. When people ask me about my siblings, I have four siblings. On my dad's side, I have three siblings—two brothers and a sister—all older than me. My oldest sister and oldest brother are old enough to be my parents, which affected the dynamic of our relationships growing up. We didn't really get close until I got older. On my mom's side, I have . . . had a younger brother.

I had moved to DC and had been working for about three years when my younger brother was killed back home in Alabama.

That's what made me shift and move back down South. I decided I wanted to be closer to my mom. So, I switched business units and moved to Marietta, Georgia. I loved it there, and I enjoyed being close enough to home to drive home anytime if I needed to. Then, my company moved my entire program to Fort Worth, Texas. It was a big move for me at that time because of my personal situation. I was in Fort Worth for seven years before I made a recent move back to Georgia. I'm now close to home again. My mom still has a house in Alabama, but she's been staying with me for a little bit to help us with the baby.

That was one of the things that made me stay with my company.

They afforded me the opportunity to move when I needed to. It was simple as me telling my manager who knew what had happened with my brother. She looked for positions for me and found one in Georgia, then reached out to the manager, and the next thing I knew, I had an interview. That was very big for me. Not to be biased, but the managers I've had in my company, the ones who I feel have always had my best interests at heart, the ones who have really promoted my growth and helped me have been the women. They've been the ones from whom I've gotten the best opportunities. Under their leadership, I feel like I've grown the most.

When life happens or other personal things affect my work-life balance, they can relate and are more helpful in those aspects.

Senseless Tragedy

About what happened to my brother... I can tell this story now because it's been about eleven years, and with the healing process, I'm now okay with talking about it. It was Labor Day weekend. Back then, I would only go home maybe twice a year, once during the summer because my family went on a big summer vacation every year, and I'd also go back for Christmas.

This particular year, I didn't go back to Alabama that summer for a family vacation, but I flew down for Labor Day weekend. After I landed back in DC, I talked to my mom to let her know we had landed and that I would call her when I got home. I remember driving home from the airport when my mom called. Usually, she doesn't call me before I call her, so I knew something wasn't right. She asked, "Hey, what are you doing?" And I was like, "Mom, I just told you, I made it to the airport, and I'm on my way home." She said, "Call me as soon as you get home." And I was like, what's wrong? Because I could hear it in her voice.

I kept trying to get her to tell me, but she wouldn't.

I figured she didn't want to tell me while I was driving. When I got home, in typical fashion, I started doing everything else and forgot to call her. I wasn't thinking it was that important. So, she called me back again. At this point, I think she was trying to tell me before she told anybody else because she didn't want me to hear about the news from someone else. She basically just told me, "Your brother was just shot and killed." I remember saying, "What?!? No, it can't be!!" I couldn't believe it. It took a minute to settle in, and I think I just kinda sat there and blanked out or something. It was unreal because I had just seen him before I flew back earlier that day.

He had been with the girl he was dating at a park by her house. Some guys were trying to rob him. They told him that if he pulled off, they would shoot him. It was just very senseless. There was nothing for them to rob him of. I don't know if they were trying to take his car. He was really a good kid... that was the hard thing.

I thought about WHY and all of that. It took some time. It was very hurtful because this was the city we had grown up in, the city we'd grown to love. My entire family is from the city. Then I'm like, this is the same city that took his life. So, you kinda gotta go through all of that. It is definitely one of those tragic things that happens very unexpectedly and changes your entire life.

I had just gotten back to DC, but at that point, I wanted to be home with my mom. I was rushing, trying to find flights. I ended up flying right back out the next morning. It was very good that we had a support system. My mom is very strong, but at the end of the day, that's her child. I wanted to make sure that I was there, taking a lot of the load off of her. To give her time to grieve, heal, and go through her process. I think for me and my mom, it brought us closer because I had been away for so long.

I was yearning to be closer to her because I was now her only child.

For a while, she went through a phase where she would give me all the love she had— I guess she had enough love for two kids. She got very overprotective and overbearing. I think she was just scared for me sometimes. When I was just going out, traveling, or going on girls' trips with my friends. I was fine with it for a while, but then I thought, "Okay, you have to loosen your grip." I had stayed at home for a month when everything happened, and every time I went somewhere, she would walk me to the door or call me so many times while I was gone. I think it took a toll on her, too.

But we got through it.

Having a good support system within my company was one of the reasons I really fell in love with them. I had only been there a few years at the time, but everyone was so supportive. It was just the things they did that made me feel supported and comforted; they made sure I had what I needed. It was the thoughtfulness as well. As I mentioned earlier, even when I returned to work, when I told my manager that I wanted to be closer to home, a week later, she called me. "Hey, I found some jobs in Georgia. I know you were looking. I reached out to the manager." And I was like, "Oh my goodness." That blew my mind. She had taken the initiative to find positions on my behalf, and that's how I ended up moving to Georgia.

That was the closest death to me as an adult. It was a tough time, but we definitely got through it. It's a part of life; you learn from it and grow from it.

On-the-Job Training

I was in grad school at George Washington in DC studying for my master's when all of this happened.

My company had programs with many colleges in the area where I never had to go on campus. They brought the classes to our work campus. They made it so easy for you. I would literally leave my desk or leave the lab and go down the hall or to another building and sit in a conference room, which would be my classroom for the evening. The company also reimbursed us for attending these colleges or pursuing higher education.

It was such a blessing.

At the time, I was starting to think about pursuing other options and looking into another field. I still wanted to do software, but maybe in a different industry. I was thinking about going commercial, doing consulting, or teaching computer science or software development in a high school or junior college. I was just trying to pave an avenue for myself if I needed to move back to Alabama and couldn't find a corporate setting.

When I left Virginia and moved to Marietta, I changed business units to Aeronautics. It was very interesting because I had never worked on any fighter jets before. It was definitely a big learning curve. I ended up in a group that worked on displays and the different things that go on a fighter jet. We did the sensors, radars, and communication (COMM). When you think about fighter jets, it's the same thing as commercial airplanes, where you have the airplane and the pilot who communicate with a ground station. We did a lot of the ground station work—they have their machines and communication links to talk back and forth to the aircraft or the jet.

The learning curve wasn't really about the software.

I tell this to anybody now, even when I'm interviewing for positions on my team, especially for newcomers coming right out of college. If you have the foundation and the basics, a lot of the stuff that we do, you will have to learn on the job. We call it on-the-job training. We work on very complex systems, huge projects with all these different systems that make up one big jet. So it's hard to expect somebody to know or understand any of that. But as long as you have the basic foundation of software development, whether it's on C plus, Java, or Python, then you can learn the rest about aeronautics as you go.

That's how it was for me in that transition.

Space to Grow

I was in Georgia for about three years when my company decided to move my entire program, the F-22 program, about three hundred people, to Fort Worth, Texas. I liked that my company afforded us a lot of different opportunities, but this was one opportunity I wasn't looking for because I had just moved to Georgia to be closer to home. Now they were moving me about ten hours away from home, about the same distance away as I was in Virginia. So, this was another torn moment where I had to make a decision quickly that affected my career.

It was very hard to figure out what to do because we only had a few weeks to decide. Since the move affected about three hundred people, I knew that maybe 30 to 40 percent of them who decided not to move would all be out looking for jobs in the same area at the same time. There were not a lot of defense companies in Georgia, so if I decided to stay, I knew I might have to go commercial. I also realized that I wanted to stay in the aeronautics area. Even if I found something I wanted to do, I was out there competing with at least another hundred people at the same time, because we all had the same time frame. Additionally, a lot of people had families they didn't want to leave behind and kids in school.

For me, I sat back and started thinking about coworkers who had kids, who had spouses, who had a house. I was like, it's just me. I live in an apartment. The company is going to pay for everything. Maybe I should try it for a year or two, and if I don't like the area, I'll just try to get back. It's not like they're sending me to Utah or Canada. I started changing my thought process and realized I'd never been to Texas.

So, I looked at it as a good opportunity.

My mom was okay with the move. By then, it had been almost four years. She had gotten a little more comfortable. I think she might've had a little anxiety at first, but she understood it was for work. So, I decided to go.

That was another career-changing move, and honestly, I will say it was one of the best things for me. Once I moved to Fort Worth, Texas, my career blossomed. There were so many growth opportunities. That was the company's reason for moving our program there, and it aligned very well with me and what I was trying to do.

There was no growth opportunity in the previous program I was on in Georgia.

That was the way it was structured. The people who were in leadership had been there for so long. Nobody was leaving the program, so it didn't present new or upcoming jobs. When I got to Fort Worth, the program I ended up on was more of an international program. I worked on the F-16, an earlier model that we sell internationally to countries like Taiwan, Singapore, and Greece. That was a lot of growth for me because we interacted with our customers. Some of them were here in our lab, and we co-developed with the Singaporeans for two years. These were new programs where they wanted to do more sustainment, modernization, and add-on contracts. That afforded me those opportunities I had never had before to work with international customers and do co-located cross-functional development.

I felt like I grew a lot.

There was also a lot of room for growth and chances to lead because we were winning so much work. That's when I started leading. I got into more of the business side of things with the company instead of just technical. I saw other people in these positions, and it just opened my mind outside of software to see how everything ties together for a business. I saw how the program manager, project managers, and project engineers work with the system engineers. When I got to Fort Worth on this other program, it was set up so that the software engineers just did the software development. We got our requirements from our system engineers. And then, we did our development and our own software testing. But we also had a system test team that did all the testing before you release it to the lab and deploy it to the jet.

This exposed me to the many different parts of the organization and how everything works together.

As I got more opportunities to work with other disciplines, I became responsible for the program execution of our contracts. I started managing our schedule, the budget, and the technical execution. I was still very software-oriented– the technical part, but I got into the business part, too. The move to Texas gave me that opportunity.

When you work across disciplines, I believe you understand the bigger picture, the system as a whole. When I was just doing development, that was all I knew. I was heads-down, just developing. I didn't understand how what I did tied into the program releases, or how we needed to meet our milestones to make sure it was released to test on time so that there was enough time to do the statistics in the labs to verify it and get it on the jet. I think that seeing the bigger picture and understanding it helps you perform better in your work.

Part of why I got my master's in systems engineering was for this reason. My bachelor's was in computer science and was software-focused. But my mentor told me, "Instead of taking software, do systems." So, I got my master's in systems because I wanted to understand other parts of engineering and how they work with software. My master's taught me about the program management side of things. I definitely think seeing how it all works together is very beneficial when you're trying to move up to the next level.

The Manager Thing

In software, there's a methodology or process called Agile that focuses on small teams with iterative development and delivery that allows for continual improvement. Within Agile methodology, you have a scrum master and a product owner. I became scrum master for one of our teams, a small team of eight engineers. I led the technical execution and kept up with the schedule, the technical, and the budget. That was my first opportunity to manage the team. A scrum master wasn't an official manager position, but it opened the door for me to lead more things.

We were bringing in more people at the time, so there were opportunities for new management positions. The next progression was to get into more of a leadership role, where I was responsible for the program execution and everything. At first, I wasn't thinking about managing because I'd always thought I would be someone who stayed technical. But once I started being the scrum master for this team, I actually enjoyed the leading part of it. I enjoyed the program execution, making sure the team was on schedule, laying out the milestones and tasks, and making sure they had all the resources they needed. I actually liked the managing side.

So, I said to myself, "Okay, maybe I'll try the manager thing."

My company did give people opportunities to get into management. They created an associate manager. Part of it was still technical and part of it was managing, where you managed a smaller number of people, anywhere from ten to fifteen. The regular managers had about thirty to thirty-five. With the associate manager, you could still do technical work during the rest of your time because you managed a smaller subset of people. I liked this arrangement because I was still torn. I didn't know if I wanted to give up my technical side. So, I tried that avenue first as an Associate Manager, which gave me a lot of the experience I needed.

I loved having my own team because I had a lot of the new engineers.

We were constantly hiring because we were winning so many contracts and programs. So, I ended up with way more people than I was supposed to. My manager saw that I was doing very well in the role, especially onboarding our new people. He liked the extra effort I was taking with the interviewing, the hiring, and bringing people up to speed. I realized career development is one of my strengths. I like helping people figure out their strengths, weaknesses, where they want to go, and what kinda path they want to be on. Then, I put a lot of the training in place to ensure they felt like they were getting what they needed.

I started taking on more because it was natural for me. I wanted to make sure they succeeded and had the tools, the training, and the opportunities. I created this whole thing, and it became like a flow. So, everybody started coming to me when we had new people. I created folders to give them all these things. I guess I created a new position, and we needed it. A lot of this protocol was missing. I had been working at Lockheed for probably about seven years at the time, and there was a team that hadn't had any new people for over ten years, probably closer to fifteen. So, they had none of this in place.

You can't just bring people in, sit them on a team, and expect them to excel.

That's how the opportunity presented itself for me to be promoted to the next management level. It was just God's timing, and it happened really quickly. The opportunity came, and I was already filling that need. I already had almost the amount of people that a regular manager has. My manager created a position and asked me to apply for it. He was like, "I need another manager with all the people we're bringing in, and you would be a perfect fit." At that point, I became open to it because I liked the manager position and the leading side of things. As long as I still get to manage a software team, I'm perfectly fine with it because that keeps me close enough to the technical part. I liked that if one of my team had issues, I could actually get in there and help them. I understand what it takes to get a release out, what happens during testing, or if we need to go back to requirements.

And that's how I transitioned from the first management level to the second level.

Georgia on My Mind

While in Fort Worth, a senior manager I had worked for in Georgia reached out to me. They were going to move some work back to Marietta, Georgia. I was now a manager, and they needed a manager out there to start up this team. However, I really wasn't interested. I had been in Fort Worth for seven years at the time, and I was comfortable. This place was where I had been the longest. I actually loved it there and had no intentions of moving. He asked me twice. I was like, "No, I don't think I'm interested."

In the meantime, I had just gotten engaged.

I actually met my husband when I was nineteen in college through my roommate. It was one of those love stories that comes back around. My roommate was dating one of his friends. One weekend, she and her date wanted to go to a basketball game. She didn't want to go by herself because they had just started dating, so she called me. He brought his friend as well, and that was how Greg and I met. We exchanged numbers but didn't talk for a while, and then he finally reached out. We dated for about two years while I was in college. We lost touch when I moved away. We ended up with a mutual best friend, which allowed us to stay in touch. About two or three years ago, we ran into each other again and started dating. At this point, we were both ready to settle down, ready to get married, and start a family.

That's how we reconnected and rekindled our relationship.

After we got engaged, my senior manager came to me a few months later and asked again if I wanted to move back to Georgia to start up a team. At that point, I still wasn't interested. My fiancé just loved everything about Texas. We had talked about staying until we started a family to be closer to home so that our kids could have a relationship with our families.

A few weeks later, we found out that we were pregnant. It definitely changed the conversation. We started saying, "Oh, maybe this is the opportunity to get back home. We might need to consider it." I talked to mentors and others, and they said it took seven years for this opportunity to come up. I should consider how much longer it might be for another opportunity to move back. I was like, "That is very true."

I had to start looking at it differently.

I called him and asked if the position was still available. They were going to go ahead and put the job req out. Luckily, I had caught them just in time. The position kinda fell into my lap, and it was a really good opportunity. It made perfect sense, especially not knowing then that COVID would happen soon. I'm just so grateful that I got a chance to return before all of that happened, get settled, and be closer to home.

I took the position in November 2019 and moved at the end of February 2020. March 2020 was when COVID got really bad.

So, I missed it by two weeks before they shut everything down.

Making It Work

With the baby, I'm figuring out how to make things work with what I'm dealing with now.

I had been working from home since March 2020, my last trimester. I didn't want to expose myself because of COVID, but it was very hard because I was building a new team. There's never been this type of team in Marietta. It's a software team, but we all work on classified programs. It's very hard starting a new team. You have to be more engaging; you want things to fit your expectations, and you want to build the culture and environment. That's been very challenging even now that I'm back because I had been out of the office for a while. When the cat's away, the mice will play.

I had to clean up so much stuff.

I've been talking to other people I know—friends and mentors—to get advice and feedback on reentering the workplace after having a child. I'm starting to get into that mommy guilt a little bit. It's mainly because we work four ten-hour days, and I'm usually working maybe eleven or twelve hours. I get up, take her to my mom downstairs, and by the time I leave, I've really not spent much time with her. When I come home, it's time to give her a bath and get ready for the next day.

So, I'm trying to decide on a few things. Am I going to take a break? Am I going to go part-time? Maybe just until she gets a little older? I don't know, honestly, what the deciding factor will be. It's been just a month right now. I'm going to try to give it to the end of the year. I'll see how I feel and decide at the beginning of the year. As a mom, I don't want to miss those precious moments and don't like the mommy guilt of working too much. I don't get to spend as much time with her as I would like.

But I also love what I do.

I like going to work and spending time learning about what my team is doing. We work on some cool things, some inspiring things, and some very innovative things. I don't want to miss that, either. So, I'm very torn when I'm asked, "Are you going to stay?" Those are the things that would make me stay—the work that I do. But now, having a little one kinda changes my priorities. Luckily my company is very flexible, and we have the option to choose our own schedules. I will say that if I do anything, it would be to switch to part-time or just take a break. I don't think I would ever totally leave 'cause I really enjoy work.

If I didn't like what I did, it probably would have been easy to decide to take a break or even leave or find something else.

Daphne's Reflections

On Diversity and Cultural Shifts

We have so many baby boomers retiring this year that we are preparing to bridge the gap by having potential backfills in place and starting knowledge transfer. In the last three years, we've done a lot of hiring and are going through a cultural shift right now.

We saw a little more diversity push in hiring.

I remember we organized a lunch for all the women in software. At that time, we had a female director, and one of the young ladies who had just come in said that when she first saw that her manager was a woman, she knew she was in the right place. It made her feel better. She fit. Then she met her manager's boss, a woman, too. Also, our director at the time was a woman. Having that many women in leadership positions opened up many possibilities, making her look at the company differently. I think it did something for her confidence too. When she told us this, we were like, "Wow." I was thinking that if I had seen that when I'd first come in, it would have changed my start, also.

It would've given me the confidence to know that I was in the right place, that, oh, I can be in these positions, too.

It says a lot when our company really promotes diversity. I think diversity comes in all colors, shapes, forms, everything. With diversity, you bring in different backgrounds, cultures, and just the different ways people think about things. You have different sets of eyes, which is very beneficial because it adds value to your company and your product. Because of my background and where I've come from, I bring something to the table that somebody else might not, and because of their background, they bring something different as well. Being open to all that and having it all in one place makes the company stand out and be even more creative and successful.

I went through a transition with my team too, where I went from a relatively older team to bringing in ten new engineers. Of course, it was a huge culture shift. Sometimes the challenge was because the more seasoned engineers had been there for so long, and they would say, "We have a certain way of doing things. This is how we've always done it." And then you have these bright-eyed, bushy-tailed, creative-thinking new hires who are fresh out of school, wanting to challenge all that. At first, it was a struggle, but the seasoned engineers ended up loving it because the young engineers brought so much life and new thinking to the program that had been missing.

I think that's what you get when you have so much diversity and people who can bring in so many new perspectives that can help change the culture, make the product more innovative, or come up with better ways to do things more efficiently and effectively.

On Role Models Like Me

Even in the workplace now, not many people look like me, but especially when I started my career, I would always be the only female or the only Black female. There are only a few women in engineering, especially computer science. So we encourage each other and figure out how to get more women interested in our field.

And when a young girl sees somebody who looks like her in the workplace, it gives her another option.

When you're exposed to seeing female engineers, now you know that's an option for you. It's like, "Hey, if they did it, then maybe I can do it, too." It also provides a different kinda confidence. When you see somebody else in a position who is like you, it just really sticks.

When I started work, I had questions about whether I would fit in my company. In undergrad, I attended an HBCU (Historically Black Colleges and Universities). It was a predominantly Black school. So, everybody looked like me. But when I started in the workforce, it was totally the opposite. There were not a lot of people who looked like me. So, it was that confidence thing. I would be in meetings wondering if I fit in, feeling that loneliness, like, there's nobody who looks like me in the meeting. So, just trying to figure out how to fit in and how things are going to go, can affect your confidence. If I could have walked through the door and seen somebody else like me, even if it were just another woman or a woman of color, I would have had more confidence starting out.

On Building Effective Relationships

When I was straight out of college and had started at my company, I knew I wanted a mentor. I wanted somebody to whom I could talk to and ask questions, somebody who could help guide me. At that point, I really didn't know anybody in the company but my manager and the people on my team. So, I just asked my manager, "Hey, I'm looking for a mentor." He asked me if I had any kinda preference. Did I want a man or a woman? What type of mentor was I looking for? He actually sent me a list of names. I reached out to about three of them and really hit it off with two of them.

One of my mentors, who was at my company for forty-plus years, just retired last year, but we've still kept in touch. She has been around for so long that she has mentored other people. She would introduce us if they were in my area or working at the same site. It was a networking thing. I like having that relationship, that guidance, and that opportunity to network. Because of our relationship, my mentor got me into a really good program when I told her I wanted to try some different work.

I'm such an advocate for having a mentor.

I've always had unofficial mentors growing up—I was in Girl Scouts and did those types of things. Since I've had mentors throughout my career, that's what I try to do now for others. For about ten years, I have always mentored with Big Brothers Big Sisters or Girls, Inc. That was one of my main goals before having kids. I knew that once I had my own kids, my focus would be more on my family than on these girls. When I was a freshman at Tuskegee and in Texas, Girls, Inc. had a STEM program for young ladies in middle and elementary school. I would teach them about robotics, airplanes, and different topics every week. I love that we can start them young. The program piqued a lot of the girls' interests. I think without them being exposed to STEM at a young age, sometimes they may not even know about something or that it exists. If you remember using a computer to make a robot go across the room when you were nine or ten, it's more likely to make an impact.

I also did Code Quest, where we taught high school students about simulators, coding, and those types of things.

In anybody's story or life, there's always going to be some turning point, times when you have to make tough decisions, whether it's about life or something in life that happens and changes or shifts your career. Those are the times when you weigh your priorities and what's important to you at that moment. Always seek out advice. My mentors have helped me get to many different places in my career that I probably wouldn't have gotten to. They have gotten me opportunities I wouldn't have had if it hadn't been for them. Every story changes every couple of years based on whatever the family or work dynamic is at the time. So I would say be open to those turning points. Be open when it comes to your career.

Don't be afraid to try new things or make big changes.

I always try to talk to my network when I'm making decisions. A lot of people in my network work in different companies. So, I'm always curious to see how their own companies handle things or what opportunities they provide for their employees. I have a really good friend who's a VP of human resources. So, whenever I have conversations with HR, my boss, or even my employees, especially if it's a serious topic or a crucial conversation, I'm sure to talk to her to get her side of things.

That's why it's very essential to build those effective relationships.

Your performance plays only one part in your career path. A lot of the opportunities and positions that have come my way have been because of my mentors. Even when I get new people on my team now, I always stress to them to get a mentor. It helps them to have someone to talk to, to guide them, and to help them navigate through their career. The relationships you build with your mentors and network will help you in those turning points. That's important.

You've also got to be there for each other, so it's not just one-sided in the relationship.

On Letting Go of "I'll Do It"

My friend and I had our daughters around the same time, like a month apart. My daughter is almost four months old; I had her in June. My friend had her daughter in May. And she said to me in a text two or three weeks ago that she's either going to have to transition to extreme part-time or quit her job altogether. It's really because of COVID because her husband is working, and she doesn't want to put her kid in daycare. It's all these circumstances that contribute to it.

Usually, these things fall on the woman, and we're more likely to stop working to take care of the kids or do whatever we need to do. I've heard of quite a few people adjusting and changing their schedules along these lines, especially with virtual school. A lot of parents who can't work remotely have to find different avenues or options. Sometimes people expect the mom to stay at home versus the dad. I think for many women, I won't say we would prefer to do this, but we're more of the nurturers and the ones who are gonna take care of the kids and ensure they have everything they need. So, sometimes, I think the mom feels like, "If I stay home, I'll get it done."

It's like that in the workforce, too.

We had this same conversation about women leaders. When I was in Fort Worth, my VP started a network and a forum with women leaders, where we all got to know each other and had an outlet to talk about things and help each other grow. One of the topics one time was just how women think, "I'll do it because I know I'll get it done." Somebody was like, "Is this because we like to do it, or is it because we just think we should?" When there's a female leader in the room among other leaders, directors, or VPs, they say that the woman always naturally goes to the computer and starts typing, even though everyone is a peer and at the same level. It's not like somebody is there as a scribe. Yet the female leaders always end up at the computer doing the typing or writing, like the secretary. This came up, and it was just so funny, but it made us ask the same thing: "Do we think it's because we feel like we should, or does it just come naturally?"

One of the directors said she does it because the others type too slow, and she knows she'll get it done.

I think that kinda goes back to the same thing. Some women want to take this on because they know they'll get things done. I think a lot of times, too, with gender roles, society expects women to be at home. If the woman makes more money, maybe it makes sense for the husband to be home. I believe it depends on the household dynamic, and honestly, it can be a little bit of both.

We need to let go of thinking we have to be the person to take it all on even though we know we can and will get it done.

Epilog

Fast Forward to May 2022, last month, I had my second child (another girl) and am currently on maternity leave. I am still with Lockheed Martin and, surprisingly, will still work full-time. My husband has adjusted his schedule and is home more to help. So, I am getting the support and help I need between him and my mom. My company and role continue to grow as our site has grown from eighty ADP team members to about 300. Of those 300, the software team has tripled, so we are hiring more managers to help me with the Marietta site.

My responsibilities have grown a lot as I'm responsible for not just staffing the site but overseeing the stand-up of our labs, supporting over three different programs, and managing other leaders and leads.

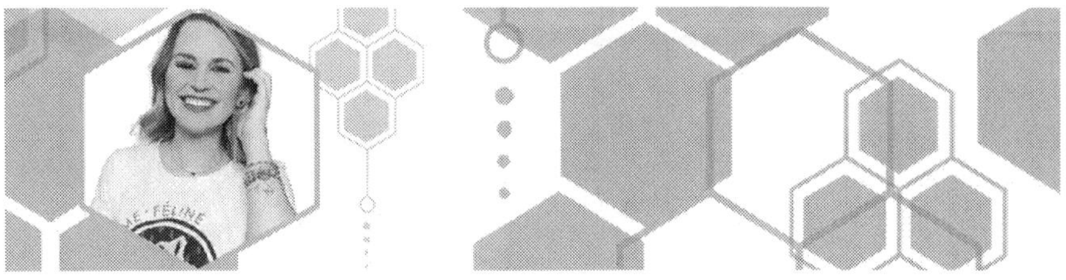

Andrea (Andi) Ruda

Founder & CEO at Rainbow CFO

My company provides fractional CFO consulting services while promoting diversity in the C-suite. Prior to founding Rainbow CFO, I was CFO at international jewelry retailer ALEX AND ANI where I led the finance organization through a full debt and equity restructuring.

An Enabling Education

At age two, I started going to Montessori school. Their philosophy is that you're not in any one grade. You're in a room with kids up to three years older than you, all being educated independently. You might be getting a math lesson while another student's doing English, then you're self-teaching yourself Spanish, and then you decide to pick up a book.

You quickly learn how to work independently.

I stayed in Montessori through fourth grade. There were only three kids in the fourth grade at that time. It was very different from traditional elementary school. There were times, though, I would ask, "Why don't I go to a normal school?" But now I know it was the right place for me.

So many kids thrive off the group and are measured against everyone else. At Montessori, it was about what you were ready for and gravitated towards. I gravitated toward math and was doing it at the level that best suited me. The more challenge I needed, the more I got.

My time there really developed me as an independent thinker.

Instead of just going to school and doing the work because I was told to do it, I came to school every day thinking, "I want to do this today, and here's why." It instilled in me a thought process of not just doing something because you're supposed to do it. I thought about every action and why.

Interestingly, this is a problem at a lot of companies too. People come in and do their job without thinking because it's always been done that way, or someone told them to do it, so they just did it.

After fourth grade, I went to an all-girls school, Kent Place, an independent school in New Jersey. I have only great things to say about why I am the way I am from going there. Their mission is to build young women to be leaders in the world. I love how their goal was to prepare you ethically and tactically to get out there and make a difference. They sent the clear message that women aren't gonna see change until they lead that change.

Going to an all-girls school, especially in the middle school years when people are insecure, was great for me. I felt supported at school and didn't have those awkward middle school feelings. I was always taking on a lot and trying new things that I probably wouldn't have tried if it wasn't an all-girls school. I would have been more self-conscious around guys at that age.

I have very positive memories of my childhood and high school. I was very blessed.

I was a big painter in high school. And every weekend, I would go to the city to take classes at the Fashion Institute of Technology (FIT).

For a while, I thought I was going to art school. My mom's an oil painter, and I was going to do the same thing. But when I was applying to school, there was this part of me that thought, "If you go to art school, you're hanging your hat on art, so you better want to do art because that's what you're setting yourself up for."

I wound up applying to business school because I realized every career, even art, would come down to my understanding of how a business works. And that knowledge would be helpful no matter what I did. I ultimately went to Stern business school at New York University where I did wind up minoring in art.

My Business and Creative Sides

My dad, mom, brother, and I are incredibly close.

My dad is an anesthesiologist and was also the CEO and Chairman of an anesthesia group. I learned a lot about leadership watching him deal with tensions, problems, and growth as he took the group from one hospital to a multi-hospital group. I admired how he treated his colleagues and how they respected him for it.

His job was actually life and death. He would say, "It's not about putting people to sleep; it's about bringing them back awake." So as much stress as I feel in my job, it's not life or death like his.

My mom is extremely creative and is a fantastic artist. Growing up, she volunteered at my school for the art gallery and was on the board of an art association. She taught me so much about love, loyalty, and how passion will bring you fulfillment.

My dad gave me my business side; my mom gave me my creative side.

My brother is three years younger than me. We're best friends. My brother's a great musician and an athlete. We all had different things we were good at in my family, and we were all supportive of each other.

They helped me believe that I could actually do anything I wanted to do.

College Internships

I was excited about the idea of work. So when I got to college, I was determined to start working right away. In my first semester of freshman year, I got my first unpaid internship for a fashion company.

In addition to class, I commuted to Brooklyn a few days a week for that internship. I was in total intern mode, getting coffee, running errands, and so on. I took a lot of the art and fashion experience I gained from taking classes at FIT during high school and merged it with what I was doing in college. I didn't want to feel like I was giving up on art.

I was aggressive about school but didn't love school. Going to class and doing homework doesn't energize me. However, I was excited to be at NYU because of the endless opportunities to get work experience. I was always aggressively looking for new jobs.

In my first full-time internship the summer after freshman year, I was a project manager at Thomson Reuters. When my boss, Susan, first met me, she was like, "Oh, did they make some kind of mistake? You're a freshman. This is a different kind of internship". But I said, "No. They didn't make a mistake. I'm ready to do the job." I was very positive. Very all in. She and I have kept in touch. It was such a great experience. I often think, "I got a head start. It was the right time, right place."

Thomson Reuters delivered loan pricing on debt in the market to all of their customers. Previously they were sending automated emails. I moved all their debt customers to an integrated platform where they could go in anytime and check it themselves.

I coordinated the initial calls, worked with technology to move them, with legal to draft contracts, with the banks to do demos, and then moved all their emails onto this new platform. It was the most holistic project management role, and I had no idea what I was doing. I was Googling everything as I went. And so I learned on the job!

My boss Susan was incredibly supportive and believed in me, "This project is yours. Go." She's a strong woman and is greatly respected. She was very firm, not a pushover. She didn't back down when she had an opinion. If something didn't go right, she didn't shy away from giving direct feedback. I noticed that right away.

As an eighteen-year-old, I was like, "Wow, I want to make sure I'm like Susan." I saw the authority she would take and the way she directed conversations. She stood out to me as a leader right away.

Susan was my first career role model.

I admired what she was doing and the way she carried herself. She had a level of authority and no-nonsense that I hadn't seen before in my prior internships. She was a woman commanding such authority and living her life how she wanted to live it.

She seemed very happy.

And she was very happy to give credit where credit was due.

She had an all-male team. It was Susan and me and then a team full of men led by a man. They were all very supportive of me. They would take me to clients and let me lead the demos as an eighteen-year-old. The support I got from the team started and ended with Susan because she set the tone.

That internship set me on the path of believing I could do anything I set my mind on. It familiarized me with so many of the basics of business. And set me up well for all the other internships I had after that.

It was more than just being given authority. I worked with contracts. I did demos. I arranged client meetings. I got to do and learn so much in that short summer. I learned more about the tactical fundamentals of working than I did from business school. Coming out of NYU, I could do a bunch of calculations. But the internships taught me how to be a functioning, confident, likable businessperson.

To get internships, I leaned into networking to find opportunities. I would reach out to a friend of a friend at a company I was interested in. I sent cold-call emails. I reached out through hiring boards and things like that.

My boss, Susan, was ahead of her time with LinkedIn too. In 2010, she told me, "LinkedIn is going to be huge," and she helped me build my profile.

I'm a big fan of moving around a bit in your career because you're forced to work overtime to prove yourself those first few weeks of a new job. So, in college, I did a different internship every semester. Every time I was hustling to show them that I could do the work really well, and at the same time, I was finding and interviewing for the next role. I always had to have my A game on and be prepared to articulate the value I'd created in my prior roles.

Talking about tasks and not value is the biggest mistake I see now that I'm on the other side of hiring and reading resumes. The biggest difference between someone I'll automatically talk to and someone I will pass over is, "Can you demonstrate the value you created?"

So, I think I stood out as a college student because I would say, "I moved ten clients over to this software." "I found a hundred-thousand dollars of missed monthly billings." You put those amounts in, and it's like, "Wow, I see the impact she made."

I didn't discover all this on my own. Everywhere I've gone, I've had someone who's given me sound advice that I take to heart, write down, and try to live. So that's another reason I'm a fan of moving around early in your career. You learn things from so many different people.

I had a finance engineering internship in college that wasn't great. I learned a lot that prepared me to be a much better Excel wizard by the time I got to consulting. But my manager was awful. It was a guy, and he would constantly make jokes about not wanting to be in the same room as me because I was a young girl, and he didn't want his wife to think he was harassing girls.

That was funny to him.

I also worked as an art director assistant at a TV show. I interned at Accenture in my junior year. I did all kinds of other internships, too. I learned a lot of different skills and what the day-to-day in different companies looked like. It helped me rule out certain things too.

When it comes down to it, I really love the business and strategy side. So, in the same way, that I can advocate for myself, I can do that for a business, which always felt like my value-add.

My consulting internship at Accenture was my favorite, so I took their offer when I got it.

Being the Squeaky Wheel

After graduating college, my first full-time role was consulting at Accenture. People go to consulting to get a bunch of experience at different places because you're on project after project.

Early in my time at Accenture, a manager told me, "If you can be the best person at Excel, you'll be invaluable to every single person you meet." So, I took that to heart when I was an analyst and got really good at Excel.

Then I built the business case for my first project and started to run a bunch of functions in my first year. Next, I started building my little team. I quickly had a few people reporting to me, including MBA-level consultants. Then, I pushed aggressively for myself to get promoted. Because of the value I was providing and articulating, there was no way someone could really say no.

You have to push for yourself – always.

But there were times I was overlooked at Accenture. You have to be the squeaky wheel for yourself. Otherwise, it's easier for people to just pass over you for someone else.

I stayed in consulting for four years. That's longer than most people stay in consulting out of college, but I had a lot of fun with it. I had a great mentor Gary who ran finance and risk for North America. He was on my project on my first day at Accenture. He wound up being my biggest advocate there.

I pretty much only went on his projects. He gave me so much exposure to the business side of consulting, which was really rare. I stayed as long as I did at Accenture because I was working for someone like him. Consulting can have its pros and cons. It can be excellent for experience but frustrating because you often lack control over the project you're on. But I really trusted him, believed in him, and admired him. I liked how much he valued communication.

He was the busiest guy. He was running finance for Accenture in America, but he had this monthly town hall. I helped him plan it, which was cool for me to see the higher-level strategy.

I admired that he never skipped it, whereas many leaders think, "Oh, it doesn't matter if we skip a communication here or there." He taught me a lot about transparency, consistency and trusting your people with information. As a leader, I now see how important it is to be transparent and what happens when you're not.

He also really believed in women. Some of his top partners were women. He was never someone who pursued diversity just to check a box. He believed in us. He knew we were his top talent. It wasn't in a patronizing way or because HR was telling him to support diversity. He truly was really great that way.

I'm fortunate. At a large company, a lot of people felt very lost. So it was great to have people who looked out for me and believed in me. It was never lip service.

Obviously, you have to play your cards well. I wasn't asking for a promotion every day. But when I felt like I deserved more responsibility, felt strongly about not going to one project, or had an opinion I felt was worth saying, I acted on it.

Belief is huge. My ability and desire to perform go through the roof when people believe in me. It's bigger than salary increases or a bigger title. It's the belief that we are going to accomplish something together.

On the other hand, sometimes you work with leaders who don't believe in you or believe, but because of how they communicate, you don't see it. So in those situations, you have to figure out how to avoid taking it personally.

Do not let others destroy your belief in yourself.

Becoming a CFO

Accenture was a great place to learn and grow early in my career. But ultimately, it's a big consulting company, and you have very little autonomy over your projects.

I worked on many great projects, but the final one was unfulfilling.

It was for a different leader at the company, and I didn't feel valued. Even though I was running a big project for a global payments company, I wanted more autonomy and was ready for something different. At a big company like Accenture, you are just a number. You can form a good network and feel like you're part of something smaller, which I definitely did. But I wondered, "What is it like to work at a smaller company?"

After reporting to CFOs and working in the financial services industry as a consultant, I was mostly qualified to do internal strategy roles at a bank. Not just finance for any industry, but finance for finance. So I started applying to a bunch of relevant jobs on job sites and interviewed for roles within banks. Smart people, nothing to complain about, but they were with big companies where I didn’t feel like I’d really own something start to finish. I wasn't feeling excited.

I was thinking, "I may as well stay at Accenture. I have a great network here. I have somewhat of a mini family." I was disheartened. I wanted to try something different. but what I was qualified for wasn't matching what I had imagined.

So I was lucky enough that my path crossed with my next boss Mark who became a life-changing mentor of mine. Mark has a law firm and many other businesses and needed a CFO.

I talked to Mark about the role and finally felt that jolt of excitement. I knew it was the next right choice for me. And I knew that learning a thing or two about the law and working at a legal services firm would be extremely valuable to me for the same reason I went into finance – every business needs to make money, and every company needs to follow the law. So, learning a thing or two about law wouldn't hurt.

So, I joined Geragos & Geragos, which led to one of the pivotal moments of my career.

Mark was another awesome mentor who took a huge chance on me. So at twenty-five, I started working for his firm as the CFO.

Taking the CFO title felt like a stretch at first. But I very quickly got the lay of the land overseeing all aspects of finance for his various companies. I hit the ground running in the first few months, enjoyed the team, and enjoyed learning about hospitality and law. Every day I was learning through doing.

It was awesome!

I finally didn't have to make a PowerPoint deck to get the most minor decisions made. At first, I sent him slides, and he would say, "We can talk over email. Or call me, and we'll just figure out what we need to do." So we would talk and then do things. It was definitely a transition from Accenture!

At Accenture, you always worked with others and learned because people told you what to do. But at Geragos & Geragos, I learned as I tried things out, seeing what worked and what didn't. And Mark believed in me no matter what which was the best intrinsic motivation.

It was really liberating to see that at smaller companies, you can just make decisions and get shit done.

Prejudged

Alex and Ani, the jewelry company, was one of Geragos's legal clients. That's how I got to know Carolyn, the CEO. Then only ten months after I started at Geragos and Geragos, Alex and Ani's CFO left. Carolyn asked if I could come up and help fill the gap.

Carolyn is such a warm, talented person. And she's another person who took a big chance on me. I hit the ground running, taking it day by day, making sure things were running as they should. I took a deep breath because when you're a twenty-six-year-old stepping into the CFO role at a billion-dollar company, you're shaking in your shoes a bit. I had a song I listened to every morning before work to hype myself up.

The intent wasn't initially for me to fully take over the CFO role, but I'm so grateful it evolved into that.

Carolyn told me that she had hired quite a few CFOs with years and years of experience, but she was really looking for someone who would work hard and whom she could trust. I knew that I could do that.

I leaned on the Alex and Ani leadership team tremendously. It was a women-led company, and I felt so supported there.

But a lot of external people weren't thrilled to see an unfamiliar face in the CFO role. So I had to deal with a lot of conflict because I was a different profile filling a traditionally male role.

When I was dealing with X, Y, or Z or feeling like someone didn't think I should be in the CFO role because I was a woman or talking down to me because I was younger, I knew I had the support of my team and the leadership team. So that was my coping mechanism.

I was very supported by the people who mattered. And very unsupported by the people who I deemed didn't matter.

I was met with a lot of confused looks.

Some didn't know how to deal with someone like me being in a CFO role. Others embraced the fact that I was young and a woman, "Wow! How cool. Here's a young woman with a great opportunity and working hard as she can for it!"

I was commuting from New York City to Rhode Island for two and a half years every Monday through Friday. Aspects of my job that I could do in my sleep now were things I was still learning. So, everything was a lot of work because I was doing them for the first time. And I had to ramp up quickly. So, I would work until 2:00 AM every night and start up at 7:00 AM the following day. I think about that time, and I feel tired and energized all at the same time!

The retail industry was new to me too. I was trying to stay two steps ahead as my inbox blew up. I was managing a team of seventy people. I had previously managed people, worked in finance, and had a CFO title. But everything at Alex and Ani was multiplied.

So, the idea that there was such a tremendous amount of work to do with such an enormous amount of responsibility on my shoulders on top of being met with such, I'd say, prejudgment – the belief that I couldn't do it – made it a lot harder. A fifty-year-old man in a new CFO role would have stress. But there was a second job on my shoulders: convincing people that I could do it.

Men walk into a room, and people assume they can do the job unless they prove otherwise. But I walked into a room, and people assumed I could not do the CFO job until I proved to them that I could.

So, I had to work very hard to prove to people that I was qualified and could do it.

Dealing with all the doubt was more challenging than any work I was doing at Alex and Ani.

There are many differences between being the CFO and being a person on a finance team. When you are the CFO, the most important thing is to look at the overall financial picture every day. Where did money come in from, and where did money go out? How is that all coming together? From a skillset perspective, that was a shift I learned to navigate quickly. But for me, it was also about having the toughness to wake up every morning and continue to push through when people doubted me every single step of the way.

I'm super tough now because of it. If you had talked to me then, I probably would have said something different, but the experience shaped me in profound ways.

The proposal

It never ceased to amaze me as to what would come out of some people's mouths. Once, when we sought consulting support from experts who'd gone through a restructuring, we wanted guidance on negotiating with the parties involved. We had been introduced to one consultant who came by the office and met with me and our CEO. Just an ordinary meeting. We walked him through everything and told him the support we were looking for.

He shook my hand and said, "I'll get you a proposal in the next few days."

As the approving CFO, he sent the restructuring proposal to me and added a note that said, "Just to keep everyone happy, we'll bring in..." And then he referenced a man who'd been in finance for years and years but didn't have any CFO experience, "Andrea will still perform her duties; however, her title will change to Assistant to the CFO. That will be an amazing opportunity for her." He was banking on the fact that an older male would put external parties more at ease. So this guy would come in and be the frontman.

A consultant who expected me to hire him actually sent me that proposal. Didn't think twice about what he was saying.

I remember opening it and crying. It was on a Sunday. I remember sitting in my apartment; my friend was over.

I was upset and offended.

Then I thought, "Wait, I'm just going to respond and tell him I am not going to use his proposal." That's what was so ridiculous. The proposal was sitting in my hands to decide. Not anyone else's. So I replied, "I'm not going to go that route. Thank you." You have to realize they were trying to sell consulting work to me, the CFO.

The bias that you need a man to do the job is so ingrained in people's minds that someone sent that ridiculous proposal to me. It was one of the most startling days in my whole career.

What was so crazy was the exchange between this man and me was so respectful. He was not trying to offend me or showing up to attack. He didn't realize he was being discriminatory. He was showing up to try to sell work to the CFO of Alex and Ani. He actually thought it was normal or helpful to suggest this. I was just in shock. I told so many people, I'm like, "Wow, I got a proposal to demote myself in exchange for money."

Like WTH?!

That moment will be etched into my brain forever.

Whoever says women don't have a harder battle than men, I dare you to find a man who would have sent that proposal to another man, "Hey Bob, I think you should demote yourself and become the assistant. You can still do all the work, but we'll make it look like someone else's."

It's ironic and sad because the consultant was probably right. Certain people probably would have felt more at ease dealing with someone just like them in the role. Does that make it right? No. But that's what we were dealing with – people would have felt more comfortable with that man in the role, who had never been a CFO before, rather than me.

The thing is, I did have that confidence where I knew I could do the job and nothing was going to stop me. I was confident, "No, I'm doing this role, and I'm going to keep doing it!" It was one of those moments you remember, "Oh, this is all very real. I'm not making this up in my head."

Sometimes for your peace of mind and comfort, you tell yourself maybe the mistreatment you're experiencing is in your head. You don't want to believe that people are biased or don't want you to succeed. So it was a transition for me to accept that not everyone would like me. Coming to terms with that has really helped.

I remember thinking, "Okay, the good news is you're not crazy. It's not in your head. But the bad news is that discrimination and bias are very real. Your worst fears are true. These people do not believe in you and do not want you to succeed. They would rather see you taken out of your role." So, it was one of those double-edged-sword kinds of days,

I got that email on a Sunday. I was commuting to Rhode Island from New York City Monday through Friday every week. I would get home Friday night and begin packing to leave again on Sunday. I was never totally relaxed. I remember thinking, "Damn it! It's Sunday. The one day I'm supposed to be able to sit and chill and pretend like some of these problems aren't happening." And then that proposal comes in and hits me. I was like, "I just want to lay down."

Sometimes you get so tired from fighting.

Then something else comes up, or someone surprises you with a nasty comment. It's exhausting. "Can't I just do my job?! Can't I just look at the financials and focus on the company?" As a woman in leadership, doing your job becomes a small part of the work.

Men can't really appreciate that side of what we deal with when we show up at work every day.

Taking a Public Stance

Like I said, I always felt very supported by my team at Alex and Ani.

But I faced many instances of discrimination, especially when interacting with people from traditional finance outside the company. For example, one external consultant treated me like an assistant, not his boss or even as a peer. He would ask me to print out his travel reservations, call a cab for him, and things like that. He'd make demeaning requests all the time without thinking twice.

I faced ongoing bias and dealt with challenges above and beyond normal CFO responsibilities. Unfortunately, this is the burden that women carry when they're in leadership roles traditionally held by men.

Ultimately, we brought a lawsuit against an outside party for their treatment of our female leadership team. I can't get into too much of the legal detail, but it was an extremely difficult time for me personally. It was the culmination of two years of being up against people who didn't want me to succeed every single day.

On one hand, it felt empowering to see my company taking a stance on this issue and acknowledging what I was going through. At the same time, it was all very public. The whole time, I was wondering, "How will this be perceived?" At the end of the day, my name appeared in articles about something very personal. For most people struggling at work or being discriminated against, it's rarely in such a public forum.

That year was so hard.

I had tons of finance work as the new CFO during a pivotal time in the company's history, I was under tremendous pressure dealing with the emotional side of everything, and I was navigating all of our other external parties and lenders who were hearing about the lawsuit because it was so public. The good news is that many women saw the whole ordeal as empowering because it acknowledged what so many women and people of color face in boardrooms and meetings all the time.

They appreciated that we took a stance.

I believe so passionately in fighting for those issues. I'm working hard for women to have an equal seat at the table in finance and in the working world. But, at the same time, all these experiences of discrimination made me feel incredibly vulnerable. It took its toll. At times I'd go home not believing in myself.

It was a really trying experience.

But I realized "the people who matter to me are supporting me! The others didn't really matter." It didn't fix the situation, but it helped me get through it and become stronger. Going through something like that, especially when it's so public, makes you so much stronger.

That was a pivotal moment for me.

The whole experience gave me a sense of purpose. Before, I had loved work. I loved the tasks I was accomplishing as CFO. But that situation instilled in me this burning desire to make changes and take on whatever I could to work towards a better environment for everyone.

Bad Timing

While all this was happening, we got a new CEO named Bob. He became another amazing mentor to me as he had been CFO of a major jewelry company before. From him I expanded my hard skillset much further that I was able to before. So, even as things changed at Alex and Ani, I found new ways to learn and grow beyond those issues I was dealing with. That kept me there and motivated day in day out.

Every week for two and a half years, I commuted to Rhode Island. Then, one day, my twenty-eight-year-old self realized, "You know what, I love my job, but time is passing. I am not near my friends or my family. I'm not really dating. I'm not doing the things I want to do in my personal life because work has taken such a front seat and was all-consuming."

I decided I didn't want to relocate to Rhode Island and wanted to get back to New York City full-time. So, I started looking for jobs closer to home and was put in touch with the founders of Resonance, a fashion technology startup. They were a big draw for me because Resonance is changing the retail industry by making clothing on demand. Knowing the inventory issues we faced at Alex and Ani, going to a place that was trying to change was really enticing to me.

Becoming the CFO of a technology startup was super important to me too. If you can't keep up with the pace of technology, you'll get automated or become redundant someday.

At Resonance, I worked on putting processes in place to measure performance. I was looking at our factories to see how we were measuring the cost of every single item coming in and out, setting up corporate processes for payments, figuring out everything we needed to run the business, and, ultimately, keeping an eye on where every dollar was coming in and out of the company.

That was different from my prior role at Alex and Ani, where they had already had explosive growth. Alex and Ani was a well-oiled machine that had been around since the early 2000s. So, finance itself didn't need an overhaul from a process perspective.

The work I did at Alex and Ani was more restructuring, changing what we were spending money on. It was putting the governance back into the business to rope people in and start to look at vendors and sourcing, how we're negotiating contracts, and what we actually needed versus what was nice to have. I might be rusty on the numbers, but we cut about forty-five percent off the P & L operating expenses during my time there.

At Resonance, it was totally different. We were in startup mode. Everyone was very thrifty. No one was spending where they shouldn't be. But we needed to have the right processes in place. So, it was more process-driven than wrangling negotiations or product sourcing.

I learned so much at Resonance about technology and how to think differently about doing things the way they should be done going forward versus how they have been done historically.

The funny part of all of this though is that I left Alex and Ani to move back to New York City to regain my life in my twenties. But this was in February 2020. I started at Resonance about four weeks before the COVID quarantine started. The worst timing ever to reclaim my "normal life" back in NYC!

Over the Rainbow

I was working at Resonance for about a year when I realized I could take the skills I learned in my CFO roles and optimize them for my own life and the value I bring to companies. I believe full-time CFO roles keep most people so in the weeds of the business they don't see the bigger picture like a CFO needs to do. I also believe companies should nurture more young talent from within.

I was really passionate about those two ideas and decided to start my own company.

So, here I am today, in the first few weeks of founding my new fractional CFO venture, Rainbow CFO. The concept is to support businesses as a fractional CFO but then train the more junior resources to become CFOs so they can run the finance function themselves.

I've put a lot of time into networking, got the entity set up for my new company, the website is underway, and I have a half dozen or so potential clients lined up.

The value proposition of my new company Rainbow CFO is twofold.

First, it is an interim or fractional CFO consulting service. For someone less familiar with that space, it is offering the service, the knowledge, and the experience of an experienced CFO to smaller companies who can't afford the full salary and benefits and all that comes with hiring a CFO full-time.

For a startup, for example, it's to put the structure in place to get the company off the ground properly, to forecast growth and expenses, and to help establish governance. The fractional CFO also holds teams accountable and gets people trained on how to read a P&L, manage a budget, and think financially.

A lot of companies are founder-led when they first start. The budget is almost the last consideration because everyone is so focused on "What's our product? Can we do what we want to do? Who is our target buyer?" Then they think, "Let's figure out how to manage the financials once we know if these other things are even possible."

At some stage, the company will need a CFO. But they may not be able to afford or need one full-time. So, the first part of Rainbow CFO's value proposition is that we offer fractional CFO or interim CFO services.

The second value proposition, which is really exciting for me, is nurturing young budding talent. There are a lot of startups and smaller companies where there is some really incredible promising finance talent. Maybe they're a director of finance, a finance manager, or they've worked at a bank or in consulting. They have some solid experience, and they're hungry to learn, but they don't have the years of experience or mentoring to get them to that head of finance or CFO role.

In this situation, the company would hire Rainbow CFO for a few months so that we can help get things set up from the fractional perspective. But in addition, we'll work alongside the existing finance talent to help groom them into a more senior finance role.

It comes down to teaching them a CFO mindset versus a junior finance mindset. It's about where to look every day and where to direct their attention so that opportunities or challenges are pushed to the various business experts who can focus on fixing those challenges or taking advantage of the opportunities.

You hire Rainbow CFO for a few months, and then you're left with finance talent who has a good idea of what it takes to grow the business. In an ideal world, you make them your head of finance and keep Rainbow on for some ad hoc consulting for restructuring or fundraising or what have you. The goal is to enable more young, diverse talent, men and women. Helping young talent grow and not having to take a back seat to someone who's done it before when they're perfectly competent, capable, and hungry for the challenge.

I know personally, it's an uphill battle being a woman in finance. And I don't have it even half as challenging as many.

I could have stayed on the safer path working for other companies in CFO roles. But someone needs to change what that role looks like because it's so uncomfortable for people who don't fit the traditional "CFO profile.". That's my motivation. The CFO role doesn't need to be as heavy-duty a paid role as it used to be. Nowadays, finance is pretty automated, so you don't need in-depth manual audits anymore. As long as you have someone with a good head on their shoulders who understands how to scale, it doesn't have to be someone with fifty years of experience. You don't have to go through twenty-five years of being the finance manager to become the senior manager or get to this or that level.

People will tell me, "It's crazy that you had a CFO role at twenty-five." But I don't want that to be crazy. I want more and more people to be able to take these stretch roles when they're hungry, willing to work, and willing to make changes.

If I can help companies identify young talent and help them figure out a more creative way to build their teams to get different voices into the C-suite, then I've done my job. Success for Rainbow CFO is changing the cultures and structure of a lot of companies. It's the perfect way to use my strengths, skills, and experiences to create opportunities for others.

That's where my head's at, "How can we make finance more comfortable for anyone who wants to have a career here?" It's been very uncomfortable for too many people for too long.

We have to change that.

Andi's Reflections

On Owning It

I would rephrase "Fake it till you make it" to "Own it." Own your role and own your value.

I've always owned that I am a competent person who can figure things out. At Alex and Ani, there was a song I would listen to every morning to pump myself up and remind myself to take it one day at a time and trust that I would figure it all out.

So, let's not say "fake it till you make it" anymore. Instead, let's say own it and be confident that even if you don't know how to do it today, you will know soon.

Be confident in yourself that you will learn how to do it. Trust that people hired you in your role because they believe in your capability to figure it out.

But you also gotta be aware of what you don't know, own your blind spots, and raise your hand for help. Otherwise, your blind spots can become problems. Especially in finance, if you're not transparent, things can come across as wrong or dishonest. When you don't know what you don't know, seek advice from a colleague or use a consultant. I owned the problem, raised my hand for help, pushed through, and learned.

Owning it is advocating for what you're good at, being transparent about what you're not, and trusting that you'll figure it out on your own or with help.

On Confidence

I remember the first day of my finance engineering internship was all coding. I was like, "What the…?" But, it was just a routine task by the summer's end. My mindset is to believe that my brain is as competent as the best in terms of firing on all cylinders. So then, why can't I learn anything? I don't know how to do computer programming, but why wouldn't I be able to learn it if someone else could?

My confidence comes from people believing in me at an early age. And because people thought I could do X, Y, or Z, it paved the way for me to believe it too.

Confidence comes down to believing you can learn anything. And once you acknowledge that, you realize that you can do anything.

So when I stepped in to be the CFO at my third company after Alex and Ani, I felt very confident. One, because I'd done the CFO role twice before. And two, I was eager to step into a new company and learn a new position and industry. To be pushed and challenged.

My parents would tell you that I have had an innate forceful and independent streak since I was a kid. I always wanted to do things for myself. To figure things out. That's been helpful to my career. I hope more women understand that confidence is a journey. So, apply for that role you want. And if you're genuinely not qualified, it'll come out, you won't get the job, and then you apply to something else. No one's gonna fault you for applying. And you'll learn in the process.

On the flip side, we don't celebrate our successes as much as we should. I'm so focused on getting better at my roles that I rarely stop and think, "This is cool that I have this role," or, "This is great; let me celebrate it."

Again, I was very lucky in my foundational years that I had more support than lack of support. Sadly, many people come from a place where they haven't been supported, which puts them at a disadvantage. Believing that others believe in you and support you is critical to enabling you to take risks.

Unfortunately, as a woman, there will be times when people will not believe in you. But guess what? They are not the only people in this world with a voice or an opinion. So find a way to believe in yourself more than you believe in the people around you.

I know that's easier said than done.

The good thing about today's world is that seeking coaching, therapy, and support is okay. A while back, that wouldn't be something you spoke about. I'm very open when talking through problems. I talk to my Chief core group, mentors, and therapists. Not because I couldn't do it on my own but because it's better to get a second opinion and have someone to talk to. It takes a village.

Companies are starting to push getting support as well. So, if you get stuck with a shitty manager, hopefully, your company is providing you with resources to find mentoring elsewhere, whether within the company or with a professional.

It's a slippery slope when people don't believe in you, or you're unsupported at home or work. But believe enough in yourself to seek out the resources you need to go after what you want.

Many women in this generation did not grow up believing they would become a CEO or a CFO. Women will only realize they can go after roles like CEO once they are taught to believe they will be one someday. And they need to see more examples of people who look like them who have successfully gone after power.

Confidence is believing you can learn to do anything. That belief comes from feeling supported and seeing people like you in power. When you don't have that, you must figure out how to find that belief in yourself anyway.

On Pushing Boundaries

Women not only have to do their job but also tune out the haters, deal with the people who want them to fail, and then be overly thankful, gracious, and appreciative of the opportunities they are given. On top of all that, they have to change the world.

It's such a burden having to take care of your own feelings and also take on the feelings of the people around you. You are expected to make people feel comfortable at the same time that you have to make people feel like you're fighting this fight.

I'm the most confident person. I can't get much more confident. But when you act too confident, you're scrutinized for that as well.

Sometimes we're exhausted and are just not looking for another battle where every stride is met with pushback or scrutiny or people questioning our ability. Somedays, you're just like, "Life is short. I just want to enjoy my day." But you have to keep pushing. You have to keep making others uncomfortable to bring comfort to everyone else more broadly.

This is my whole vision for Rainbow CFO. There are plenty of women out there who are confident in their skills but are sitting forever in that more junior finance position. And they're not being considered for the head of finance or CFO roles.

My goal is to say, "Hey, consider your internal talent!" Even if they don't have that CFO title, their experience is different than the person who's been doing it for thirty years or came from a different background. Your internal talent can rise to the occasion if you believe in, support, and recognize them.

When companies pass around the same executives with the same pedigree, they miss out on great internal talent. That's where Rainbow CFO can come in.

On Your Brand

Confidence in how you are perceived by others is your brand.

There will always be people who can do something better than you and worse than you. So, just be yourself.

I don't spend time thinking about how I compare to other people. Actually, I never do. No one has my exact background, my exact experiences, or wants to do what I want to do. There are no longer concrete paths that everyone has to take. So, you can't compare yourself to anyone else.

At least, I don't.

Before, if you wanted to work in finance, you had to be an analyst, then an associate, then move up and up specific levels for X amount of years. You had to have graduated from Ivy Leagues. A lot of people went to investment banking and the more traditional route. They might have a stronger pedigree than I do, but I never think about that. I definitely don't let that hold me back.

The world is more fluid now too.

A hard lesson to learn is that not everyone's gonna like you. In high school, everyone wants to be liked. Then you start to get into the working world and realize you're not everyone's cup of tea. And that's okay.

Someone said that if there are people who don't like you, it means you're taking a stance on something.

When I am in situations where I'm nervous or reluctant, I ask, "What's the worst that can happen?" Often, we're lucky enough that the worst that could happen isn't physical harm or danger. But thinking about that helps me take risks, "Let me take a stab at it."

Some people spend a lot of time thinking about all the people who might be better at something than them. But at the end of the day, I wake up thinking about myself, and I go to sleep thinking about myself. It's not that I'm the most selfish person on the planet. That's just innate human behavior. So, you have to trust that other people aren't going to bed and waking up comparing you to others. Instead, they think about themselves and how you fit into their lives. And you're doing the same.

So, as soon as I realized how selfish people are, and not in a bad way, it was a huge weight off of me because I stopped stressing over that one thing I said, or that time I got that thing wrong. People are innately focused on themselves. No one is going to bed thinking about what you said or did. They are thinking about themselves during that work call or whatever they said.

That's why it can be very freeing to acknowledge that humans are selfish. Selfish may be the wrong word, it's more like self-oriented.

And I love people.

I truly love hearing about what other people are doing and genuinely want to help people. So, it's not selfish or self-centered, but I still would say I am definitely self-oriented. Even the causes I choose to help with come back to what energizes me. There was a Friends episode where Phoebe was convinced that she could do a selfless deed, but along the way, all the characters were pointing out how everything was actually self-serving in some way. Like if you help someone, you feel good about it.

So, self-oriented is the better word.

A piece of advice I give people – whether they're talking about work or talking about a guy they're dating is that "People wake up and go to bed thinking about themselves. So, stop stressing over it. There's so much better stuff to worry about." Instead, it's better to think about what you want to learn and how you will do a good job.

Another thing to remember is that the people who are different tend to be the ones who end up being recognized more than others trying to fit a mold or be like someone else.

I don't want to have the exact pedigree of someone else, as impressive as they may be. I don't need to compare myself to every model on Instagram. If I did, I wouldn't be me. People find me interesting enough as myself, and I know I have something I can bring to create value for their company. So, I like being different. My parents must have done a good job teaching me that in middle school during those awkward years.

To sum it up, just get comfortable with the idea that people wake up and go to bed thinking about themselves and not you. So, you need to wake up and go to bed thinking about yourself. Think about your strengths and think about the ways that you can make yourself better and better each day. Know what you can and can't do and what you want to learn. Then, be open about those areas to yourself and others. And don't overthink anything.

Just do your thing and keep pushing forward.

On Doubters

I may have cared early in my career about how people perceived me. But somewhere along the way, I realized that what others think about me doesn't matter. Many people doubted or perceived me as inadequate until they actually worked with me, and I changed their minds.

I now know that it'll be okay if I don't fit the mold. If I think I can do it, then I'll be able to do it. So, if you know you can do it, you'll be able to do it too.

You have to believe in yourself.

I learned to put that shield up so that if someone doubted me, I wouldn't be sitting at home in tears thinking about their doubts. Of course, early in my career, I had those teary nights, many of them. But I learned to say, "Yeah, but I'm still here! I'm still continuing in my role. I must be doing a good enough job."

If I had spent all my time thinking about what others think, I would not have taken the roles I did. I probably would have been sad and believed them and said, "Oh, you're right." when people would question me or try to knock me down. But I'm like, "Do you expect me to quit my job because you think I can't do it? That's not going to happen here. I want to do this job. And until someone tells me to stop doing it, I will keep doing it."

The doubters don't matter.

On Taking a Stance

People still say things to people that are condescending, biased, or old-fashioned. So, the more you call people out on things, the more people will start to acknowledge it's happening.

I started thinking about ways I may have biases I didn't even realize. So, I decided to be more aware, change myself, and call people out. It doesn't have to be as dramatic as a lawsuit like Alex and Ani's. It can be as simple as saying to people who I love or to others, "Hey, that's not okay. That's condescending, or that's this or that." People respond and take note. Usually, it wasn't intentional. It's the way people grew up and were trained to think. So, they're not registering it as malicious or trying to discriminate against women or any group.

But it's still wrong and needs to be called out, and people's behaviors have to change.

Like the guy that sent me the proposal to demote myself at Alex and Ani, it is so accepted in the banking world that others would deal better with a male CFO and that the woman would be in an assistant role. It's how he was born, raised, and taught. So a lot of the discrimination that women face may not be intentional, which is crazy because when you're a woman, you're like, "How could anyone not see this?!"

When people are like, "Yeah, discrimination is real, but I don't discriminate," they aren't looking inward enough to know that things they have said or done have led to someone going home crying and questioning herself. And women make undercutting comments to women just as much as men do.

So, people have to get comfortable with being uncomfortable.

They have to realize inequities are definitely out there, and they must also recognize their own bias. That can be uncomfortable. All of us must make changes right now so that the next generation will not be raised with those biases. We have to push through and work towards being more inclusive.

And we must have more women of all backgrounds having power, money, and a seat at the table.

There's a lot of hate and racism in the world. We can't tolerate it anymore.

And we can't tolerate unconscious bias anymore, either. Sometimes that's worse because it's just so ingrained in our culture that we don't feel mean or bad about regurgitating them or acting on them. People may not even be aware of the impact of what they are saying or doing. So, we have to call it out and get comfortable making people aware, even though that can be awkward for them and us. Think about it; it's already awkward, uncomfortable, and even dangerous for the people experiencing bias.

So, we have to flip that mindset about who we make uncomfortable.

On Evolving the CFO Role

I love being a CFO. It is really cool to get a seat at the table and see how a company works from start to finish. I love presenting at board meetings. It can be such a rush to know you're representing an entire company and talking to the people who have their own dollars invested and are doing everything in their power to make it work.

Being trusted to have that voice is a really cool experience.

I also love being part of the creative meetings, going through the factory, and learning how a product is made. When your role involves owning all of a company's budgets, it gives you front-row seats to areas you would otherwise never see. That is really cool.

And the CFO role is changing.

There's always going to be a need for finance strategy, and there's always going to be a need for good management. So, there is a need for a CFO in companies. But traditionally, it is very boardroom, conservative, and not hands-on. So when you think of a traditional CFO, you think of someone who's just seeing the very top line, not rolling up their sleeves.

Automation and other technologies are doing so much of that function for companies already. They don't necessarily need a CFO to conduct a traditional audit and work with like a big four firm anymore. The future role of a CFO is going to be more of a problem solver, someone who can direct the company to where they need to look. Even larger companies are using more of a fractional CFO model in the same way their board members might sit on multiple boards versus having to be in the weeds every day.

In the CFO role, or any corporate finance role, you have to understand where the money is coming in and leaving the company better than anyone else there. That is the heart and soul of finance operations. So, whether or not you are in government, retail, financial services, or any industry, knowing that simple principle enables you to be valuable to any of these organizations.

Since deciding to study finance as I applied for college, I've always understood that.

You need to understand business and finance for any company because every company's goal is essentially to create money or to take money in and spend less than you took in. If you understand that, you can work for any kind of company you want, whatever interests you and is exciting for you.

That's why I love the CFO role and don't envision leaving it anytime soon, even though it will look a little bit different in my new venture.

All organizations, even nonprofits, need to be more effective with the funds they're taking in. So, there will always be a need for people who understand the numbers and how to make more money.

Automation will streamline some of it, but at the end of the day, going into a finance career will enable you to go into any career you want because that operational finance role exists across industries. I love finance as a gateway to continue taking on new experiences and to feel prepared to take on a CFO role in a new sector tomorrow. I could perform the function of managing cash, of projecting for the future anywhere.

That's exciting to me.

When you're the CFO, you know where every dollar is coming in and leaving, so your opinion goes a long way. People want you to push back. That's what the board wants you to do. And that's what your CEO wants you to do. So having that bird's eye view of what every team is spending enables you to bring that all together and make sure it's all complimenting each other, it's not redundant, and it's one cohesive strategy.

The difference between a really good finance operations person and a more strategic CFO is the ability to bring that all together and see more than just the numbers on the page. You need to have a strategic operations lens more than just a finance lens because if you're just looking at the numbers on the page, it'll tell you one story. But if you're able to understand how a corporate strategy works, how marketing works, how customers are influenced, and how demand works, you can use the numbers to work with the teams to understand and measure progress on the broader vision.

That's a bigger story.

The CFO helps craft and approves a lot of the budgets in partnership with the CEO. Let's say the CEO or board says we need a stronger diversity and inclusion initiative. We need to really focus on our recruiting to be more holistic. The CFO enables that. A board or a CEO will ask, "How do we put a more diverse workforce in place? How do we strive towards that? How do we grow our teams that way? How do we instill this in our values?"

The CFO will put the plan in motion.

Often, the best ideas don't have dollars behind them to start.

The CFO's superpower is to enable ideas, "Oh, we want to do this. We don't know how we're going to do it. We don't know what it looks like, but we know this is important to us." So then the CFO starts to be the foundation of that plan by saying, alright, "Here are the buckets we can spend in to enable that. Here are the sources of the funds. Here's the stuff that doesn't cost any money that I'll pass to someone else to figure out." Working through a financial plan can raise the most critical questions that need to be answered to execute successfully. The CFO doesn't need to answer all the questions on his or her own, but by asking he or she is putting the right wheels in motion to be successful.

The CFO identifies where the money will come from and how to make the idea a reality.

On Embracing Risk

To make moves in your career, you need to get comfortable with taking risks and being open to failing.

In my short career, I've taken a lot more risks than most other people my age have, including this most recent pivot to starting my own company. The reason I've been able to do that comes back to people believing in me and supporting me.

When I look back on the best decisions I've made, I wondered at the time, "Is this right? Am I taking too big a risk here? Will I fail?" During the first few months at Alex and Ani, I had a bit of imposter syndrome, "I don't have enough experience." It's easy to let that fear weigh on you.

They say men apply for jobs that want way more experience than they have, but women tend to apply within the guidelines. For example, if a job description asks for five to ten years, women will only apply if they meet that guidance. But a man who has only two years would apply anyway. So often, the biggest battle is pushing past that hurdle, believing in yourself, and believing that if you need to fill in the gaps, you'll figure it out or raise your hand for help.

People trust me because I believe I should be trusted. I believe in myself, carry myself confidently, and always do the right thing. That shines through more than you realize in the hiring process.

I wouldn't have gotten any of my roles if I didn't apply for the job or just prayed a CFO job would land in my lap. All of this comes through building relationships and helping people out when they need help and not doing it to be self-serving. I try to make others successful, whether that be people or businesses, and through that am able to achieve my own goals and meet my own definition of success. Believing in the process, relationships, and other people enough to know that you'll help each other. We all have to work together; we all have to be in this and put ourselves out there and support others when they take risks.

As much as I've taken risks, there have been people to support me I've known I can rely on if things don't go exactly as planned. Do I have a recipe for exactly how my story unfolded? No, but there's a reason my story tends to stand out to people. And what I do know is that I was enabled by great mentors and my own internal belief that I could do it.

That's why I feel so strongly about what I'm doing with Rainbow CFO: providing that support to junior talent at companies and helping them find these opportunities to start to own things, take on leadership positions, and push themselves out there.

If companies are willing to invest in their people and Rainbow CFO can offer them support, there can be more stories like mine.

On Staying in STEM

For any of us women to stay in STEM, we must be there for each other.

And we need to be here in these male-dominated fields because these careers can change our world. So, I want to shed light on the different types of careers women have to give hope and inspiration to those who are figuring out what they want to do.

We spend a lot of time talking about the challenges we face, but at the end of the day, I love what I do. I want more women to feel supported so that someday we can just come in, really kick ass with the work, and have fun doing it without this extra burden.

I also want to tell women who are dealing with these issues and are fighting the good fight that they're supported by other women.

They are not alone.

People will say women need to just be more confident. But it's not that black and white. We still face too many challenges. All I know is pushing forward is worth it. It's so worth it. So, we need to stay and keep fighting and supporting each other till many more women have a seat at the table. It's like the message I embraced in high school that women aren't going to see change until they are the leaders.

My resounding message is that I love my job. It's fun and exciting. The challenges I've faced and worked through have strengthened me, made me more excited for what's next, and given me a greater sense of purpose. I am even more confident and ready to face the next set of challenges that come my way.

I want the reader to take away the importance of taking risks and opportunities when they're presented. My career is the culmination of the unique experiences presented to me. It results from trusting my gut, jumping at opportunities, and never thinking I'm not qualified. Or waiting around till I'm more experienced. No, go for it now and learn as you go. Trust your intuition in taking opportunities and knowing when to walk away from them.

And try to have fun along the way.

Francesca (Frani) Esquenazi

CEO/Cofounder at Future Club

I'm the CEO and executive producer at Future Club, a co-op game company specializing in 2D animation, engaging gameplay, and crafting memorable worlds and characters that people can fall in love with.

Valentine's Day Gift

I was born in Peru. I'm Peruvian. Ethnically, though, I'm Irish American on my mom's side and Italian on my dad's side.

The people in my mom's family have a lot of Irish features. My mom's blond, with blue eyes. She was born in the US but grew up in Peru, so she has a very thick Peruvian accent. People always ask her, "Where are you from?" My granddad, my mom's father, was from New Jersey. In the 1950s, in the hopes of traveling and getting out of New Jersey, he joined the army as an engineer and was sent to Peru to set up antennas to track Sputnik for the US government. He didn't speak any Spanish–that's how he met my grandma; she was the Spanish teacher assigned to him. They got married and moved back to New Jersey, where my mom and one of my uncles were born. My grandma hated New Jersey, so they moved back to Peru, where my mom grew up.

My older sister and I were born in Peru. My dad was a special ops fighter pilot in the Peruvian Air Force.

My mom and dad made me on Valentine's Day, but a month later, on March 13, he died in a freak accident during prisoner-of-war training. My mom told me, "You are the reason why I didn't kill myself. I was pregnant, but I was so depressed." My mom couldn't handle living in the same city where everything was a reminder of my dad. So, when I was two since she was a US citizen, we moved to California.

My life has been marked by one tragedy after another. There have been constant challenges. I'm thirty-five now, so at this point in my life, I'm like,

"Bring it on. I'm ready for whatever."

I grew up in LA until the age of about ten. My mom was a teacher. We had a preschool in our home. We had a cool backyard for all the kids to play in and a music room. Even though we didn't have a lot of money, she was very much into providing spur-of-the-moment types of experiences for us. We weren't able to go to Disneyland, but she'd say, "We're going on a road trip to the beach," which was always awesome.

LA was where I got my first taste of video games. I grew up in the nineties, right on the edge when kids still played outside and explored things on their own. Video games weren't necessarily endorsed at that time, but I definitely played a lot of them. Every day after school, I would come home to my Nintendo and Sega Genesis and play Sonic and Mario.

My sister and I would always fight over the consoles.

I was really into puzzles and figuring things out – video games were the thing that helped me develop my critical thinking, "Okay, I can't do it this way, and I can't do it that way; how can I do it?" Today, games are almost too easy for people. There's always an easy mode or a button that shows you how to do it. Whereas back in the day, those earlier games forced you to explore and figure things out on your own.

Before the internet, there were guides on solving these puzzles, but you'd have to go into a store to buy them. If you were stuck, you couldn't just go online to a YouTube video to see how to get through a level on a game. I think that persistence, "I'm going to solve this," definitely played into my personality.

I'm one of those people who stick with stuff for hours until I figure it out; I actually prefer it.

A Tough Childhood

In 1996, when I was around eleven, my mom sent us back to Peru. She was having issues with her school and had to file for bankruptcy. So she couldn't join us in Peru. When you're eleven, you don't understand situations like this. I always knew that we came from Peru, and I kind of understood Spanish from my mom, but I never spoke it myself, and I didn't know how to read or write in Spanish.

It was really daunting and scary. "I'm not going to have my mom, I'm going to be in a country where I don't speak the language, and I'm going to live with a bunch of people who are my family but who are also technically strangers," I thought to myself. I had met my granddad and some uncles and aunts for a few days at my uncle's graduation in Miami. They were cool, but there was no connection, really. None of our family lived in California.

It was very just, "This is it," and I hated that this had to happen.

My sister and I basically flew alone at eleven and thirteen years old from LA to Miami and then from Miami to Lima, Peru. It was definitely a culture shock, being completely immersed in this entirely new environment. It was supposed to only be for a couple of months initially, but we ended up staying for eight years.

I had a tough childhood.

We lived with my aunt, my mom's sister, who was a producer for TV commercials. She was single and didn't have any kids. She was very Irish; I guess *Irish* is the best word to describe my family–with a lot of yelling, screaming, and overreacting to everything. When we lived in LA with my mom, things were tough because we were poor, but at least she tried to make the best of it.

After about five years, my aunt sent us to live with my grandad. She just wanted to have her life back. It definitely felt like, "Okay, no one wants us." There was definitely a lot of abuse, not so much physical abuse but more so mental abuse from my family. I now know this was because they had also been abused and just didn't know how to deal with it.

None of them had ever gone to therapy.

High school is hard enough when you are in your teens with teenage angst, but this hardship was multiplied by a hundred because we didn't have my mom. I was definitely depressed in high school. As an adult now, I can look back and think, "That experience was actually good. Even though it was very difficult, it made me more independent. It would have been nice if my mom had been there, but I didn't actually need her." I realized that I could still survive emotionally without having her around.

My mom was afraid of flying, and she didn't have the money to visit, but she was able to come a few times. When she came out for my graduation and prom, she was there for about two months, the longest she had ever stayed. At that point, though, it had been about six years since she had last visited. I remember after a month, I was like, "Okay, you need to go back because I just can't be around you. You drive me crazy." I was older, around fifteen or sixteen, and it was like, "Why are you coming and trying to be my mom when you haven't been my mom for the last five years? How can you tell me what to do?"

It was definitely a kind of power struggle between us.

It was challenging growing up, especially without my mom, but that drove me to be more involved in art, painting, and drawing. I would get lost in art because it was how I could escape the chaos at home.

Los Angeles Times

The way we moved back to LA was crazy.

Let me back up. Even though my mom and grandfather were American citizens, my sister and I were not. We are Peruvian since we were born there. So, when my mom moved us to the States when we were very young, my sister and I were permanent residents, not citizens. When we moved back to Peru, we lost our US residency, which meant we couldn't fly back to the US to see my mom unless we got a visa. It was such a hassle. So, my mom went through a ton of paperwork to help us apply for US citizenship.

The US is constantly changing its immigration laws.

There was a law around 1999 that said you could get US citizenship if you were born abroad and could prove that your grandparents were American citizens. So, my mom applied for that for us. My sister was able to get her citizenship that way, but they lost my paperwork. So, I had to come back a year later, in 2000, after they finally found it. But then they told me, "Oh wait, your dad died before you were born. So, technically, when you were born, your only parent was an American citizen. You should have automatically been a US citizen." I thought, "I waited fifteen years for you guys to tell me this?" But I was so grateful, especially when I suddenly had to move back to the US.

When I was eighteen, my sister, who's a few years older than me, had been in university in Peru for a few years at that point. She was having authority issues with my family in Lima, especially my grandad. One winter break, we were supposed to visit my mom in LA for the summer. I had my bags packed with two weeks of summer clothes.

When we were on the plane, my sister told me, "By the way, I shipped all my stuff to mom already, and I'm not going back." I was like, "What?!" She said, "I'm not taking the return flight back to Peru." And I'm like, "Okay, and you chose to tell me this now?" She was like, "I didn't want you to tell anyone. So, I kept it from you." I was so mad at her. "Well, now I can't go back either. If I go back, everyone's gonna yell at me because you stayed."

So, we both stayed in LA.

All my stuff was in Peru, and I had only done about a year of college. I really wanted to be an animator, but they didn't have animation schools in Peru, so I studied graphic design instead. My granddad was pissed because he had already paid for four years of college for my sister, and she only had one year left to graduate (in Peru, there are five years of university).

So, that is the crazy story of how I decided not to go back to Peru while on a plane to LA.

Luckily, it was a good decision because it got me to where I am now. But it was very scary at first. "Where are we going to live? What are we going to do?" My mom didn't even have a house for us to stay in. We stayed with a friend of hers who lived out in Hollywood Hills. He had a big house that used to be Marilyn Monroe's. Occasionally, he rented it out for big reality shows. So , we lived in this little cottage in the back.

I had also never had a job.

When I was going to school in Peru, there was no expectation from my family that I had to work. Now all of that was out the window. I got a job at a hat shop on Third Street Promenade, selling hats for seven dollars an hour. I came from a third-world country, so I knew nothing about US labor laws. They definitely exploited people in that hat shop. I didn't realize I had gotten a job where all of my colleagues were from Bulgaria, Russia, or Thailand–all working under the table for this guy who paid in cash. Because I didn't know any better, I worked fifteen-hour days, sometimes without breaks; I worked there for a couple months.

Around this time, I met my future wife, Zoe.

I became friends with one of the guys who was staying at the Hollywood Hills house when they were filming a reality show. He helped me move to a new apartment and introduced me to another friend who invited me to a house party. Little did I know that this was where I would meet the person I would spend the rest of my life with.

I was eighteen at the time, just a few months after I had gotten to LA.

When we met, she was male. She's only recently transitioned and gone through that whole process maybe five years ago. We just hit it off and started spending a bunch of time together. She would come to visit me at the Promenade when I was working. She would watch the cart while I ran to the bathroom at the mall. She said, "Do you know that this is illegal?" And I'm like, "What? They're paying me under the table?" She's like, "Yeah. And you should get breaks. And they can't make you work these many hours." She added, "You're an American citizen. You don't need to work illegally like the rest of the people you work with. You could get a job anywhere, and they will treat you better and pay you better."

I was so clueless when I moved here. I didn't know how to do anything; I didn't even know how to write a check! So, she really helped me with a lot of stuff.

It's all very funny now because today I'm a CEO running a company.

In-N-Out Burger

Because my new apartment was near UCLA, there were a lot of international students, and this was one of the few places that didn't require a credit history. The apartment had only one room with a bathroom, basically a bachelor. There wasn't even a kitchen, and it was still crazy expensive.

Across the street from my apartment, there was In-N-Out Burger. It paid a dollar fifty more than what I was making at the hat shop, it was legal, there was a bathroom, and I could get breaks.

So, I applied and got the job.

In-N-Out Burger is probably the best place to work as your first job. They made things super clear. You start at level one with a set salary. You got a twenty-five-cent raise if you progressed to level two, level three, and level four. You ascended to these different levels by proving that you could complete tasks on the checklist. It was very gamified in my mind: "Oh, I need to learn how to do those five objectives, and if I do, I get a raise."

I was very motivated by having a clear path to getting promoted. Within a few months, I was a level four, making $9.50 an hour. It was very gratifying to see that as long as I was able to prove that I could do these things, I could get promoted.

At the same time, I decided to enroll back in college.

I had my one year of graphic design back in Peru, but this time I wanted to pursue being an animator. I checked out ArtCenter and CalArts, and Art Institute—but they all cost tens of thousands of dollars a year tuition. I thought, "This is crazy. How do people afford schools? Everyone told me, "Well, just get a student loan. It's fine. You'll get approved." I was very scared of getting loans. It seemed like a huge commitment. So, I figured out that I could take the same animation classes at CalArts with the same teacher at Santa Monica College for free instead of paying fifty thousand dollars.

I enrolled in SMC and started taking my general classes.

Because I was working full time, it took me five years to graduate instead of however long people usually take to finish community college. I would schedule all my classes within two days out of a week, from 8 a.m. to 8 p.m. In any chunks of time between classes, I did my homework. The rest of the week, I worked so that I would have an income. If there were classes I could take on the weekend or paid work I could do, I did that too.

But I ended up leaving my job at the In-N-Out Burger because the managers started guilt-tripping me about why I didn't stay until three in the morning, "You live across the street. Why are you going to make someone who is supposed to commute home stay and close the store? SMC is not that hard." They were making me feel bad about prioritizing my school over work. That was not going to happen. I could only get a better job if I went to school.

So, I quit.

A Date With Fate

My next job was at GameStop. The store was two blocks from where I lived in Westwood, so I could still walk to work. I had been renting games from Blockbuster because I couldn't afford to buy them, but then I was getting late fees because I wasn't turning them in fast enough. So, I decided I could work at a GameStop and play all the games for free.

GameStop was pivotal to my whole career.

It was across the street from the game developer Pandemic Studios. They developed the very first *Star Wars: Battlefront* game, one of my favorites at the time. I remember seeing people wearing shirts with the game logo coming into the store all the time. So, I asked them, "You're from Pandemic Studios? You guys did Battlefront, right?" So, they're like, "Yeah, we're right there across the street."

I was really lucky to be in the right place at the right time.

I was at GameStop for about nine months and had been telling the manager that we needed more security, but he'd say, "It's Westwood, it's UCLA, it's safe." No one listened to me because...what do I know?

Then one morning, two teenage kids came into the store. I had seen them before. Long story short, I got held up and held hostage. They took the only other customer and me into the back room. I felt so bad for this guy. He was a super sweet guy who would often come in and play on the consoles in the store. He was like, "Do you want my Game Boy? Do you want my watch? He was trying so hard to give them whatever they wanted so they would leave us alone. I thought, "Please don't say anything."

Then they duct-taped our hands and our mouths. When they had me turn around with the gun to the back of my neck, I remember thinking, "Please don't rape me." I had just gotten engaged and had my engagement ring on. I didn't want them to steal it. Looking back, who cared if they took the ring? But it was brand new, and I wanted to keep it.

I was so lucky that the UPS guy had seen them coming in and asked someone at the newspaper stand to call the cops. Since I only lived two blocks away, he was also my UPS guy. He knew where I lived. He drove to my house and called my then fiancée. By the time he came back, the building was surrounded.

There were snipers on the roof and helicopters and all this craziness.

The entire time, I had such a weird sensation. I was completely numb. My voice was monotone. I wasn't scared. I wasn't worried. I was very calm, very neutral. I was just...there was no feeling. I was out of my body. My senses were just turned off as a way to cope with what was happening.

The kids didn't know what they were doing. They had no way out and ended up stalling for three hours, doing nothing. Then one jumped out of a window, and the other walked out the front door and gave up.

After they left, the customer managed to get out of his duct tape and then helped me. He was incredibly strong. When we finally walked out, I saw twenty cops pointing their guns at us. They didn't know who the hostages or hostage takers were. As soon as I saw that, my mind went boom. It all hit me. I just started bawling. Just the sudden realization that "Oh my god, I survived."

Pandemic Studios was across the street on the 19th floor. I knew a lot of people there because they'd come into the store. They saw everything. The police, the helicopters, the news. Me.

That was the last day I played EB Games or went to GameStop. I didn't want to work there anymore. I had told them this would happen, but they hadn't listened. When the district manager for GameStop came over to check on things, he didn't come over to check on me. No, the first thing he said was, "They broke a window. We need to get that fixed." I was like, "Screw you. You care more about a window than your employees."

I ended up getting a job as a receptionist at a Pilates studio while I was finishing school. I was there for a few months when one of the Pandemic Studios guys I had befriended and who came into the Pilates studio a lot told me, "Hey, our receptionist is moving into HR, and we need to hire a new receptionist. You know half of the company already. You should apply."

So, I applied.

The Pandemic Days

As they were taking me through the office for my interview, people called, "Hey, Frani, what are you doing here?"

The guy who would become my boss told me, "Everyone has said how awesome you are, so this is just a formality. We're going to hire you." So, I thought, "Oh, okay, cool. But I still want to do the interview."

I got the job because people knew me as the girl across the street—the only girl who worked at a video game store. This receptionist position at Pandemic is what got me into the gaming industry.

I was still working full-time and going to school full-time. I finished work at seven, and my classes were from 7:30 to 9 p.m. or on the weekends. Pandemic allowed me to do homework while I was at the front desk. I would also ask the animators who worked there, "Hey, what do you think of my animation? Can you give me any feedback?" It was great to be able to ask experts working professionally in this thing I was going to school for.

People saw that I was really eager to do anything in addition to just answering the phone and sorting mail. I completely revamped the mail-sorting process. I was running the company video game tournament and all of their fun social events. I would help out anywhere I could. I wanted to learn more about production, so they gave me basic production tasks, like ordering dinner for the team or setting up the paid time-off calendar, so people knew when people were going on vacation.

I would approach all the teams doing the three projects being developed at the time. "You guys need help? What kind of help? Give me something to do."

We were developing the *Lord of the Rings* game at the time. The producer said, "Hey, we need someone to go through every *Lord of the Rings* movie and splice out all the scenes where this creature comes out, then put it together into one video so the animators can scroll through and see how the creature moves." I said, "I'll do it!" I had to watch *Lord of the Rings* a billion times. I never want to see it again.

Whatever throwaway thing that no one else wanted to do, I just did it.

I even applied for a production coordinator position that was open then, but they hired some guy instead. Years later, when I spoke to my friend John, the main producer on the game at that time, he was like, "Man, looking back, we totally should have hired you, but we all thought you didn't have the experience yet. Even though you had a lot of drive, we needed someone to come in and not need any training. But after everything I've seen you do, what a mistake that was."

It was also nice being the connective tissue between people. As the receptionist, I knew everyone at the company, what they did, and where they sat. Sometimes I would talk to people and realize they didn't know other people who had worked there for years. So, I would introduce people to each other, which would help the project. My experience at Pandemic gave me an example of what good can look like in the gaming industry. It was definitely an excellent place to learn. And it had a really good company culture. Luckily, I didn't start my gaming career at one of these horror stories companies I often heard about.

I dodged a bullet.

After I was there for about three years, around 2009, EA (Entertainment Arts) bought the company. Though they said nothing was going to change, that was complete BS. They basically dissolved the company and were planning to lay everyone off except for about fifteen people they were taking to EA.

Someone leaked the news. So, we found out that we were being let go through a Kotaku article. Everyone was on the company email, saying, "Hey, I just saw this article. Is this true?" Sure enough, an hour later, they took us all to conference rooms and told the entire company that we were being let go. Afterward, everyone ended up at the bar across the street.

At the time, it was really sad. I cried on the way home. But it was the best thing that could've happened to me. I was almost done with my animation degree and needed to focus one hundred percent on my demo project. I got some severance pay, which helped to support me financially. It was also good because everyone I knew ended up at different companies. People went to Disney; people went to Sony; people went everywhere. I still have friends all over the industry from the Pandemic days.

It really helped launch my career.

Riot & Mandalorians

Around my graduation in June of 2010, I found out I was pregnant. Now I needed to get a job for sure. I had been applying to a bunch of jobs doing whatever, but nothing was working. Then, out of the blue, I got a message from the person who had been the HR director at Pandemic.

She had gone to a small new company called Riot Games.

At the time, I had never heard of them. I had never heard of their new game League of Legends. I couldn't even play it because I didn't have a PC. It had been out for maybe ten months. It was gaining popularity but wasn't a household name like it is now.

My contact said, "I remember you helping with a bunch of production stuff. Would you be interested in a production assistant role?" I'm like, "Yes, please!!" She said, "But first, we need an HR office person to help us with a bunch of paperwork. If you need a job immediately, I can bring you in to help me with that. Then I can set up the technical production coordinator interviews for the engineering team." I was like, "Whatever, I need a job."

When I started at Riot, I was literally just scanning in people's offer letters. So again, I got to know every single person at the company and what they made. At the time, it was less than a hundred people. The engineering team was the biggest team at the company, and the art team was maybe eight people—one person per discipline–one animator, one effects person, and one modeler.

When I left Riot five years later, there were over two hundred people in the art department alone.

Being at Riot was my big game-development education, my game industry university, in a way. It was five years of lots of different types of challenges and problem-solving. After the HR job, I worked for the VP of technology. Five technical directors handled different parts of League of Legends—gameplay, gameplay engineering, the store, the actual backend server stuff, and the head of the entire tech department. However, the team didn't know what they wanted when they hired me. When I was at Pandemic, my job duties were very clear. Now, I was coming into this new job where my direct boss was like, "There's no one at the company who has this role, so we don't really know what we're looking for."

"We just need someone who can come in and support our team."

Funny thing, I think what really helped me get the job at Riot was that my wife and I were really into Star Wars cosplay. We kind of launched a mini business with a sculptor friend of ours to create Mandalorian helmets, like the Boba Fett helmets. Everyone knows what a Mandalorian is now because of the TV show, but ten years ago, no one knew what it was. We were just this small nerdy group of Star Wars fans who wanted to make their own Mandalorian characters.

Before we got into our business, the only people making the helmets sold them as kits. They were super expensive, would take six months to reach you, were not made well, and you had to customize and paint them yourself. It was also the worst customer service I had ever experienced in my life. So, we were like, "What if we made our own helmets and gave people a better customer experience?" We were tapping into this niche market of customers paying two to four hundred dollars for a helmet that wasn't even painted and fell apart.

We found a sculptor to sculpt the model. We figured out a way to cast it out of resin. We built a rotocast machine out of two-by-fours and bicycle chains. Then we figured out a way to daisy-chain them together so we could make three helmets simultaneously. We could create a better product and sell them for less, around a hundred dollars apiece. Suddenly, we were the new people selling these Mandalorian helmets. Probably eighty percent of the Star Wars cosplay community were wearing our helmets. We were known as the "prop people who knew how to make good stuff."

What I had done on the side as a hobby became a business.

We were making so much money compared to what I was used to earning as a receptionist. Plus, I was able to use that experience when I was interviewing for the job at Riot. "This is what I've been doing since my last job." They were like, "Oh, that's so industrious of you to figure that out."

Figuring It Out

I didn't tell Riot I was pregnant at the time, "If they hire me and think I'm the right person, then hopefully, they'll be okay with the fact that I'm going to have to be off for a few months." So, when I told my boss, he was like, "Okay, cool. But you'll have to help hire the person who's going to replace you while you're on maternity leave."

I was never given a "here's how you do your job" talk.

I had to come up with what my job was, figure it out, and solve problems. His management style gave me a lot of freedom and made me feel more confident about what I was contributing to the team. I would go to meetings and absorb stuff. If I noticed that this person was also having the same problem as someone else, I thought, "What if I put together this process and share it with everyone?" Just from listening to the issues that people were complaining about across the multiple teams within the engineering department, I was able to figure out patterns and help provide team-wide solutions. That was the type of stuff I was doing as a production coordinator, just going around and solving issues, like when I was younger and playing games and figuring out, "How do I solve this?"

I also made it very clear where I eventually wanted to work at Riot.

I wanted to get into animation and be in the art department. I liked the engineering team but didn't want to be an engineer. They were very clear, "Okay then, talk to whoever you need to talk to and figure out how you can get into that department. But you need to make sure you can backfill your role before you leave."

So, I took the receptionist to lunch, interviewed her, and felt she could do my current job. I had been in her role as a receptionist myself–eager to do whatever, and she was such a huge fan of League of Legends too. So, we hired her as my backfill before I went on maternity leave. She ended up being one of the best producers at the company.

When I returned from maternity leave, I moved into the art department, doing the same job as a coordinator. They had a whole other set of problems around recruiting. "Our team is too small, and we have ten thousand unread emails in the recruiting inbox of people who want to apply for a job. We don't have time to do our work and look at all these demo reels, of which eighty percent is crap anyway."

One of my first jobs as an art coordinator was going through every single email in the art department's recruiting inbox, looking at demo reels, and going, "No, this sucks," or "Oh, this one's okay." I would make a list of the okay ones and ask people what they thought, but no one answered my emails, ever. So, I said to them, "Once a week, I'm going to get all the department heads—of animation, concepts, illustration—and sit you together in a room. We're going to look at my list of people, and you guys are going to tell me 'Yes or 'No.'" Over time, I was able to get through all those emails. In the process, I developed an eye for what they were looking for from these artists' demo reels, for example, in terms of composition or animation. That helped me grow as an artist. It also helped me shortlist the applicants further because now I knew who they would reject.

After I supported the art department's recruiting efforts, I handled outsourcing because there still weren't enough artists in-house. The department worked with a lot of contractors and a few vendors, but no one was tracking anything at all. Some assignments were being done without a contract. And if there was a contract, the finance department would be like, "This person's contract expired six months ago, so we don't have to pay them." Or the art department would go, "I made the contract once, and I don't need to look at what the deliverables are. I'll just keep assigning them stuff." I'm like, "Guys, this is not even legal. This is bad." My job became a liaison between the artists, the art managers, the people assigning the work, and the legal and finance departments.

Basically, I created the outsourcing pipeline for the art department because it became clear to me that it was such a mess.

Once our outsourcing protocol was in a better place, I started managing vendor relationships. One time, one of our artists was on his honeymoon, but he was the one guy in contact with the vendor who was supposed to deliver a bunch of assets for one of our releases. No one could get ahold of him to reach the vendor. After that, I said, "Okay, we can't have one person block the game's entire development." So, I went to the engineering team. "Can we set up some sort of portal where the vendor can upload their work, and someone can log in, look at it, and give comments directly there without having to have so many emails or it all having to go through one person's email address?" So, we created a vendor portal that automatically sent notifications to the various internal managers. I was able to get that portal done because I had made all these great connections within the engineering department. So, there was also an internal confluence that evolved over time.

After that, I did a lot of tools development for the art department.

We would figure out a way to turn any issues that the artists would have into an internal tool that all artists could use across the department, regardless of which team they were on. We optimized our processes—how we communicated and gave visibility to what was being worked on. I created this producer role for myself within the art department, which was growing so fast and hiring people all the time. My starting salary as a tech coordinator in the engineering team had been fourteen dollars an hour. Then they bumped me up to seventeen dollars after maybe six months. I don't remember what I made when I moved to the art department, but it wasn't very much.

I was getting benefits though.

There wasn't an art director for a long time, so there was no department head. When they finally hired the studio art director, he was like, "Yeah, you should be getting paid more." That's when I got a big bump to being a salaried employee.

Princess Leah

I've been talking about the work part of my life, but you have to look at all of this in the context of my personal life and what was happening with my daughter at the time. My daughter, Leah, was born healthy.

My pregnancy and maternity leave was good.

Then about a month after I went back to work, she had a really high fever in the middle of the night. We had to take her to the hospital because she was having very weird eye movements. They were rolling to the back of her head, and her eyeballs were fluttering really quickly back and forth and up and down.

They had to do a spinal tap. Leah was three or four months old.

Before I knew it, I was in the hospital again. They did a special test at Cedars Hospital and kept her overnight for a few days until the fever went down. They couldn't find an infection. They did an MRI of her brain; it was normal. There was nothing obvious they could point to that may have caused those weird movements. I was worried about something more biological. They said, "We've been watching it for three days, and the fever hasn't returned. She probably has some sort of viral infection that gave her a fever. She seems normal, so you should just go home."

So, we went home.

A few weeks later, we went for her first round of vaccines. They told us, "She might get a little temperature. So, just keep an eye on it." We're like, "Okay."

That night, she started having these weird movements. She was like someone with Parkinson's, just moving and moving. So we took her to the ER again. They did the MRI again and the spinal tap again. It was just so heartbreaking to see this tiny baby going through all of this for the second time in a few weeks.

Leah was also born with tracheomalacia and had this weird "eow, eow, eow" sound when she breathed. The doctor said, "Oh, what's happening is that her trachea is a little floppy. They grow out of it. It's nothing to be worried about." So, we got used to this little sound that she would make and didn't think it was much of an issue. But now, while she was at the hospital, it was getting worse and creating problems with her breathing. Then suddenly, she was having a lot of trouble breathing. You could see her little rib cage deeply pull in when she was trying to breathe.

Within seconds, there were fifty people in her room.

They took Leah to the ICU and had to intubate her. This time they kept her longer. No one could figure out what was going on. They did more tests and more brain scans. She was in the ICU for two or three months and still had the movements. They did an EEG, thinking those weird movements might be a seizure, but there was no seizure activity.

I was grateful that Riot told me, "Stay at the hospital, be with your daughter. You're not going to lose your job." However, I was paid hourly at that point, and I wasn't making any money being at the hospital.

I had a blog that I would write in every day. It kept track of the medications they were giving her, the tests they were doing, and the results that had come back. They thought they had done every single test that they could. They thought she had cancer. They thought it was a tumor. They thought...they didn't know. Nothing was coming back.

At that time, everyone in the Star Wars community knew us for making the Mandalorian helmets, and they knew about Leah. She was known as Princess Leah (pronounced like Leia) in the community. When we started telling people we were in the hospital, the Star Wars community started fundraising for us. They raised about thirty thousand dollars in a month–just strangers on the internet who knew about her through my blog. So many people connected with her story. Someone made a Facebook support page for her. It was amazing. People from the news also showed up, wanting to interview us.

We were happy to be interviewed because we thought, "Maybe there's a doctor who will see this who can figure it out."

While Leah was in the ICU, they extubated her at some point. But then they gave her something that made her really sleepy to the point where her heart rate dropped. So, they had to intubate her again because she had gone limp. She remained intubated for a few weeks. They were afraid of extubating her again in case she would not be able to breathe. That's when they asked to put in a trach, "At least with the trach, she can still get ventilation. If she has trouble breathing, we can bag her manually and access her airway."

It was a tough decision to say, "Yeah, get the trach." But it was honestly the best thing we could have done. With the trach, she could move around, and we could pick her up and hold her again.

Coming Home

This whole time, we were living in the ER. We didn't go home. We had to get used to the sounds of alarms going off at all times and all the hospital activity. We weren't sleeping very much. There was only one cot, so one of us would sleep on the cot while the other would sleep in her bed or on the floor next to her.

We became really good friends with the doctors and the nurses because they would see us there every day. In the very beginning, we didn't know what was going on. Finally, after three months, because we were going to go home soon, we were trained in how to put in the trach and take it out and clean it. They also told us, "She's going to be on oxygen and need these machines. So, you can't take her back to a one-bedroom apartment. Do you have a big enough place?"

No, we didn't.

So, we had to find a two-bedroom apartment and move within the span of a week. Boxes were everywhere. The only room that was set up was her room. On our first day home from the hospital, the nursing agency met with us, introduced us to our nurses, and started her round-the-clock care.

We were in the apartment for literally fifteen minutes when the smoke alarm went off. There was a giant fire in the kitchen. A nurse had somehow bumped against the stove, and something had caught fire. Since we were still in the process of moving in, we didn't even have a fire extinguisher. So, I thought, "There's a huge five-foot-tall oxygen tank in Leah's room. If that catches on fire, the whole building goes up!"

We ran outside with Leah, with all these tubes and everything, screaming. Our neighbor ran across the street and put out the fire. By the time the fire department reached us, it was over. The apartment was a mess. There was smoke everywhere. They told us, "You can't stay here tonight."

We had to go back to the hospital. Luckily, we had scheduled a sleep study for her that evening, so we had already planned to stay overnight. Also, my wife had gotten bad smoke inhalation while trying to put out the fire. So, my baby was in the sleep study room on the third floor of the UCLA Santa Monica Medical Center, and my wife was in the ER downstairs with smoke inhalation.

That was just an extra thing that was thrown at us.

The Diagnosis

We brought Leah home the next day and began looking for the right nurses. We went through so many home nurses who weren't competent. One of the night nurses fell asleep. Another nurse accidentally pulled her trach out. At three in the morning, she knocked on the door, "The baby's blue." I'm like, "You're a nurse; aren't you supposed to know what to do?" She didn't know what to do. So, I had to run in there and put the trach back in. And it wasn't going in because it was all dried up. I had to stick it in my mouth to wet it so I could shove it back in and start bagging her. Thank god she survived.

Leah was born in February 2011.

She was in the hospital between May and August, more or less. Then in November of that same year, she got meningitis and started having seizures. We took her to the hospital again. I had to fight with the doctors. "These are not her normal movements. These look like a seizure." They're like, "Oh, but it's a Sunday, and we don't have the one machine, and we don't want to have the person have to come in." I was screaming at the ER doctors, "You need to get an EEG on this baby now." They finally ordered the EEG and admitted that she was seizing. They had to give her a bunch of drugs and induce a coma for her to be out of the seizures. She was in a coma for about a month.

Every time they tried to take her out of the coma, the seizures were still so bad that they had to adjust her seizure meds. This was in November of 2011 when she was about nine months old. From that point on, she never quite recovered. She was always very sleepy on the seizure meds. We did get her on a keto diet, which helped a lot with the seizures.

At that point, we still didn't know what was causing all these problems.

She had also developed cataracts in her eyes. The first time she was in the ICU, I noticed it, "Her eyes are really cloudy. Something's wrong." The nurse told me, "No, she's fine." I'm like, "Trust me. I look at her eyes all day." So, finally, I got a doctor to come and look at them. He said, "She has cataracts. We will have to remove the cataracts and the lenses from her eyes. She's going to have to wear glasses." So, Leah had glasses with really thick lenses, like Mr. Magoo.

I also noticed she wasn't quite responding the way she used to. And she was getting mad all the time. They tested her but couldn't find anything that could have caused the cataracts. But she was going blind. So, she was having issues with seizures, issues with her sight, having gastrointestinal issues. No one could figure out what was going on. So, finally, they said, "We want to put her in this study." It was a human genome experiment that would test her genome sequencing. Normally it would cost thousands of dollars to do her whole DNA sequencing, but because UCLA was doing this study, it would be free.

We were like, "Yeah, go for it."

They did the study thinking they would find out what was happening, but the results came back inconclusive. "We couldn't find anything in her DNA that could point to what's causing these issues. Her DNA has about the same number of abnormalities as anyone."

So, the study didn't give us any answers either.

When she had the big seizure with the meningitis, they took a new brain scan. That's when they said, "Okay, it looks like it could be a mitochondrial defect in her genes. We're going to specifically test for mitochondrial disease." It wasn't until they put the new scan of her brain together with the DNA stuff that they figured out it was a new mutation of mitochondrial disease that they'd never seen before. Your mitochondria are the parts of your cell that generate energy in all of your cells. They said, "There's a defect in her mitochondria where it doesn't make enough energy. That's why it is hitting multiple systems because it's in her DNA. It's not a specific brain issue; it's in all of herself."

Finally, they confirmed that it was a mitochondrial disease.

There was no cure, and there was no treatment. It would just be about managing her symptoms and providing quality of life. There were a lot of really horrible doctors who questioned why we were keeping her alive, "She's getting worse, and there's no cure. Why are you even bothering with this?"

"What's wrong with you?" I thought. "How can someone tell somebody that?!"

In fact, going back in time a bit, the first time we took Leah to the hospital when we didn't know what was going on was in May 2011. It was Mother's Day, my first one. The doctor said, "She's probably not going to make it past six months." I was like, "Do you even know what day it is today? Do you even have any idea what you've just told me?" He had no concept. He wasn't saying it to be mean. He was just saying it very matter-of-factly.

But that was just not something I wanted to hear on Mother's Day.

Life in the Balance

By the way, all of this was happening at the same time that I was working.

One reason I was doing as much work as I was because I felt I had to keep working just as hard to show that although I was taking a lot of time off to be with my kid, I still wanted to be useful. I didn't want to get fired. They were letting me keep my job because I was still providing value. And I needed my health insurance to cover what was going on with my daughter. But insurance didn't cover everything. Just the electrical bill with the oxygen tank on twenty-four-seven was crazy expensive.

At that time, I didn't care as much about how I was progressing in my career. I never really pushed for a raise or for any extra money. My thought was that I would do the best I could at my job, but I was not going to try to climb the ladder. My priority was my daughter. They even told me that there was a position open for a product owner, which would have been a promotion. But I had to tell them I couldn't do it right now.

I turned down more responsibility and pay so I could have the flexibility to leave whenever I needed to. I would be in meetings, and my wife would text me, "We're going to the ER." I'd text back, "Okay, I'll meet you there in twenty minutes." Everyone knew already, so there was no need for any explanation. They even got me an iPad to work from my room when I requested one. In the beginning, I was still being paid hourly, so I could clock my hours from the hospital, which helped pay the bills.

Leah died in 2013 when she was two years and three months old.

With this disease, she would have to go to the ICU every time there was an issue, whether it was a UTI, a respiratory infection, a cold, or something. The nurses at home weren't cutting it. Everyone knew at that point that there was no cure. So, it was about making sure that she was comfortable.

That she was not in pain.

She couldn't really move on her own. She couldn't sit up. She was really floppy. How awful to be just lying in a bed, staring at the ceiling your whole life. That's not a life.

When she wasn't in the hospital, we would take her places. We took her out to the park. We took her to the beach. We took her out for strolls around the neighborhood. We had a little wagon that we would sit her in and prop her up in a therapy chair. We would put in her oxygen tank and her suction machine, and the vents. We took her to the California Science Center in LA, where this huge dark room was like a theater. It had footage of volcanoes, the ocean, and different elements like fire and water. She had problems with her sight and wore these thick glasses, but we could tell that when she was in that room, all of a sudden, she could finally see. You could see her face reacting.

She was in awe, just staring at the massive screen.

Those were the kinds of things we would do. When people heard the alarms of the machines while we were out and about, they'd freak out. "Do you need help?!" We were like, "No, we're fine; go ahead. We're just suctioning her trach. That's normal."

We learned how to resuscitate a baby and had to do it multiple times. We learned how to care for someone with a trach and a Broviac tube, which was how she would get medications directly into her artery. We had to care for that and keep it clean. We got very used to being her nurses, doing all the things that the nurses they had sent us didn't know how to do.

We quickly figured out the medical system was atrocious.

Insurance covered two weeks of nursing care, and then we had to pay another three thousand dollars a month to get round-the-clock nurses. I was constantly fighting with Medicare and Medi-Cal. No one told us that there was a whole program with Medi-Cal that she could have been on from the beginning called the Long-Term Care program. Long-Term Care required a diagnosis, and she didn't have one for so long. We could've paid nothing.

Even within Medi-Cal, they didn't know that these departments existed. I finally found out by calling and calling and talking to someone who knew who to call and set it up. But by the time I figured out what that program was and had enrolled her, she had died. Literally, the week before they approved her, she died.

She had a UTI, so we took her to the ER. We always took her to the ER when things went wrong, so we didn't expect that to be the last time. We had just gotten so used to this being how it was.

Her lungs weren't working well anymore.

This ER visit turned into a month-long stay at the ICU. The doctor said, "She's having this and that and whatever. And we can do this procedure." We were like, "Okay, we'll do it." The nurse had to be the one to step in, "Do you understand what's happening right now? The surgery the doctor is talking about doing, yes, it'll probably help her, but it's going to be very painful, and it's not really going to make that much of a difference. You have to make a decision if you want to do that or if you want to face the inevitable."

Thank god for that nurse.

We really didn't realize that we were finally at that point. It was something that my wife and I had talked about previously. "When that time comes, we can't be selfish. We have to do what's best for her. We don't want her to be in pain." It was a difficult decision, but ultimately, it was like what we had always said: "We're not going to just let her die unless it's clear that there is no other way."

Despite having thought about it before, it was certainly still a shock.

"Oh my god, this is the moment."

I had dealt with a lot over the past few months. I had been getting more into meditation. Once we had her diagnosis, it became clear that it was more about her quality of life and spending time with her. I started to be much more mindful whenever I was with her. I was totally there, memorizing everything.

I can still close my eyes and transport myself to that moment.

In a way, we are luckier than many people who lose their kids, maybe in a freak accident; they don't get a chance to say goodbye or savor those moments. I feel because we knew that she was so fragile for a long time, we were just right there in the moment every time we were with her. I can still smell her; that's how focused, and in the present I became. Because I knew, "This isn't going to last forever."

Twenty-seven months. A little over two years.

It felt like twenty-seven years. Each month felt like a year; each day felt like a month. Time slows down when you're going through something like that. Now when I think about it, it's been longer since she passed away than when she was alive.

It changes your concept of time.

Because it's a genetic disease, we adopted twins two years ago. I'm so grateful. Even just seeing them sleep and breathe without a machine, I think, "Oh, thank god they can run. Thank god that they can cough and chew and do all the things that she couldn't."

Leah's Impact

A few weeks after she passed away, I was in the process of organizing an art show with the artists at Riot. People wanted to do an auction and donate all the money to mitochondrial disease, which was really sweet.

I threw myself back into work and didn't really process her death at the time. We were so used to our lives being about the hospital, the doctors, the nurses, and insurance—then, all of a sudden, that part of our lives was gone. Now it was all about work, organizing this and that. I kept busy because it allowed me not to focus on the pain.

We got a donation from this amazing family in Kansas City, who sent us a check for a lot of money. They said, "We want you guys to go on a vacation and use this money for yourselves." We were okay with accepting donations to help pay for Leah's medical expenses, but we felt we couldn't take this money. It was too much. But they insisted.

Since her death, we had tried to meet some of the people we had gotten to know through Facebook because of Leah's story. We thought, "What if we buy a camera and interview people to see how Leah impacted them?" So, we used the money not only as an opportunity to take a vacation but also to connect physically with the people who had been in touch with us throughout this whole journey.

We decided to go to Europe since we'd never been and because there were people in Spain who had heard about Leah's story. Their community was helping to raise money locally for another kid with mitochondrial disease. So, we were able to meet the family who was in the same boat that we had been in.

Around the time Leah died, a woman in England had also sent us some money she had raised from a bake sale. We met up with her and heard her story. "I wouldn't be sitting here talking to you on camera years ago," she said. "I was in such a deep depression for the past six years of my life." She had been diagnosed with this disease where her teeth would fall out, and since then, she had very much been a hermit. She closed herself off from her family and her kids.

"Your daughter changed my life."

"I saw this picture of a baby with all these tubes and smiling the biggest smile. She was so happy. She made me realize that if she can do it, then I can get out of bed and do it too."

She found that the fundraiser motivated her to get out of her depression and do more to help others. "I've realized that by helping others, I can help myself." She had always liked and commented on our photos. But she was just a picture that you see on the internet. You forget that there's a real person there. It was incredible to hear her talk about Leah and share the life-changing effect that our daughter had on so many people.

It is an amazing story, and it restored my faith in people.

We decided to make a documentary about it. We interviewed more people in England. I visited my family in Peru to interview the Star Wars community who had also helped us out. We captured so much footage, but when we tried to put it together, it was so painful to relive the whole thing. Looking at the footage of her or the interviews, I couldn't do it. I needed to hire an editor who was not so close to the subject.

It's still something I want to finish, a personal project to tell her story once I'm ready to relive it. There are so many aspects of it that it's hard to figure out what we want to say, but it has now been some time, seven years since she died in 2013. For a long time, I didn't know how to end it. But now, our life has changed so much. We have our two kids, and I have a new wife.

There's so much in our lives that has changed completely.

A Career in Gaming

My entry-level gaming job started when I was a receptionist at Pandemic, doing whatever production work I could get my hands on.

I did a lot of game testing. At the time, we were working on *Mercenaries 2: World in Flames*, which takes place in Venezuela. Because I'm a native Spanish speaker, I did a lot of QAing (quality assurance testing) of the Spanish translations. QAing required playing the game, finding bugs, writing them down, and telling people what needed to be fixed. Besides *Mercenaries 2*, I also worked on the first production support for *Lord of the Rings: Conquest* and *The Saboteur*.

I was in a support capacity, not on the development team. But having access to and being involved in the game to some degree and getting a surface-level understanding of what game development entailed was really helpful for me to decide whether I wanted to do game development for my career.

Initially, I was very much thinking that I wanted to be an animator and work on animated films with Disney or Pixar. I had never considered going into video game development. It wasn't until I was in a position where I could learn more about it through people at work that I realized, "Oh, this is really cool. It looks like there's potential for me, whether that's with animation or on the production side."

My biggest takeaway from my early career was how important networking is in the games industry.

This is probably the case in any industry, but in entertainment, it's essential. I knew every single person at Pandemic by name–all 250 people. Every job I've gotten in my career has been helped by the fact that I already knew someone at that company and had a relationship with them—that's how I got my job at Riot and later at Lab Zero. I wasn't just one more person in the pile of résumés. Even when we all left Lab Zero to start Future Club, the team stuck together because we had all worked well together.

For people who want to get into the games industry, half of it, yes, knowing and developing the skill to be a designer or an artist or whatever. But a lot is going to networking events, meeting people, and getting involved in that community. It is much easier to get into the industry when you know people. People I haven't worked with since 2007 or so at Pandemic still contact me.

Today, the roles have reversed, and I am now in a position to help them out by getting them into a company.

People Are People, Not Resources

When I started at Riot, the art team consisted of just ten people; then, it became hundreds. A lot of artists would get hired on one project, and people on different teams would never get to meet each other. As a result, I organized a lot of fun stuff for the artists to do together outside work. The point was to create opportunities for people to bond and get to know each other as people. One time, I set up a scavenger hunt at Disneyland. People were put into random groups with different people they hadn't met before. I still remember one of the artists telling me, "I met one of my best friends on that Disneyland trip. I would never have been able to meet them if it hadn't been for you, Frani."

Those were the things that made me really happy.

I spent a lot of time thinking about how I could improve people's work environment and improve their workflow, which included providing spaces and opportunities for them to get to know each other better. Once, we also brought in ex-Special Forces military guys to do leadership training. We went out into the woods, flipped tires, and did this whole scenario where you had to rescue a hostage. We had people blindfolded and led through a path in the forest by a teammate who could only give them verbal instructions. The exercise really highlighted how important communication was. If you don't communicate the exact thing you are trying to do, or if someone doesn't hear it correctly, your team will fall apart.

At Riot, I turned my role into an entire multi-person department–Art Operations. It became a discipline for all the team activities and processes I had started, like recruiting and outsourcing, with me coordinating everything. As a hiring manager, I looked for people with initiative, drive, and a positive attitude. Did they want to be there; were they curious about figuring out how they could help people solve problems–that was more important than where they went to school and what their degree was. I would have hired someone who was less skilled but had a positive attitude, made the effort, and was willing to learn over a brilliant rockstar who was a jerk.

Who wants to work with a jerk?

These are the things people call soft skills, but they are also simple, basic skills that everyone needs to have to work as a team. You have to be able to work with others and understand that different people communicate in different ways. I can't talk to person A in the same way that I would talk to person B. Being able to form relationships with people, to know them so that you can learn their language and how to best communicate difficult feedback to them, makes such a huge difference. It's positive and makes things more productive because you start to form mutual respect. When conflicts come up, and they will come up, it's much easier to resolve them when mutual respect is established because you know where you're both coming from: "Hey, we are on the same team. We're not going at it as me against you. We both want the same thing, but we maybe want them in a different way."

It helps to have that relationship with people so that you don't think of them as just a resource. Instead, they're a person who is bringing skills, value, knowledge, experience, and perspectives that are probably different from yours. And that's a good thing. Having different perspectives, and not having everyone who always thinks exactly like you, is really good because it helps you to catch the blind spots that you might not have spotted.

That's why when people talk about diversity, I've never thought about it as having to hire someone by their race or whatever. It's not just about that. It's about the unique perspective that this person can bring to the team that others may not have. In a lot of cases, people from different ethnic backgrounds and cultures do bring that unique perspective, too, but it's not the only way to have a diverse group of developers. So, this approach is more critical than a quota or thinking about people as "human resources." I hate that term because it's so dehumanizing, and it treats you like a thing.

No, you are people. People are people.

They're going to have their personal experience and perspective. That's why I think taking the time to have team-building and bonding activities helps to form deeper relationships that aren't just about "work, work, work" all the time. It helps you collaborate better because you develop mutual respect for each other's unique points of view. And that's really valuable.

Pivoting to Production, Sort Of

At both Pandemic and Riot, I did similar things, helping out wherever I could and bringing organization to chaos.

At that time, I was still thinking, "I'm eventually going to be an animator." At one point, though, one of the more senior producers pulled me aside and said, "Look, production suits you. You need to decide soon whether you want to go to art or focus on production because they're very different skills. And if you don't focus on one or the other, you're not going to get really good at either."

Maybe a year into my role at Riot, I decided I was okay with not being an animator. I was really happy doing what I was doing, and I want to keep pushing toward learning more about production. I still love animation. I am still an artist. I still paint and draw in my free time. But professionally, I was more interested in developing my production skills.

So, I made that decision.

As the team grew internally, they realized that the artists, in general, needed tools to be developed so that the art department could function better across all these different pods of feature teams that were doing different things. So, one of the things I helped to build was an internal art-share tool and portal that created more visibility for the different art styles used by each feature team.

With the tool, across all the disciplinary teams—whether you were on Skins, Champions, the new client team, or whatever—people could now see and give feedback on art that was being created and realize, "Okay, cool, they're making this. By the way, we're also making this other thing. So, let's make sure that's consistent." I was proud of my impact on the art department.

However, things were still weird.

My role had never existed at the company before, and it didn't have a clear career path. That's ultimately part of the reason why I eventually left. I had this outlier position. It was production, but it was *for* the art department, ensuring that the department itself ran smoothly with recruiting, outsourcing, and team building. My production skills and role were not applied to a feature team like Skins or Champions. I wasn't a producer on any of the things that were features for the game.

It was challenging for me to move into a full game production role at Riot. I don't know why it was so difficult for people to see a path for me. Maybe because I was there as a production assistant first and then as an art producer for the art department itself. It just wasn't clear to them how I could make that move from doing art department production to actual game production.

I definitely did also feel a little bit of unconscious gender bias.

I would tell some of the more senior producers that I wanted to move into the production discipline, and they'd say, "We're not really hiring junior people. We want to hire more senior people first so that they can help train people." Then, a month later, I'd see that they had hired a junior producer anyway, a guy. I would find out because the artists would say, "Can you come to our team and be our producer? The guy they just hired doesn't know anything." So, I knew people wanted me on their team. But for whatever reason, it didn't seem possible for me to make that transition at Riot.

Yes, there were opportunities that I bowed out of when my daughter was alive and sick from 2011 to 2013. Perhaps I could have made that transition more easily during that time or at least gotten my foot in the door as a producer on a feature team. But those roles came with responsibility, and because my daughter took priority, I knew I could not commit at the time. I made this really clear to my team, and because of that, maybe it was more difficult for people to see me in that producer role later on, or perhaps they just saw my capabilities as being limited to that particular time in my life.

During those two years when Leah was alive, I missed the boat on getting into game production and lost out on opportunities to show people what I could do. Then, after Leah died, I was ready to move into that role and began aggressively pursuing the positions I wanted. But the landscape had changed—maybe the process for hiring was different, or perhaps the department had shifted in how they were transitioning people into that department.

As I was changing focus, Riot was changing and growing too.

"Don't Take It Personally"

I had other issues as the company was growing.

I had always been managed by the art director. I helped hire and then train two production coordinators to work as colleagues of mine, and the three of us all reported to the same art director. Then, without telling me, my manager made one of these guys whom I had trained my manager.

The way I found out about this was really disappointing and disheartening. I was doing one of those 360 performance reviews when I realized the system wouldn't let me review one of these guys as my peer. So, I contacted the HR department. They said, "Oh yeah, you can't review him because he's your manager now."

I confronted my manager about it, and he was like, "Oh, I had too many people reporting to me, so I just needed someone to be the manager for the group of you guys." I couldn't believe it. I had been there from almost the beginning of the entire department, even before him. "Why did you not consider me to be the manager?" I asked him. He was like, "I had conversations with him about wanting to be in a more managerial role, but I never had those conversations with you. I didn't think you were interested." I said, "You didn't even ask me. I didn't even know that was a possibility. If I had known, I would have definitely been interested. You assigned him as my manager, and you didn't even tell me. That is really insulting."

He said, "Don't take it personally. It wasn't meant like that."

That attitude made me start to think about where I really wanted to be in the long term. I realized I had been drinking too much of the Kool-Aid. Maybe Riot wasn't this perfect place where I would be forever. So, I started to wonder, "Is there really a place for me here?"

My new manager was not great. My monthly one-on-ones with him were so frustrating. So, I asked to be moved to a different team called the Foundations Team. There, the artists put consistency to the characters and develop the lore and the world for League of Legends. Today, there are so many different League of Legends products, such as one-offs like short, animated films, blog posts, or comics about the lore and character backstories. All of those came from the work we did on the Foundations Team. Even now, a lot of the work in some of the games was solidified by that initial Foundations Team. Before we did that type of work, the Champions Team would make characters without thinking about how they all fit together in the same universe. That was our job, to create consistency.

The Foundations Team was one of the last teams I worked with before I left Riot.

The Point of Exit

The issue I had toward the end of my career at Riot was around feeling like I was contributing a lot of value to the company but not feeling like I was compensated appropriately for what I was doing.

I had started at a really low salary as a production assistant. It had gone up slightly, but I knew people were doing the same work I did but getting paid way more and who hadn't been there as long. So I would push for more money, and they'd come back to say, "Okay, if you show that you can do X, Y, and Z, then maybe I can put you in for a promotion or a raise." So I would do those things, and suddenly, it was, "But you also need to do A, B, and C." Every time they'd tell me, "Jump this high," I would jump that high, and then the bar kept getting higher. It affected my mental health because now that I wanted to go all in and focus on my career, it was almost all-consuming. I felt like there must have been something wrong with me if I was not moving up. There must have been something I was not doing. So, I had to work harder and prove myself even more, and I had no work-life balance.

Riot's philosophy was, "We're a meritocracy, so as long as there are results, you're going to do well." For a while, I believed that. I felt that if I just kept providing good results and jumping higher and higher, they'd eventually notice me. But I was not supported by the people who could actually make anything happen.

And I knew I deserved more.

I started to feel that this wasn't the company for me. That I needed to go somewhere else. I made it clear that I wanted to be more in the games production part of things. I thought, "I don't know if it's because people still see me as a coordinator. Or maybe they don't see the potential that I have to be doing more. Perhaps that's why they don't see me in that role.

I don't know what they see.

"What am I going to do? How am I going to move forward in my career? Do I have a career here? "

I definitely also had those thoughts of, "Well, maybe I'm not good enough to be a game producer. Maybe that's why I'm not in that role."

Space, Grace, and Confidence

After my daughter died, I had only taken a month off work. At that time, I told myself that I needed to focus on my career one hundred percent. It was like I pushed the grief away and compartmentalized it. So now, after I had put all this effort into focusing on my career and it wasn't going anywhere, I started having panic attacks and anxiety attacks over it, on top of not properly grieving for my daughter.

It was so very anxiety-inducing that my doctor told me, 'You need to take two months off work. Just stop."

It was good for me to take that break. We traveled a little bit and went on several camping trips. I'm really into nature, so reconnecting with the earth helped me reset everything. I disconnected from work and did weekly therapy. I was on medication. It wasn't long-term, and I was able to get off of it after a year. I'm very glad that I did therapy. It really helped. It made me realize there were a lot of things I wasn't confronting.

The break and all of that eventually helped me resume going back to work.

It also made me realize that I needed to look for another job. I finally knew I deserved more. I didn't have to stay at Riot. I had other options. I started applying for other roles at different companies. After one company, in particular, didn't hire me, I realized, "Thank god. I shouldn't have taken that job anyway." I would have gone from the same thing to something just slightly different. That's when it clicked. It was not that there was something wrong with me; it was something wrong with them for not seeing what I had in me.

I realized, "Okay, I'm going to do these job interviews with that confidence that I know I can do this. I'm going to tell them bluntly, 'If you hire me to be on your team, this is the role I'm going to have to be in, or else it's not going to work. I am not going to be your assistant. I will be in a leadership role because that's the type of person I am and where I operate best." They really didn't like hearing that at a couple of places. They were looking for someone to be the maid, to clean up their messes, but not necessarily be in charge. And when I didn't get the job at those places, I was like, "Cool. You're going to pass. I'm *also* passing. No hard feelings."

Around this time, I was contacted by the co-founder and owner of Lab Zero. I had known the co-founder since our Pandemic days. We hadn't seen each other a lot while I was at Riot, but he had been involved with the stuff that was happening with Leah. As a friend, he had come to the hospital a couple of times to show support during a very challenging time.

I talked to him a bit when the whole manager thing at Riot happened. "I'm feeling really frustrated at Riot. Can you believe they did this?!" So, he knew I was unhappy and looking to leave. He contacted me around the end of 2015. "Hey, we just did an Indiegogo for our new game *Indivisible*, and it got funded. You're the first person I thought of because we need a producer, and you'd be great."

I was like, "Yeah!" Here I was, trying to prove myself and get myself seen at Riot, but why did I have to put in all that effort when another team wanted me? Lab Zero had done *Skullgirls* previously, but they had done it without a producer. It had been really difficult, with a lot of challenges, and so I was the first person he had thought of. It was very validating after the last year I'd been through to finally feel like there was a team that saw my worth and value.

It was perfect timing for me to leave Riot too. Lab Zero was going to start preproduction on their new game in February of 2016. So I joined them as a producer.

At the time, we were a team of twelve or thirteen. I was going from this giant company to less than twenty people and was THE producer. There weren't any senior people around to advise or guide me. At Riot, at least I had the safety net of other people who had more experience and could help me, but now the training wheels were off. I had to do the role by myself now. It was a little bit daunting, but also really exciting to feel that all my efforts had paid off. That people saw my worth.

Looking back, I'm now able to see that there were a lot of issues with Lab Zero's leadership from the very beginning.

I had come from having worked on a leadership training course at Riot and implementing a whole leadership academy. I had spent a good year thinking about what makes a good leader. Toward the end of my career at Riot, I interviewed many different leaders around the company for a mini, internal documentary about what leadership meant. Riot tried to instill leadership qualities in everyone. There was a big push for people to understand that leading also means knowing when to be a follower. Even if you're not a lead or a manager, you can still have leadership qualities, and you also benefit from knowing what good leadership looks like so that you can hold leaders accountable.

I came into Lab Zero where leadership was very broken; the team was fractured. Culturally, there were a lot of issues with communication, trust, and fear among the team. People were afraid to talk in front of others. And because I was the new person and the producer, everyone would come to me with, "So and so said this."

So, my first problem to solve was getting people into a room where they could talk to each other. I was used to having monthly one-on-ones with people at Riot, but here I had one-on-ones with every single person on the team almost every week. I needed to understand all the dynamics among the people and where the conflicts were coming from.

As soon as I joined Lab Zero, I could put into practice a lot of the things I had learned about leadership at Riot. I was helping people understand that you can be upset and frustrated, but at the end of the day, you need to be able to communicate with the people on your team so that you can work better together. Otherwise, it's not going to get better. You can't build something if people don't trust each other.

Over the next month and beyond, things did improve. We had more regular team meetings where people could bring things up. We started to talk about the schedule and how we wanted to work.

However, there were still some issues with the company.

Becoming a CEO

My transition from producer to CEO of Lab Zero happened because the previous CEO had the title but wasn't performing in the role. A title is just a title. If you're not doing the work that the role requires, then you are not that title. So, when the CEO stepped down, I was asked to step up.

Going from producer to CEO was a big shift. It was very daunting and scary. I wasn't sure if I wanted the job. I thought, "Oh my gosh, can I actually do this? I don't know if I'm the right person for this." But the team said, "Yes, you need to do this. You've been running the company for years anyway without the title."

I became CEO in December 2018 when the twins were six months old—*and* I was still the producer. I couldn't hire another producer because we didn't have the budget, and the game was beyond schedule. It was a huge challenge to do both of those roles on top of being a new mom to newborn twins.

In October 2019, almost a year after I became CEO, we shipped the game *Indivisible*, which was nominated for "Character Design" and "Game, Original Role Playing" at the NAVGTR Awards. Then we started work on a new project. But we had unresolved legal and IP issues left over from the prior CEO's tenure. I was dealing with all that when the friend who hired me, the sole owner of Lab Zero at the time, made very inappropriate public comments, which brought to light a pattern of abusive behavior within the team that I was unaware of. He had become a huge liability for the company, and people didn't want to work for him anymore. We had to ask him to resign. After trying to negotiate with him for weeks, he fired another person and me from the board.

Then basically, everyone left the company.

That whole experience was really hard for the team. We realized we couldn't continue working with someone like that, and we never wanted to be in such a position again. So, we started our own new company, Future Club, an employee-owned game development studio. We set it up as a co-op, so everyone would have equal equity and a say in the organization.

Future Club is a brand-new company, and I'm in the process of getting money and setting up all the basics, like payroll, HR, contracts, NDAs, social media, and a million other things. But it's been great. The team is focused on the work and building a pitch for the next game, whereas I'm focused on how we will run things.

Basically, we are starting from scratch.

I believe in the team's abilities, skills, and experience. And publishers realize we have a proven track record of shipping games, so I'm pretty optimistic. It's been a good couple of months and really refreshing for the team, who are very motivated. I think this whole painful experience has bonded us to become even closer. We've created a very positive environment to work in, and it's very freeing to be able to collaborate in a healthy way. It's scary but also exciting because we know that whatever we do next, we'll be able to own it.

It won't be in the hands of one or two people.

The type of games we're making are still focused on 2D animation. That's one aspect of how we are different. We have a certain look and style that isn't very common in video games, which are mostly 3D. We can be the best 2D animation game studio because there aren't many. A lot of people see this and realize, "Okay, you've done *Skullgirls*; you've done *Indivisible*. You clearly have very high-quality production value on the artistic visuals."

The advantage of working in 2D is that it's timeless. It's not stuck in a time where certain graphics look like they belong to a specific era. Realistic games were only cutting edge in the year 2000. Instead, 2D doesn't really age, so I think our games will be able to last longer. That's the benefit.

We're also in the process of creating new IP, pitching, and developing prototypes to fund a new project, and we have been able to attract investment and get the community to fundraise a little bit. One of the other aspects we're focusing on is diverse representation. One of our pitches is very diverse—the audience is mainly women. We want to have a diverse cast of women characters with different skin tones and body shapes. We've all seen the white European knight dudes.

Now we want to tell stories that haven't been told before.

We're trying to create stories that are not usually heard of or seen in games; we want to bring more representation to other cultures that people aren't so familiar with. That was something I was really proud of with *Indivisible*—it was steeped in Southeast Asian culture, which you don't see in a lot of games. By giving people a way to engage with stories, cultures, and issues in a different world, we can highlight them without beating people over the head with them. We also want to highlight the things we care about that are happening around us and parallel the issues we live through in real life.

When you communicate these things in a fantasy world, people can suddenly see them in a different light and draw inspiration from them.

The fact is a lot of gamers want these stories. There's a big push and interest in stories that are outside the norm or what you typically see, like transgender, nonbinary, gay, or lesbian characters. Gamers who identify with these characters exist and want to see themselves represented in the content. There are probably people who are cynical about what we are trying to do: "You know that's not going to draw a lot of money or sales." Yes, it probably won't be as big and profitable as League of Legends or Fortnite; it won't appeal widely to millions of people. But we're not trying to be Riot Games. We're trying to be our own thing. It's not that we don't want to be making money; we obviously want to make money. But we don't want to do it at the expense of our values and the things that we care about.

At the end of the day, when people can see themselves and their culture represented, that will make a significant impact for them. And there will also be many other people who will learn about and appreciate these stories.

We have all the colors of the rainbow represented in the company and many different cultures. We care about ensuring enough candidates in our pool of people to bring in unique perspectives that we may not otherwise have on our team. It's more important than just ticking a box and saying, "Oh, we have this percentage of this race represented; therefore, we are inclusive." We want to give people a chance to have a say in the company, the games we make, and the stories we tell.

The gaming industry really needs that now more than ever. So many people feel there isn't a place for them in the gaming industry because it's always been so white male-dominated. But now there is a market, and we're starting to see more interest and support from the funding and publishing side, and from audiences in general, for games made by people of color and women.

It's less about money and more about, "What are we trying to say? What are we trying to leave in people's hands? What are the experiences we want to create? How does the game make them think about the stories that we're telling?" Maybe it'll make people think differently, in a good way. Our games provide another perspective.

And if that content is not being made, then we can be the ones to make it.

I'm really excited to see what we do next.

Frani's Reflections

On Being a Co-Op

The way we've structured our company is as a cooperative. The group of fifteen developers that we have on the team and I are all equal owners. I don't own half of the company because of my title. I own the same amount as everyone else, and all our salaries are transparent.

We're also having a lot of discussions about how we want to handle conflict resolution and how we want to handle voting as members of this company on big issues. Everything is openly discussed, which I really like. We all become more accountable to each other rather than just deferring responsibility to someone else at the top. In the type of structure we have, you directly influence what your career or your salary can be.

It's a very new way of working, and something that is a direct response to what happened at our previous company. That was a situation where, philosophically, there was this idea that everyone was open to talking about things, but at the end of the day, there really was one single company owner. He made the decisions and structured the company around people doing whatever he wanted to do, even though he was the person that was creating a lot of problems.

In our new entity, we're all equal.

This structure doesn't give anyone an advantage over others. We really want to try to retain as much of the ownership of the company as possible for the people who are actively contributing to it, rather than just some investor who's giving us money, then expecting to reap the benefits of everyone else's hard work. It's a new process that we're all getting used to, but it's really exciting. I think it's a good test case–does this co-op model work in game development? Many of the studios we've been in touch with are smaller co-ops than us. They're either a team of four or six; very few are more than ten.

It'll be interesting to see how things work out—how we scale and keep the cooperative philosophy as we grow.

On Open Communications

I love getting negative feedback from my team. Not that I enjoy the facts, but I actively take the time to schedule meetings with people to say, "How am I doing? What can I do better? How did that meeting go?"

Spending time understanding how people work with you ultimately helps you work better with people. There have been times when, initially, people on my team said, "No, it's fine. There's nothing to report." Then six months down the road, out of the blue, because I took that time to talk to them, they're like, "Look, I didn't want to say anything to anyone else, but I want to tell you that this thing is really bothering me." People will come to you with their concerns or worries: "I'm not sure this is the right thing for the project. And I'm not sure if I should say it in the team because I don't want to offend people."

There are a lot of people who feel that they don't want to step on anyone's toes. So, they won't say anything. But that might be the person you really need to hear from. If you don't spend the time helping them understand that they can be heard and that there's a space for them to be heard, you might miss out on something important. In the five years, I've spent with this team, I've developed relationships where people feel comfortable coming to me even if they don't feel comfortable saying things in front of everyone else. Then it's an easy, "Okay, that's an excellent point. Let's talk to so and so about it." I work with a lot of people who are more introverted, which is a big contrast for me because I'm the most outgoing, extroverted person.

I've done research on how people communicate. I've read a bunch of books about introverts and how critical they are to teams. Someone might be the quietest person in the room, but they could also be the person who sees something that no one else is paying attention to. It's really important that they have the space to raise those concerns. They might not bring it up in a meeting, but maybe they communicate better in writing, and they need space and time to sit down and think and write their thoughts rather than just be on the spot.

I made the mistake, initially, of thinking that things were cool when I didn't get instant feedback. But, once I learned more about how people communicate in my one-on-one conversations, I started leaving the door open. "If you can't think of anything now, but you think of it later, feel free to message me on Slack or email me." Then I would get these very well-thought-out, analytical messages on potential issues. We've seen things coming so many times because I helped create a place where people could bring those things up and even talk about the mistakes I've made.

It's all a process; we're all learning.

On the Value of Servant Leadership

I was able to see a lot of really good and really bad examples of leadership style at Riot. Because the company was so big, I could learn from different types of leaders and think about what I liked and didn't. It helped me become a better leader. The things that I did or failed to do in retrospect have also made me become a better leader.

Ultimately, for me, as CEO of a company, I'm less invested in having people do things my way. The title of CEO can be interpreted in different ways. People assume when you're the boss, you're the one who makes the calls; you're the head. I see the CEO role differently. My job is that I'm no one's boss. I work for my team, and my team does the work. I'm not necessarily the person to tell people what to do. Instead, I provide the focus and motivation, then, people do the work.

We are a team. It's teamwork.

I care more about how I can make the working environment for my team the best it can be, which will lead to the best product. So, for example, ultimately, when it comes down to it, my job is to make sure my team gets as rich as possible doing what they love to do. So I focus on making sure we get funding and good terms and that the schedule is set up so that people can do the work at a pace that's not killing everyone. So as CEO, that's my primary function.

Leaders must focus on making the team and work environment as healthy and positive as possible while providing direction for where you want everyone to be in five or ten years. Leaders need to have the big vision but not get too caught up in wanting to be involved in the project so deeply that they are not letting the people they've hired—the subject matter experts who know more than them—do the best work they can. Leaders have to provide enough direction, trust that people will know what to do, and let them do their work.

You can't use that top-down control model in game development, technology in general, or any kind of creative effort. That may work well when you know exactly what you're trying to build. If you're trying to build a house and have a blueprint, it's okay to hire the guys to do the work and dictate how they do it and in what order. But in game development and technology, you often don't even know what problem you're trying to solve, and you don't know how exactly to solve it. Part of how you solve the problem is by collaborating with a team of people and creatively problem-solving over time—trying things, testing them, and tweaking them. That can't be done in a very top-down way because you can't predict things. So, you really need to allow a bottom-up approach.

You lead from behind.

On Evolution & Relevancy

I'm pretty certain no project that's ever been pitched in game development was the same thing when they put it out in the market.

The game evolves and changes. You can't quantify fun until you actually play it, and you have to allow for that free flow of creativity and problem-solving among the team. That's why agile development in games is so critical.

You are reinventing the wheel in different ways. Even though there are the same game genres, each game experience can be so different. "These systems are kind of similar to this other game, but there's this whole new mechanic that we've never seen before that's super fun."

That's why I love video games.

A lot of values were instilled in me at Riot that I still carry—focusing on talent, and the team is one of their core values. Putting the player first is one of Riot's manifesto points. It wasn't a fixed "What do I want to put in a game?" It was fluid, "What does a player want?" It's not about, "I'm some genius creative director, and everything has to be my vision and what I want." It was about, "What do we want people to feel when they play this game? What do we want that experience to be?" And then working backward from that: "So, how do we achieve that?"

Although I had management issues with my personal career trajectory at Riot, there were a lot of positive things that I learned there.

Even now, as our team is building prototypes and pitching our game ideas to a couple of publishers, we've gotten interesting feedback that's evolved the concept. Different people will say, "Oh, have you guys thought about this and this?" Then we put it in the game and the engine and test it out, which then leads to, "Oh, what if we tried this other thing from some other game?" That's part of the really cool process of finding that fun and not getting stuck micromanaging people as a leader. It doesn't help the team be more creative if they have those constraints coming from above. It's about not getting too deep into the "how" but more about the "why we are doing this." It's: "You're the team. You figure out how, and you tell me how we're going to build it. Then let's build it, play it, talk about it, and then go back and see how we can improve things."

Providing a vision, the "why," and not micromanaging the subject matter experts but letting them evolve the game is how League of Legends has been so successful for as long as it's been. If you look at what League of Legends looked like when I started working at Riot ten years ago and what it is now, there's a huge difference. You can see that it's evolved.

Staying relevant is about evolving.

On Being Grateful and Present

Leah's life changed my entire outlook on everything. Yes, it's been a painful experience. But it's given me an outlook where I'm more grateful for what I have.

I'm so much more grateful every single day because I know nothing is guaranteed. None of us are guaranteed to make it through the end of today. We could get hit by an asteroid tomorrow. We don't know. There's been so much that's happened in my life—you haven't even heard half of it. But it's taught me that you have to do the best you can and be in the moment. To stay present.

The present is the only thing you know for sure.

It's good to have accomplishments. It's good to have things that you can be proud of, that you worked on—and I do have those. I'm proud of the fact that I worked at all the places, even In-N-Out Burger. Ultimately, that's what I hope to do with my job: make games that people can play and create memorable experiences that will exist long after I'm gone.

It's very important to me to keep my career from consuming all of my identity.

Yes, I have career aspirations, but I also have personal aspirations. I don't want to live to work. I want to work so I can live and have other experiences. For the people who are close to me in my life, I don't want it to be, "Yeah, she was a CEO of a game company, and I never got to spend time with her." When I'm gone, I want my kids to have fun memories of spending time with me. The people in your life, the ones you care about, will only be there for a limited amount of time. You, too, are only going to be in their life for a limited amount of time.

You're not going to take your bank account with you when you're buried. If you are so focused on work, and work consumes you to the point where you let go of your family, friends, and life, what is it for? Yes, you may be able to leave them an inheritance so they can be comfortable, but at the end of the day, your bank account is not what really matters to the people who matter to you.

Our careers are important, definitely. And it's good that women can have careers. But it's not everything. We aren't defined by our jobs. We're whole people who, at the end of the day, go back to our relationships.

The way I think about my career is that it allows me to have my life.

On Being Your Child's Best Advocate

Through our experience with Leah, I've realized that advocating for your kids when they're sick is so important. Because we were so involved in all of her care and we learned everything we could, we became her best advocates.

There are so many doctors who don't listen to the parents. By the end of our ordeal, the doctors realized we knew her so well that they'd tell the nurses, "Just do what the parents said." They ended up respecting us because we knew what was happening and because we spoke up.

A lot of people tend to get scared and only rely on what a doctor tells them. People have this misconception that doctors are all-knowing—even some doctors think of themselves that way. But doctors don't know everything. As a parent, sometimes you have to be the person to tell doctors, "This is what's going on. We know her best."

You need to stand up for what you believe in, especially when it comes to your kid's care.

People tend to get frozen by what's happening if there's a serious medical issue: "I don't want to know. I don't want to hear it." But you can't advocate for your kid if you don't know. If you don't learn as much as you can about how to care for them, do a lot of research, and really be involved, then you're going to let someone else make a decision that may not be the best. You have to raise hell for your child because your baby can't do it. The baby can't speak; she can't even move.

You have to be the one to advocate.

That's a big part of what I took away from that whole experience. This is not to say that doctors and nurses don't have value; they're obviously very knowledgeable and experts in their field. But they don't have all the answers.

And they don't know your child as well as you do.

On Home Life

I'm very lucky to have an amazing wife who's been able to support my career journey and be there for me whenever I'm feeling down or doubting myself.

Right now, my income is the primary one. But in terms of division of labor at home, we still do stuff together with the kids and pick up the house when it's a mess: "You do dishes, I'm going to get them ready for their bath." It's very ad hoc, whatever needs to be done. I don't expect to always be like, "You need to do all these chores because I'm the one who's working." Instead, we share the load. I take breaks at lunch to help make lunch with the kids. But today, for example, I had a meeting during lunch, so she had to do lunch with the kids. It depends on the day, and we make it work as best as possible. It's all about making sure that we're communicating what we need from each other, compromising on certain things, and trying to keep that up so that we don't start to have resentments.

Sometimes we trade turns: "Okay, tag, you're it. I need a break from the kids. You'll have to take some time off so you can be with them for a bit." And that's fine. I love hanging out with my kids and being a mom. But, at the end of the day, I do my job because I want to have professional accomplishments and also because I want to be able to provide the quality of life that I want for my family. For women, the question that often comes up is, "How can you be a mother and a CEO?" I think men who are parents go through similar challenges; however, there is no social expectation for them to take care of the kids.

People don't tend to ask men, "How do you balance your work with your life?"

The truth is none of us really know how; we just do it. You do your best, and as long as you're thinking about having a work-life balance, you're probably doing a good job. I do always feel like I'm out of balance, but I put in the effort to try.

That's what matters.

On Loving Who You Love

That whole experience with Zoe's transition has taught me that when you love someone unconditionally, it doesn't matter what the outside looks like or what changes people go through. We all go through changes. Even if it's not a gender change, people change physically or otherwise.

I realized I am in love with her soul, which was about who she is as a person, not what she identifies as. I hope that if there are people who are in relationships with partners who are trans or partners who are trying to figure things out, they realize that the person inside is what matters. That was what I could see and the one thing I cared about.

That's what love is, right?

There are probably people who might not be able to get over that. They might say, "No, I don't think I can see myself with a woman," and that's fine too. It's better for that person to know so they can also move on with their life.

On Advice to My Younger Self

My advice would have been to believe in yourself.

Looking back on all the things that I've dealt with in my life, in that moment, that thing always felt like the worst thing I'd ever experienced. I'd think, "It can't get worse than this. I'll never recover from this." But I've been able to overcome so many struggles in my life. It shows me how strong I am. You're stronger than you think you are. Just keep believing in what you can do, just keep going; just keep trying.

After my daughter died, I didn't think I'd ever be a mom again. And now I can't imagine my life without these kids. On top of it, to be in a place where I'm now my own boss and lead a team of people. It is amazing. Before that happened, I remember going through that feeling of, "I can't do this; I am not cut out for this."

It's okay to make mistakes. That's how you learn, and that's how you grow. These things will pass. One thing my daughter taught me is that everything changes, always. Either for good or for bad. So, you have to appreciate things when they're good and realize that when things are bad, its not going to stay bad forever. They'll get better eventually, even if it feels like its the worst thing at the time.

Don't give up.

I still get a little nervous and think, "Did I make the right decision? What's going to happen with this new company?" Then I tell myself, "Be in the moment. You've been through so much and gotten this far, and you're going to go through much more in the future. You can handle it because you've been through bad stuff before."

You have to keep going. You have to keep trying. That's all you can do.

Melynda Barnes, MD

Chief Medical Officer at Ro

I run medical affairs for a digital health company on a mission to build accessible, impactful, and trusted care that people want. I am a surgeon, licensed to practice medicine in all 50 states and DC. I'm double board-certified in otolaryngology, which is head and neck surgery, ear, nose, and throat (ENT), and facial plastics and reconstructive surgery.

I love working for a company that allows me to advocate for patients and providers across the country.

The Gift of Teachers

My twin brother, Jason, and I both had Mrs. Greenlee as our second-grade teacher. She was so dynamic and caring and loving and thoughtful. Mrs. Greenlee was such a strong advocate for my brother and me. One of my fondest memories of second grade was being "Star of the Week" and writing an essay about what I wanted to be when I grew up. I remember writing, "I want to be four things. I want to be President of the United States, an Olympic gymnast, a pediatrician, and an author of children's books." So, I created a little career to-do list at age seven. Lucky for me, life would help narrow these career aspirations and point me in the direction of my true calling.

From an early age, maybe eight or nine, I remember my mom would let me go to the polling places, and I would create these signs and handouts on different propositions and why you should vote no or yes for Prop 58 and all those things. I remember that people seemed not to be interested. I thought, "Don't you want to know more about what you're voting on?" I learned very quickly that people don't always vote for what's best for others. They vote for what's best for them, and they vote a lot of times along ideological issues and along party lines. So, even if they agree on something, like the environment is important, they might still vote no on an issue because it doesn't line up with the party they are affiliated with, or they might vote yes even though they think the initiative's not that great.

That did not sit well with me. So, politics and being President were ruled out for me.

I was on a competitive gymnastics team, but when I was then, I was already five feet, and my coach told my mom that I would likely be too tall to be a competitive gymnast. So, my dream of becoming an Olympic gymnast fell away as grew taller than my teammates.

That left becoming a doctor and writing books for kids.

I loved science and was fortunate to have all these strong female teachers who recognized something within me and took the time to take things to the next level, to really support me in my journey. They all told me that science and math were my strengths. But I also wanted to help people. I cared about issues and equity. So, becoming a doctor, they said, "would be perfect. You should totally do this."

And they all told me that I *could* be a doctor.

The Gift of Reading

While I was in fifth grade, My English teacher, Mrs. Ishii, created an individual plan for me. I had my own books and assignments– and spent most of the class completing those assignments on my own. I loved reading, being in my own world, and imagining the different places the books would take me.

Mrs. Ishii also recognized that I loved to read and was super curious about the characters' experiences in the book. She was such a wonderful teacher and assigned books for me to read that were written by diverse authors. So, the rest of my classmates were reading *James and the Giant Peach*, and I was reading *Roll of Thunder, Hear My Cry*, and *To Kill a Mockingbird*. She gave me books written by Black female authors, books centered around the Black experience in America, and biographical books.

Reading is amazing because it can transport you to different worlds and different time periods. You can meet different people. You get to see how people think and why they act the way they do, especially if a narrator is telling you their thought process behind X, Y, and Z, and then you see their actions. You're like, "Oh, that's why people do that?" It gives you some insight into the human condition. So, why not make that as diverse as possible? The human condition did not start and end in England. There are people and experiences that are valuable and valid across the world. That's how you build empathy. That's how you build people who are global citizens. That's how you build people who are able to understand that not everyone's life looks exactly like mine, but that doesn't mean that their life is any less valuable or any less worth it.

When you read and are introduced to different concepts, it doesn't matter necessarily what your skin color or ethnic background is because the human condition is the same.

My mom is really big on education. I remember her giving me a real, grown-up textbook on the human body when I was eight and in fourth grade. Could I understand everything in the book? No, but I carried that thing around everywhere I went. I was always reading it. Besides my favorite book *Matilda*, which I read like a hundred times, I also read Ben Carson's *Think Big* and *Gifted Hands*. I read all of these books before the age of ten.

In a sense, Dr. Carson became my roadmap. He was able to overcome challenges in school and being from a lower socioeconomic status, to become a neurosurgeon at Johns Hopkins. I didn't have difficulties in school, but I found inspiration in his ability to achieve his dreams when others told him that his dreams were impossible. I knew that I loved school and that my teachers were finding ways to keep me engaged.

So, I thought, "Okay, I'm going to be a pediatric neurosurgeon like Ben Carson." That was my goal.

On the Move

When I was eleven, we moved from California to Atlanta. My mom enrolled us in a program called M-to-M, majority-to-minority. It was a busing program that allowed students to enroll in different schools with a different racial majority. I was living in south Fulton County, and my home school was majority Black, so I was bused to northern Fulton County to a school that was better funded and was one of the top schools in the state. That's how I went to the school in Roswell, Georgia. The school was a little hesitant to put me in advanced classes, but after a month or two, they moved me to a special class with five other students. We took high school math and science in middle school, which was very cool. I was a part of a little community of other high-achieving kids who loved school. And the beautiful thing was that we were not competitive. There was no reason for us to be. Some of those people are still my really good friends today.

The Smart Kid

A funny story: my eighth-grade history teacher would do these trivia Fridays. When you walked into the class, he randomly assigned you a number, seated you in groups, and then began the trivia. The points you earned from trivia could be added to your test as extra credit or bonus points. It was brilliant because it made you study before the test, and everyone was super engaged and pumped for trivia.

Soon, my teacher started noticing that people were waiting for me to go into the classroom first and sorting themselves so they could try to be on my team. One day he pulled me aside and said, "Wait, I want you to come into class last because everyone's trying to figure out how they can be on your team." It was so funny. I hadn't even noticed.

I had a very positive experience being the smart kid.

People were very nice to me. People would say, "Hey, did you get that answer? Do you understand this? Can I ask you a question?" For an introvert, it was actually great. There was no pressure. I was comfortable with the way people interacted with me. I thought it was great that people would ask me if I could help them with something or be their partner on a project. It gave me a language to communicate with and meet other kids, especially as a new kid moving into a school.

There were all these cues around me that education was key to improving your socioeconomic status and achieving your dreams.

I believed if I did well, I could improve my circumstances.

A Wonderful Childhood

High school was more of the same. I really loved my school, which was a blue-ribbon school. My mom, again, worked hard for us to be able to move to Roswell and thus no longer had to participate in the Majority to Minority program. I ran track in high school and was on the dance team. I also worked as a hostess at a restaurant during high school and volunteered at a food pantry.

I took Spanish in school and really loved it. When I was at the food bank, I would volunteer to speak Spanish to the people who were there. One of my projects was translating a poster to make the people coming in feel welcome and included. Many volunteers were older women who remembered the neighborhood when it was basically just 100 percent Caucasian. We all worked together to find ways to support the new wave of immigrants moving to our community

Living in Roswell afforded me a wonderful childhood and a wonderful education. I continued to have amazing teachers. For example, Mr. Granville, my AP biology teacher, supported me, introduced me to research, told me I could be a doctor, and told me that I could go to any college I wanted. My teachers and the administrative staff were constantly advocating for me. I would come into my homeroom, and there would be applications on my desk to do enrichment programs over the summer or apply for college scholarships. One summer between my sophomore and junior year, I did a computer programming course at Clark Atlanta University. My project was to learn C++ to program models of DNA and RNA reactions. I also did a summer program at Duke University between my junior and senior years, where I got college credit to take summer session classes on campus.

All these things resulted from my being proactive, but also because of people saying, "Hey, have you looked into this? You should apply for this."

I'm really thankful for all of the mentors and teachers I've had along the way!

I Just Needed to Decide

Georgia had a great program called the HOPE Scholarship for students who matriculate to a state public college or university. You had to maintain a 3.0 GPA, and in exchange, you would get free tuition, books, and sometimes room and board. The hardest thing about the scholarship was qualifying. But I knew that I had already met the criteria. And I had been admitted into the honors college at the University of Georgia very early on. So, I knew that, one, I would go to college and, two, I would go for free.

It was just a question of where I wanted to go.

Choosing which college was a bit reactive and a bit proactive.

My dad lived in San Jose, in Northern California, and I had a couple of cousins who lived in California and really loved Stanford. I first knew of Stanford, mostly from their women's basketball team. So I was pleasantly surprised to find out that it was an outstanding educational institution only about thirty minutes from my dad. So, Stanford went on my list. Before things were digital, I remember getting printed perspectives, information guides, and applications from many schools in the mail. I did my research. I only applied to eight colleges, which was probably a tiny amount compared to what kids are doing now.

I got into all the schools I'd applied to. So, I just needed to decide where I wanted to go.

I was very much interested in how things worked and problem-solving, so I gravitated toward MIT. People need to realize the sort of change that happens when you go from high school, which caters to everyone, to a school that caters to people who want to specifically do technology and engineering. It's cool to just be in that environment. I remember interviewing with an older alum from MIT who lived in the Atlanta area, and just being so energized and inspired by his experience. The interview took place in his basement, where he had this whole workshop set up of things he liked to build and tinker with in his retirement. We talked about curiosity, innovation, wanting to know how things work, and loving things like physics, engineering, and science. And I remember thinking, "This is amazing. I hope I get into the school."

I ultimately decided to go to Stanford for several reasons. The minute I stepped foot on the campus, I felt like this was where I was supposed to be. I tell people it's like falling in love. You can't really explain everything. You just feel some magic. I loved that they had sports, that you could get involved with volunteer activities, and that you could study abroad. I loved the audacity of the institution to want to be the best in everything—have the best sports team, the best medical school, the best business school, the best undergrad, the most Nobel laureates, everything. I was impressed and inspired and knew immediately that this was my school.

It was an added bonus that my dad, brother, and sister were nearby.

At Stanford, I majored in Biology and Spanish. It was an incredible four years. I met a lot of people who positively influenced my life, and I feel like I really gained the skills to do what I do today, which is to be curious, to ask questions, to be diligent, to do research, and to know that things can be done in different ways. You don't have to follow the status quo. In fact, thinking about ways that the status quo can be changed or challenged is very exciting and can lead to innovation and ways to have a positive impact.

Supporting People Like Me

After Stanford, I went to Mount Sinai in New York for medical school. Mount Sinai was also an amazing experience. I wanted to go to New York because my oldest sister was living there, and after visiting a few times, I knew I wanted to live there, at least for a little while. Mount Sinai really understood the medical student experience, and they were doing everything possible to set people up for success. In addition, they also had a commitment to diversity before that was a popular thing. They actively expanded their definition of the underrepresented minority to not just be Black, Mexican, or Native American. They said, let's look at people of Spanish-speaking descent in general. Are we missing strong Puerto Rican, Dominican, Panamanian, or Argentine applicants? Mount Sinai is located at the intersection of Spanish Harlem and the Upper East Side. They had a lot of health fairs, a lot of outreaches, and a lot of tactical hands-on engagements with the East Harlem community. And I thought, "Well, here's a school that's talking about diversity on their tour and in their information sessions and actually doing many wonderful things in their very diverse community." Medical school is hard enough. I'd never done anything like it before, and I didn't know anyone who'd gone to medical school.

So, a program that was really looking to support people like me was the best place for me.

Letting Go

I had an excellent medical school education and just a great experience. I took a year off to do a clinical research fellowship sponsored by the Doris Duke Foundation. Ultimately, I matched my number one choice for residency, which was back at Stanford doing ear, nose, and throat (ENT) surgery.

Everything was a huge success.

The theme of my story is always, "Be open." Be open to mentorship and be open to people giving you suggestions and ideas. Initially, I wanted to be a neurosurgeon. But there were people along the way who said, "You know, Melynda, does that fit your personality? Have you looked into ENT (Ears, nose, and throat)? Have you looked into otolaryngology?" I was like, "I don't need to look into anything else. I read Ben Carson's book. This is my roadmap. I'm going to do it." And then I started shadowing physicians, and I was like, "Oh, I'm not sure I actually like this. I've been saying I'm going to be a neurosurgeon for, like, twelve years. What am I going to do now?"

I knew I wanted to be a surgeon because I like problem-solving and fixing things. Those things had attracted me to MIT. I saw similarities and parallels between engineering and surgery. Someone has a problem. You're going to fix it immediately. You can identify the problem and identify the solution. That was table stakes. Then it becomes a question of where you want to operate. Do you want to operate in the abdomen? On bones? For me, I really loved finesse—fine, delicate operating, and I loved intricate anatomy.

It was an ENT doctor at Washington University in St. Louis, where I did my clinical research fellowship, Dr. Jay Piccirillo, who said, "You really need to consider ENT. You are going to love it." He introduced me to the department chair of ENT at Mount Sinai.

Otolaryngology (ENT) is a fantastic specialty. There is a vast variety in work—you can operate on kids or adults, people with chronic or acute illnesses. The ways in which you operate are different—you can use endoscopes, you can use microscopes, you can spend a lot of time suturing like facial plastics, or you can operate deep in the neck. The neck's anatomy is intricate and beautiful; so many vital structures run through the neck. Given the variety of patients and conditions, each day and each surgery are different. And you're helping people. For example, you might do surgery to take out someone's tonsils that takes less than an hour t, but that means a kid can sleep well at night, which means that they can do well in school. The intervention is not that difficult, but the outcome and the influence on someone's life can be huge.

And I loved that.

There's no medical equivalent to ENT surgery. ENT is the medical *and* surgical field for the head and neck and the ear, nose, and throat. That was also important because it meant I had continuity of care with the patients. I could see a patient for an ear problem and see them again if they developed strep throat or couldn't breathe through their nose. I could help people in many different ways, which was very important to me.

It Has to Transform You

Residency is hard. It is five years of putting everyone and everything above and before yourself. It's five years where time is not your own. Someone's telling you, effectively, when to eat and when to sleep because your number one priority is taking care of patients, learning how to be a doctor, a surgeon, and an otolaryngologist, and learning how to do research. You also learn how to be empathetic, how to deliver bad news, how to deliver good news, and how to tell someone you were wrong.

It's such a life-changing experience.

Being a doctor is not a career; it is an identity. It is a lifestyle. And even if I'm not seeing patients every day now, I will always be a doctor. I always have that lens. People still email me and call me: "Hey, what is this?" "Can I send you a picture of that? I have to have a first-aid kit in my house and in my car in case someone needs help. I keep EpiPens in my first-aid kit for allergic reactions.

It's who I am; I can't help it.

It makes sense that the transformation process from medical school graduates to physicians is difficult. If it's easy, you wouldn't be able to do the work. The grueling nature of the training was on purpose because it needed to be difficult to build resiliency so that you could get through these days and save people's lives. There is no margin of error. We can't make mistakes. This is life and death in some cases. And even if it's not life and death, it can be a deciding factor as to whether or not someone gets back to their baseline functional status.

Look at COVID right now and the great sacrifice of our frontline workers, our doctors, our nurses, and everyone else who works in the hospital.

If the training to become those professions were easy, you would not see people being able to go to work every day and put their lives on the line to help others in this type of situation. It has to be difficult, but it doesn't have to be cruel. It has to transform you. It's difficult, but it has a purpose. To build grit. That's my positive spin on five years of working multiple eighty-to-one-hundred-hour weeks. You need that to mature and be able to sacrifice yourself for others.

You need to develop empathetic grit.

This is What I Trained For

I remember being the resident on-call one night, and I got a frantic call from the emergency room. There was a patient who had been shot in the neck. There was blood pooling, and they were having a hard time finding an airway for him and getting an endotracheal tube in. I remember saying, "I'm hopping in my car right now. Do whatever you can to find a surgical airway, meaning cut a hole in his neck, over the trachea, as best as you can to try to get a tube in." The ER attending said, "Yes, we're trying, but everything is so distorted with the gunshot wound and the swelling and the bleeding . . ." I said, "I'm coming, I'm coming." My attending was also on her way.

I remember walking into the hospital, thinking, "This is what I've trained for." It was a clarity Zen-like moment, like in the movies when time stops, and you walk slowly. There was so much chaos going on. People were yelling and screaming and trying to figure out how to save this young man.

Once I walked in, I said, "I need a lot more suction, and I need everyone to calm down. We're going to find an airway for him, and then we'll treat his gunshot wound." So, everyone started hooking up suctions, and I remember thinking, "I know what I need to do. I know where I need to make the incision. Let me find the landmarks. And if I can't find the landmarks, I'm the best person in this room to estimate where they are because I work on the neck every day."

I was able to make the incision with the ER attending and get an airway for the patient. When my attending walked in, she took over from the ER attending. We took the patient upstairs to the operating room to care for his neck wounds.

I remember finishing that case early in the morning; it was basically the next day at 7 a.m. I had to be at the hospital that same day because it was during the week. I remember going to my car to take a little nap. Then, as I walked back into the hospital after my power nap, I thought, "Yeah, this is what I'm here to do." I'd been given this unique opportunity to save people—not just the opportunity but also the skill set. It was no longer just a desire, but my hands could actually do what needed to be done.

To me, it just made it all worth it.

This is Why I'm Here

When I was at our public county hospital, Santa Clara Valley hospital, we had a very diverse patient population, a lot of Southeast Asian, East Asian patients, and Spanish-speaking patients. Our residency was very diverse, but there was a special connection I could make with patients as a person of color. It was unexpected to them; these patients were used to seeing Caucasian doctors. I think it lowers their guard a little bit because they feel more comfortable. I always made sure to use an interpreter with our patients who spoke Tagalog or Korean or anyone who felt more comfortable speaking a different language other than English. With our Spanish-speaking patients, I would speak to them in Spanish. Take the time to sit down, build rapport, and understand their needs.

The big surgeries are exciting and impactful. I also found my purpose in everyday interactions. It's the mom who comes in with her kid who has sleep apnea and needs to have their tonsils out so that they can breathe better, sleep well, and grow and do well in school. It's sitting down next to this worried mom and being able to explain all this in her native language and not make her feel like it's a burden, to let her know it's going to be okay.

I really try to make my patients feel like no question is too small or too "stupid."

Something that was very common among my patients when I was a resident, and even continuing into my being an attending, was when people said, "How come I'm X number of years old, and I've never heard this before? No one has ever explained it to me like this; I didn't know that's how the nose works or why I have to take thyroid medication. Thank you so much." It's afterward when parents say thank you so much or that this was the best doctor visit they'd ever had that makes me think, "This is why I'm here." I'm here to be a walking role model and patient advocate.

A New Calling

I graduated from residency at Stanford. I did my fellowship in facial plastics and reconstructive surgery in Portland, Oregon. They take one person a year, and I was their thirty-fifth or thirty-sixth fellow there and their first female fellow. So that narrative of "no pressure" continued with the fellowship.

From there, I got my first job at Yale. I was brought in to start their academic facial plastics and reconstructive surgery program within the division of ENT of Otolaryngology. I really enjoyed the work environment there. I also applied to be on the board of directors for Yale Medical Group, the leadership body for the physicians at Yale. There were four spots for new at-large voting members. It was a unique opportunity to be new to Yale, just out of training, and to get this spot on the board.

I really enjoyed working with the board. That experience would later play a role in my decision to move to Ro.

I was on the finance committee, working with the hospital and medical school leaders. It was an amazing opportunity to understand and learn how hospitals and medical groups work. I remember the chief medical officer, Dr. Vender, asking me, "Hey, I would love to have you on a committee around the quality of life for physicians and trainees at the hospital. And I would love to get your thoughts on how we can better engage patients." That really meant a lot. This giant and leader in the field was asking my opinion, and I'd been there only two years.

It was a wonderful opportunity to give back to my fellow physicians.

I remember leaving one of the board meetings one day and thinking, "Wow, I'm so happy. This is such a great experience. But I wonder how I can do this on a larger scale. How can I improve how healthcare is delivered and optimize that experience for more than just the Yale community?" So that's when I started thinking about leaving Yale to help patients on a larger scale, though I didn't know in what capacity I would help. Did I need to go back to school? Should I pursue an MPH or an MBA? So, I spent a lot of time talking to people and getting their input, and over and over, I heard the same thing, "You know what? It sounds like you should work at a startup that's tackling a problem within the healthcare space. That's the best way to address this problem on a national level or even an international level, depending on what the startup is.

Startups in healthcare need doctors and clinicians with experience working in the healthcare delivery world.

I didn't know how to approach finding or joining a startup. There are no manuals or roadmaps like Dr. Carson's book to follow. So, I continued asking questions. Then, I hired a business coach who helped translate my long academic CV into a business résumé. She gave me a lot of techniques to learn more about industry: "Go online, look on Indeed at the different types of jobs, start to get a feel of the language and what they're asking for, and then apply for some of them or at least talk to the recruiters and get a sense of what the day-to-day life looks like."

The job post for Ro came to my email from a job board one day, and I applied. They contacted me the next day, and we had a video chat. When I got off the phone call with Dr. Doron, I was like, "Yep, this is where I want to work." It was very clear. I was like, "I don't know if they want me, but this is the type of job I want, and if it isn't with Ro, I will find a place like it." Luckily for me, it was with Ro.

Ro was founded in October 2017. We are the patient company, and we are redefining and redesigning healthcare to focus on building impactful, accessible, and trusted care that patients want in a way that allows providers to thrive and practice at the top of their license. We use technology to lower healthcare costs, which in turn makes it accessible to all. We serve and take care of patients in all 50 states plus DC. In addition, we have a comprehensive generics pharmacy called Ro Pharmacy, which has medication for as low as five dollars for a 30-day supply.

We want to build a new way of delivering affordable healthcare that meets our patients where they are.

At Ro, I run medical affairs. I oversee four teams: Innovation R&D, Clinical Strategy, Quality and Safety, and Clinical Product Strategy. These are behind-the-scenes functions that people might not think about when they first hear about a digital healthcare company. Most people think, "Oh, you're a doctor working at a healthcare company that provides digital first care. You must see patients via telemedicine." Of course, we have outstanding providers that take care of the patients, but my job is to oversee teams that build products and services that provide value to patients and providers. I feel like, once again, I found the job I was supposed to do. It really hit all of my strengths and the things I love. I get to work cross-functionally with other people from other disciplines. I get to teach about how healthcare is practiced. I get to be a patient advocate. I get to be a physician and provider advocate in how we design how doctors work on our platform while keeping their lives, schedules, and needs in mind.

I get to be an advocate for underrepresented minorities on this large stage of speaking about health inequities and disparities.

Ultimately, we're working to change how healthcare is delivered in the United States. I get to do that. I know that the work I'm doing is touching people, literally in every state. And that's something that I would not have been able to do in traditional clinical medicine, where you're geographically restricted. Now, I can spearhead initiatives and lead projects that will help people across the country.

I feel so incredibly blessed to have found my calling and to work for such an amazing company that is working hard to deliver a wonderful patient and provider experience.

Melynda's Reflections

On the Power of "You Can"

Some teachers recognize their enormous responsibility and influence on the next generation in how they support you. But I think the worst experience for students is to have teachers who don't care either way. Sometimes people can be motivated by a teacher who says, "You can't be a doctor. You're not smart enough," and they use that to energize themselves and to say, "Look, I did it!" But it's better to be motivated by the teacher who's like, "You can do it. Come on. I believe in you." I think the worst is apathy, someone who doesn't tell you anything at all. They just pass you by and move on.

For me, there was never any question that I didn't have the intellect to be a doctor. I think it was more that my teachers were also looking at other factors, like the fact that I didn't have any doctors in my family. So they wanted to make sure I always felt included. They recognized that medicine, especially, can be kind of a club. And if you don't know the right steps, you might not make it. So my teachers were just like, "You can do this. Find the roadmap. You're going to have to find people who've done it before. Ask them how they did it. Be proactive. When you get to college, go seek out the premed office. Find a junior or a senior going to medical school and see if they can help you. Have someone you can ask questions, like 'How can I do well on the MCAT? Do I need to take a prep course? Just because you may not know all that stuff upfront doesn't mean you can't do it.

Find people who can help you at every step.

On the Impact of Gender Roles

Residency is where you see differences between what men and women go through. People start thinking, "Oh, well, if I do surgery and I'm spending all this time in the hospital, will I be able to get married? Will I be able to have kids? How will all this work out? Will I have to delay having children because I'll be in residency for so long? After I'm done with residency, will I live in the hospital all the time?" Look at our traditional gender roles in America. As progressive as we are, we still have things that are just seen as what the woman is going to do and what the man is going to do. So, without making too much of a commentary on society, I'll just give you a snapshot of some of my co-residents. While I was a resident, more of my male colleagues were married compared to my female colleagues. Of the married ones, only one female resident had children, but she had them before residency, but almost all of the married male residents had children.

Personally, I wasn't thinking about marriage and children when I was deciding my specialty. I was more concerned about finding a field that I loved where I could help people. t What was great for me was that I had a lot of female attendings at Stanford who were married and had children. They didn't sugarcoat things. They would say, "Your partner is incredibly important. Find a spouse, regardless of their gender, who is supportive of you and of your career choices. And if you both decide you want to have children, you have to think through how that will look if you are both working in demanding fields." You will have to acknowledge that things might be different for you as a woman.

I have to acknowledge that my being a mother and what motherhood means to me will look different from other women, and that's okay. It's acknowledging that equity is not equality. Things may not be a fifty-fifty split at home. And that's okay. If you have the right partner, that person will support you, and you both will figure out how you want to do things, whether it's daycare or a nanny, whether it's doing meal delivery service instead of having one person cook every night. You have to be creative, but the right person will want to be creative with you. And the right person will not think of your career as a negative but will see it as an overwhelmingly positive. They have to love that you're out there saving lives and problem-solving and kicking butt, or else it could be a source of tension. Marriage is hard even without the added pressures or demands of being a dual-career household.

Just be open and honest and say, "These are my goals. What are yours? Okay. How are we going to accomplish that together? I probably will not be the person cooking dinner every night. Is that okay?"

On Talking with Your Partner

The partner you pick is crucial. I can't underscore or emphasize it enough. If you choose to go down that route, picking someone supportive of your dreams is paramount. I'm incredibly grateful for my husband, Karim, who has been extremely supportive: being a cheerleader for and championing the achievements in my life, being a partner as we raise our family, and being a true partner in our relationship. We definitely follow the mentality of "What do we need to get done? Who has the time to do it, or has the skill set or expertise?"

And then we do just that.

He's an intellectual property litigator and a partner at his firm. He loves his career. He loves his firm. Before I transitioned careers, seeing someone who loved their job and was so passionate about it and dedicated made me realize and say, "I want that too, and I think that a job at Ro would be my equivalent." We both support and cheer on one another, which is invaluable.

That's very important to know that things aren't always split fifty-fifty. Usually, at some point, your partner has to focus on their career, and then you have to focus on your career. Or you need more help at one point, and they need more help at another. So just knowing that you are committed to a unified goal and that you both are doing whatever you need to do to get that accomplished—and that you both want each other to be happy is key.

Focusing on the other person's happiness will always make you happy because it all works out if they're focused on you and you are focused on them.

On Being a Visible Minority

My minority status is very visible to people, and I'll receive emails that say, "Hi, I saw you in the hallway," or, "I'm a college student, so-and-so told me about you. I'm wondering if I could just get thirty minutes of your time to talk to you." Yes, it would be much easier for me to say, "Oh, I'm sorry. I'm very busy." But I think about the people I cold-emailed and those who spoke to me. And so, I'll say, "Yes, I'm happy to chat."

Some things may be a burden or not, depending on how you carry it.

For me, I'm going to carry these responsibilities as lightly as I can so that it doesn't feel like they're weighing me down. I've had a lot of positive experiences where people come back to me and say, "Thank you so much for taking the time to talk to me. I wanted to let you know that I did leave my job, and I joined so-and-so company, and it's amazing," or, "This startup that I joined is totally successful, and I wouldn't have done it if I hadn't spoken to you." I had one mentee who had just gotten into medical school. Being on that journey with her, helping her with her applications, prepping her for interviews, and helping her decide which medical school was best for her was extremely rewarding. It was worth the hours of time talking to her on the weekends and at night.

I feel very blessed, lucky, and happy with my life, and I guess since I know what that feels like, I really want other people to feel that way too.

On Building Grit

You have to be able to multitask. You have to make quick decisions and quick assessments. For example, is this person in danger, or are they okay for the next hour or two hours? When do I need to call in help? Does this look right? Or does this not look right? And if it doesn't feel right, what am I feeling in my gut that's telling me something might be wrong, and how do I address that? It's not for the fainthearted.

That's not necessarily automatic in people, but it's something that can be built. You can train someone to have that grit and to be able to function well in distressing situations. That's why residency is five years and not necessarily a 9 to 5. You definitely don't want the first time you're in a distressing situation to happen when you're already an attending physician, and people are looking to you for guidance. You want to have those experiences in residency where you have a lot of support around you and where you get that positive reinforcement of "Look what I was able to go through in this demanding program. I was able to help someone or save someone's life."

My time as a resident has helped me in my day-to-day life. I tell people I'm pretty unflappable. There's not too much you can throw at me that will cause me to panic or become flustered. Instead, I'm always thinking, "How do I plan? How do I quiet out the noise? What is the real problem here? How do I assess this? How do I move forward? Do I need help? What kind of help?" That definitely comes from my training as a surgeon.

On the Other Side of Fear

At some point, I decided to leave traditional medicine. At the end of the day, I felt I had been doing so much for other people that maybe it was time for me to do something that was for me. People might see it as selfish, but like I told my husband, who was my fiancé at the time, "Look at me and what I've done in the past. Do you think that there's a chance that I'm going to make a change and not work hard to be successful at that? I know myself. I know my strengths, what I'm trying to do, and I have this feeling in my gut that this is the right task for me—and with your support, I'll be able to get that done."

An extra layer of responsibility is attached to being a woman of color in medicine. Frankly, that made my decision to leave traditional medicine harder. I felt like, "Oh no, I'm leaving the hospital. I'm leaving the medical school environment. I'm supposed to be a mentor to the next generation. Kids who want to do what I do, and now they won't see me walking the halls. What does that mean? How can I still be a mentor and give back to the community?" How I made the transition was knowing that I would always be helping people. It's just that how I helped people was going to be a little different. In hindsight, I can honestly say that I haven't lost all the stuff that I was afraid of losing.

Everything that you want is usually on the other side of fear.

Take a leap of faith. Believe in yourself and listen deeply to what you want and what you think makes you happy—just take that first step. For me, it was saying, "I think I want to do something else," even though I thought I would let people down. But I believed in myself. I said, "Well, if I do something different, I know that I'll make an impact, no matter what I choose to do. So, I just have to be brave enough to make that first step."

The startup role accelerated my path in many different ways that are important to me. I'm in a very visible position now. I've had even more people reach out to me. I have a platform to speak about issues and raise awareness around so many topics—being a woman in medicine, a woman in tech, and being a minority in those two areas. Health disparities and inequities and the lack of access for certain people. How we just accept the influence and the effect of racism on healthcare. And the need to change how we think about healthcare in our country and how it is delivered.

I'm still able to positively affect others, just in a different way.

I want to impart this value to others: be brave enough to believe in yourself and to bet on yourself. Even if others aren't in your corner, those who truly care about you will come around and continue to support you and cheer you on.

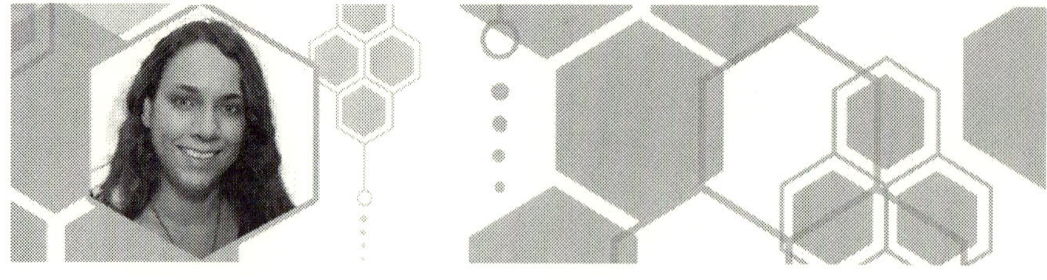

Meghan Athavale

CEO LUMOplay

I run a software company. My friends and I invented a technology to make environments visually interactive. We have about forty thousand active installations worldwide, including Google, McDonald's, Target, NEC, and United Way. We create automations, write codes, and implement integrations that allow us to scale the technology and services we offer.

None of us have parents who went to MIT. We were all community college grads. We are the epitome of a bootstrapped company.

Hard Lessons

I grew up in a poor neighborhood in a very small mining community in Northern Manitoba.

My dad was a first-generation immigrant, and my mom didn't come from a wealthy family. She didn't live with us. She lived on nearby reservations and taught First Nations students. So, she was away during the week and only home on weekends. Some of the reservations were fly-ins. So, we would only see her, maybe once a month. My dad was a guidance counselor working at six different elementary schools. So, my brother and I spent a lot of time on our own.

My dad raised my brother and me pretty much himself.

It's not easy for men. Society isn't really set up to support male primary caregivers.

I'm half East Indian and half Polish. My parents were a mixed-race couple in a community where that was not okay. I have memories as a child of people trying to take my brother and me away from my dad because they thought he was kidnapping us. I code as white. So does my brother. As kids, people always looked at us funny when we were out with our dad.

When we were young, my dad had dark skin. He's become much paler in his old age because he doesn't go outside anymore. My brother and I both have brown hair and blue eyes. So, from a very early age, we learned that different people are treated differently based on how they look. We watched this firsthand because people would treat him differently than they would treat us. It's a hard lesson to learn when you're a little kid because it's just so painfully unfair, and you're powerless to change it.

There's nothing that you can do to change somebody's mind if that's what they have chosen to believe.

Now that I'm older, I'm grateful I had that experience. I think it gives you a lot more empathy. It's very easy for people who have never been treated that way to not be able to empathize with people who have. Even if they recognize that racism is a thing, unless you know what that feeling is like, it's hard to really offer support to people and understand what needs to change.

A Very Odd Child

Growing up, I had an undiagnosed Asperger's issue. I had a tough time in school. I wasn't able to sit still. I was very disruptive. I would not have wanted to teach me.

I was a very odd child.

I would dress up as an animal, show up at school, and refuse to talk. Like, I would meow or bark for weeks on end. I don't know if that's ever age-appropriate, but I definitely did that long after I was too old for anybody to think it was even remotely normal.

Understandably, my dad was worried about me and whether I would be able to succeed in the world because I was so disconnected from reality as a kid. The thing that kept me learning was that I absolutely loved reading. I was in grade three when I started voraciously consuming novels. I was constantly reading.

We were total latchkey kids.

We didn't grow up watching TV. I think we had maybe three stations. Books were a huge part of our lives. I read a lot of science fiction. My initial interest in STEM spawned from the Madeleine L'Engle series, the Time Quintet – *A Swiftly Tilting Planet*, *A Wrinkle in Time*, and stuff. Those were the first books I had ever read where the main protagonist was a female, and there was a prominent female scientist in the series. After reading her books, I started getting really interested in science and math.

I ended up winning a science award the following year for my science project.

Trips to the library were a ritual for us. When we went to the library, I started coming home with computer books about DOS and Basic. I would look for instructions for making my own ASCII video games and stuff. That was in the early eighties. I was ten or twelve when I discovered this love of technology and interest in science fiction and computers.

The thing that started pulling me towards learning how to code was when my dad, a few years later, bought one of the first Texas Instruments computers. There was no graphic user interface. You were just writing command line code. There was no color monitor, so everything was green on black.

We thought it was amazing. It was magical.

My dad was very open-minded, but he still had a "this is what girls do, this is what boys do" kind of attitude when I was growing up. So, there were a few things he brought home that I know he was hoping my brother would get into but that I got into instead. For example, he bought my brother a skateboard after *Back to the Future* came out, and I was the one that learned how to skate.

I don't think my father was expecting me to get into the computer.

I think it's difficult for a parent when a new technology comes out to understand whether it's good or bad. Like when people see their kids playing on tablets for hours at a time, but they're educational games, you ask yourself, "What are they losing, and what are they gaining from this experience? Am I being a bad parent by letting them do this thing that they really want to do?" With my dad, it was the same.

I was also very into piano and would play for hours on end. But I was doing terribly in school, so it was a source of conflict. I think because of a combination of factors, I wasn't really encouraged to spend time figuring out how to use computers. It was more like a reward if I did okay in school.

If I didn't perform well in school, I was punished by having the piano and computer taken away. It wasn't very effective because I had a very hard time focusing. I think there were definitely moments when I lost opportunities because, in my mind at the time, computers and piano were just hobbies.

It never occurred to me that I would make a career out of writing code.

Dabbling in BBS

As a child, I didn't consider myself particularly tech-savvy. I just really liked making video games on this computer. I didn't know anybody else who even had a computer, let alone who was interested in them. Even a lot of the teachers didn't have computers at home.

I obviously did really well in computer class when I went to junior high school.

The internet had just come out, so I started to live on the internet a lot.

This new technology was just slowly becoming a part of our lives. And I had a really good window into it because it was the place I liked to hang out. But, again, there was no point at this time when I was like, "Hey, this is a viable career choice," like, "I could get into this and understand how it works and leverage it." Nor did I have a good understanding or perspective on what I knew that other people didn't know. I had pretty poor self-esteem.

I just assumed that these hobbies I had were weird. I didn't think of them as useful or something to be proud of.

Then that changed around 1987 when I moved from this tiny mining community in the middle of nowhere to a city, Winnipeg. One of my friends from Thompson had already moved to Winnipeg and lived in a house with some of her friends. She was a few years older than me. They had a BBS (bulletin board system, an early public electronic forum that allowed users to post or read messages). So I would spend time making ASCII art, putting it on their BBS, and just literally hanging out in chat rooms at night and chatting with people.

The reason this was such a draw for me was that I didn't have a lot of school friends. I had a really hard time understanding and interacting in social situations. So, having an environment where I could just chat anonymously with people was really nice.

It's worth noting that I exclusively always pretended to be a boy when I was online. I found that people weren't as accepting of me in the computer or technical circles if they thought I was a girl. Either they weren't accepting, or they were creepy. I was a young kid. I didn't want to deal with that. Looking back on it now, I think it's really sad that it had to happen like that.

At the time, I just wanted to be one of the boys, and it wasn't something I questioned. It helped me form a sense of identity that was, for the first time, separate from what my parents or peers thought of me. Like, I got to craft who I wanted to be. I think that's one of the nicer powers of online personas—it allows you to experiment with the kind of person you want to be. You don't feel the risk of being interested in something and then feeling like you have to commit—that's how people get sucked into cults, right?

Online, you can dabble. You can experiment with things.

There were a lot of communities that I would jump into and immediately jump out of. There was no fear in trying. I would have been afraid to try a lot of things if I had had to actually go to a meetup in person. But I was able to experiment in a safe way from behind an anonymous pseudonym from the comfort of my home.

BBSs were very much like that. It was pre-internet.

Every BBS was managed by a different person and had its own sort of flavor and feel. But, for the most part, the only ones I knew about were local things being run in Winnipeg. So, it was cool. I remember finding a bulletin board group that just discussed music and discovering all kinds of new music that way. There were book club ones, too. There were definitely, like, a million porno ones.

I found a lot of musicians and artists. In the end, that's what drew me into STEM, meeting artists who were using technology to either create their art or to help promote their art or just to inform others about the art they had made. That to me, was super inspiring.

A World of Possibility

If I am to describe myself as a kid, I always thought of myself as an artist, somebody that just was compelled to create things.

I didn't think of digital things like video games as art until I started spending time on BBS. Most of the ASCII art that I saw was really good. People put so much time and effort into hand-bombing these extremely elaborate graphics out of nothing but characters. That was what started drawing me in. I wanted people to see the stuff I was making.

Shortly after that, I started writing and distributing short stories online as the technology grew. Then I ended up in community college taking computer animation. Because I knew how to draw, I thought, "Computers and drawing, I'll probably be good at it."

As soon as I started doing that, I realized there was a huge world of possibility. You could make something and weren't just sharing it with your friends anymore. You were sharing it with every single person in the world who was on the internet.

I was hooked.

That was the thing. I'm shy.

I used to play music on stage but had to quit because it gave me anxiety attacks. But I still love making stuff and sharing it with people. So, this was, like, the best possible stage for me. I could hide behind an avatar or a fake pen name. I had three different accounts where I was putting up flash games. Some of them worked, and some of them didn't. I was putting affiliate codes on everything and figuring out ways to make money with my art. I just happened to be on the ground floor when all that became possible. I started to appreciate what a unique generation I belonged to because there was only a tiny little window in time where you got to see that transition and that phase change from physical to digital.

Gender roles were different at the time because digitalization was such a disruptive force.

It was easy for me to get contract work. Eventually, I got a long-term position with the provincial government because I knew how to use a computer. It didn't matter that I was a woman. There was no expectation that I would be any less good at my job. It would be more difficult now than it was then because, at that point, I had already learned things that they hadn't started teaching in school yet.

I didn't finish high school. So, I don't have a high school diploma.

I don't have any evidence that I'm academically good at computer science or anything. I'm entirely self-taught. The community college course that I went to didn't cover programming at all. We learned 3D modeling and the Photoshop suite. But I started learning how to code because Macromedia Flash was so accessible. It was well documented, and it was easy to find people who would help you. No one ever suggested that I go find a programmer to work with. Everybody was just like, "Yeah, if you're using Flash, just do it yourself." Flash was the gateway drug to learning enough Python to be pretty dangerous and learning how to use HTML, DHTML, and CSS.

I threw up websites left and right that are probably still out there somewhere and are incredibly embarrassing. I still have, like, six different websites and little projects that I run because it's so much fun.

Angry Runaway

I was a really angry kid by the time I hit high school.

I had a really rough time.

The move from Northern Manitoba to the city was a huge culture shock for me. I was really excited about living in a city. But then I got there and lost contact with the few friends that I had. I had a tough time making new friends through no fault of their own. I was a difficult kid.

My parents were deeply concerned that I was doing poorly in school.

The methods that they used to punish me were very counterproductive. I don't know what they could have done differently. But rather than reinforcing things I was good at and interested in, those were the things that they took away from me to punish me.

I was so deeply unhappy.

I also didn't really have a great sense of consequences. I wasn't like, "Oh, I can just stick it out for three more years at my parents' house, then I'll get into university, and then I can work on my own career." There was no way I could have done that kind of long-term planning at the time. So, one day I was like, "I can't live here anymore."

Eventually, I ran away from home.

My parents and I had a pretty epic fight.

I was still playing music a lot back then and had been invited to do my first big show at a women's festival. I believe it was the twentieth anniversary of a place called the Western Cultural Center, which was a big part of my life at that time. They had a lot of all-ages shows and stuff. And I volunteered there. It was a place where I actually felt I could connect with people because everybody was there for the music.

I was invited to play on stage with all these really talented women. It was my first time doing that, and I was really proud of myself. Before, I'd only done open mics.

But my parents told me they would change the locks if I did the show. They were very angry that I decided to do it. They didn't come to see it. For me, that was the final straw. I was just like, "Nobody understands me. I hate you."

We had a big falling out.

I ended up moving into a friend's basement. I went out and got a job so I could get myself an apartment. I was still trying to get through the last year of high school. But I was pretty young, like fifteen. It was too much. It would have been very hard to continue going to school full-time, working full-time, and taking care of myself full-time. I was pretty delusional. I didn't have a realistic understanding of things. I was just like, "Oh, I'll get a job and rent an apartment." I just felt like I didn't have anything to lose. In retrospect, obviously, I did. All kinds of terrible things could have happened. I ended up living with a group of friends.

Then the house caught on fire on Christmas Eve.

Occasionally something terrible would happen like that, and I'd end up back at my parents'. So, it was back and forth. But I was perpetually trying to live on my own. That was always my end goal—just to be self-sufficient. At the time, I told myself, "Once I'm out of here, I'm never going to talk to them again."

I did a lot of things independently to try and figure out who I was. It can be paralleled to, like, if you're gay and live with a family that is deeply opposed to homosexuality. Eventually, it just breaks out of you. You can't deny who you are. And so, what I found with a lot of my friends—because I obviously spent a lot of time hanging out with other artists and the technological counter-culture and the weirdos—was that there were other people like me.

I started volunteering at the Western Cultural Center when I was in grade nine or ten, and I met many other people trying to figure out how to apply what they were good at to the real world. For example, I would meet people that were extremely good at illustration. They were making posters for bands or album art. It was around that time that I started seeing that some of my skills and interests could potentially be a life choice.

My parents wanted me to go to university.

To their credit, they were the ones who saw the community college computer animation course and brought it to my attention. But, for the record, all of us recognize now that there was just this disconnect between what they thought was in my best interests and me trying to figure out who I was. Back then, there was no way my family could have known the impact of what I would be doing now. Obviously, my dad thought computers were important enough that he had invested quite a bit of money into one of the first ones. But the job that I do now didn't exist back then. So, it would have been very difficult for them to make a judgment call on allowing me to spend less time on school and more time focused on making things on a computer or learning how to process music.

I understand where they were coming from now.

My dad immigrated here. He got an education degree. My mom got an education degree. They both became teachers, which they did for the rest of their lives. So, seeing me not pursue something that offered stability was difficult for them.

Understanding this disconnect was a really good cautionary example for me when I had my son. It changed how I parented. The world is changing so quickly. As a parent, you cannot really offer your children guidance on what they're supposed to be doing with their lives or the best way to invest their time. All you can do is figure out what they are most likely going to focus on and how they can learn all these little micro skills that can be built up over time.

One of the Guys

When I was around seventeen, I was pretty sure I was going to be a musician. There was a woman at the Western Cultural Center named Robin Merit. It was the first time anyone had said to me, "Hey, that skill you have is valuable. People will give you money for it. Let's just teach you how to do this." So, she called me every couple of days, making sure I was still practicing and coaching me through becoming a musician.

But in the end, she couldn't get me over the anxiety.

One of the by-products of hanging out at the West End and spending a lot of time at shows and meeting a lot of independent musicians was that I also saw the downside. When people invest their personal creative energy into becoming larger than they are, and this is true if you become a TikTok star as well, the social pressure builds up. Some people just are not equipped to deal with it, or they're not mature enough at that point in their lives.

I certainly was not mature enough at that point in my life.

I found that the anxiety led me to smoke a joint before I went on stage and stuff. Even at that age, that wasn't who I wanted to be. I saw what happened to those people. I saw how those stories ended. So, I was like,

"Yeah, I do want to make music, but I don't want to put myself through anxiety that's going to cause me to do things that are bad for me."

Around the time I got into the community college program and was still playing shows, I got a grant and recorded an album. After that, I decided that as long as I could find a job where I could continue being creative and drawing or making stuff, that was okay. Ever since I was a very young child, I wouldn't feel satisfied at the end of the day unless I had made something. So, my career choice shifted from being a musician at the front of a stage to joining the supporting cast in production, doing animations, video production, and stuff in the back end.

I was really happy doing that. I enjoyed it. It was challenging.

In my first job out of college, I was the only woman. There was definitely sexism at the office I worked at. I just took it in stride. I just assumed it was part of the world. If you're a woman and want to work in a traditionally male-dominated field, you're just going to have to deal with sexism. It never really made me angry. In some ways, it made me feel special. I felt like other women couldn't handle those kinds of really negative sexist things. As a result, I didn't have a lot of female friends, which I super regret now. I really regret that one of the by-products of the whole "being one of the guys" mentality is that you don't get to bond as well with other women.

And as one of the guys, you're seeing the worst side of men.

It dehumanizes you after a while because you become this other thing. Like, you're not a woman anymore, and you're also not one of the guys. You're less valuable because you're not something that can be pursued, but you don't form the same friendships with the guys either. Over time, it started to make me really angry. I wasn't angry when I went into the workforce, but as the years went by, I saw people who were less qualified than me get raises, and I saw the inequality of it all. It started to make me really angry.

I was determined not to let other people's biases hold me back.

Stuff We Believe In

When I finished community college, I went to Calgary. I worked at an animation studio. At the time, I was married. I had my child, Dylan, really young, before I even finished community college. I was the primary breadwinner. It was a very difficult job, long hours, not the best job to be at while raising a small child. My ex-husband also had mental health issues.

We ended up having to move back to Winnipeg. So, I lost that job. There wasn't another job in the city that I was qualified to do. There were no animation studios in Winnipeg, except one that refused to hire me because I was a woman with a young child. That was the tipping point for me. I was just like, "Okay, I know I'm really good." I know I'm very qualified for this job." I was like, "Okay, I'll go get whatever job I need to, because we had to pay our bills, but "I'm not gonna give up being a creative coder because I can't get hired because I'm a woman with a kid. That's not okay!"

And so, very slowly, I started my first company.

I took a small business course through the YMCA to learn how to write a business plan and stuff. I went through a series of experiments where I'd throw up websites, try to sell something, and see if it worked. I had a T-shirt stand that I ran at a couple of festivals. I went and got myself a dye sub printer and learned how to make really good bumper stickers.

The bottom line is around the age of thirty after my son was a little bit older, when I'd gotten a divorce, owned a little house, and things were reasonably stable, I realized I didn't want to get up every day and work for eight to ten hours on someone else's bad idea and make them money. That didn't click for me. I didn't understand why I should spend my time that way. We have a pretty finite amount of time on this planet. So, I was like, "I might make less money, but at least I'll want to get up and do this thing every day." I just wanted to put myself in a position where the effort I was putting in felt like it was worth it. I was never motivated purely by a paycheck.

I wanted that feeling of being satisfied at the end of the day because I'd made something I was proud of.

Eventually, I ended up meeting other people who were like me and who had the same priorities. They were like, "Yeah, this is the thing I really want to work on, but no one will hire me to do it." I was like, "Let's just start a company and do the things we want to do and see if people will pay us for them."

In retrospect, we should have done it in the opposite order.

We should have found the customers, see if people would pay us, and then make the stuff. One regret I have that I think I can speak to on behalf of my entire team is that we did not include somebody who had gone through an MBA program in our initial lineup of staff. There were a lot of blind spots and unnecessary struggles. But we managed to make it work.

So now, I get to work with my friends every day on stuff we believe in.

The team is really small. Everybody has a defined role. My role is primarily in project management and account management around the technology we build.

The product that we sell is a software application that you install on a computer. You connect your computer to a display, typically to a projector, but sometimes people use touch screens, flat screens, LED tiles, or whatever. The most common setup is a projector, a computer, and a 3D camera. The projector points at a surface, and whatever's projected on that surface reacts when somebody moves.

The interactive stuff you see in airports, for example, most of the time it's our platform. Some of the applications that we've done are fishponds. Those are really popular. People will project a koi pond in their front lobby, water will ripple when you walk over it, and the fish will scatter. For McDonald's, we did something where the characters' shadows would come out onto a screen when you walked past, mimicking everything you did.

When we started the company, I made a lot of the stuff.

My business partners and I would sit down and create these one-off experiences together. As we started maturing as a company, the technology itself also changed quickly. There are new 3D cameras coming on the market every single day. There are different projectors. There are different computers. One of the biggest challenges with having software you can use for pretty much anything on the market is researching it and making sure that the people you're selling it to understand how to use what you've built. So, a typical day in my life is talking to our customers for a couple hours.

We have a help channel and a community channel where people reach out. I'll talk to people about how to use our technology. I have to know how to use everything and do everything. I have my hands in the code and understand how everything works. Then I've got to figure out a way to communicate that to people that are not as technically savvy as I am. I make tutorial materials and keep them up to date. I create trainings.

On top of that, every morning, we have a team meeting to make sure that our priorities are aligned for the day. The team is pretty autonomous. Everybody works on their own parts. One of our guys spends his whole day working on the website. For websites nowadays, you just are always improving them. He's always working on improving the shopping cart experience, creating better systems for importing SEO content to the app market, or whatever. One of the other guys works on the software platform itself—the thing our customers install. Then two people work on the games. One works on templates and systems for other people to make their own games.

That's basically our team.

Making Ideas Happen

Let me back up.

I took an animation course in college and found that I didn't really enjoy doing linear animation. I don't want to knock it. It's an awesome art form, but the thing that I liked doing most of all was creating characters that could be interactive. It just gave them a level of life that you can't get any other way. So, for fun, I would draw cute little animals. Then I'd add a little bit of code to them so that you could control them using the arrow keys on your keyboard and guide them through these little open-world scenarios that I'd create.

The best way I can describe it is as a child, I always wanted an imaginary friend. I used to really love sewing my own stuffed animals and stuff like that. Learning how to code gave me the ability to make my drawings and the little animals in my head come to life. If I had been raised in different circumstances, something like animatronics would have really appealed to me.

I didn't start our company with a clear idea of what we were doing or where we wanted to go. I just started making games out of the animations I was doing. Then the company kind of started accidentally.

My cofounder and I worked for a web design company and would get together after work to make our own touchscreens and things for fun. We ended up designing an interactive environment for a party we were throwing. Someone took a video, and it went viral.

People started asking us to make interactive display software solutions for them.

Within the first year, one of the things that we evolved into was becoming more of a service company. People would call us and say, "Hey, I have this cool idea. I want to project a countdown clock for Christmas on the side of my mall," or, "We want to put a bunch of squirrels on the wall that follow people around when they're at our party," or whatever, and we'd figure out how to do it.

So, the entire company grew out of one project after another. Like, "Can we project something on the wall that reacts when people send a text message?" Or "Can you make shadows on a wall that mimic what you do, but it's a different character than you?" I was friends with a lot of artists, so people would have these ideas in their heads, and both my business partner, Curtis and I just liked trying to make people's ideas happen.

It was really fun.

Then as we moved forward, we realized it was much faster and easier if we built ourselves tools so that we didn't have to repeat the same processes over and over again. But then, we wanted to know if anyone would want to use those tools. We didn't know if this was something we should continue developing for other people or as a product we could potentially sell. So, we made the original version of our interactive display software free and just threw it up online with a few examples.

It was a custom platform for creating content for touchscreens and large-format projects. And these tools ended up being useful for other people. Gradually, people started downloading and using them, and a community formed around them. It wasn't how we made our money. We were just like, "Hey, we made this cool thing. If you want to use it, here it is."

We went viral again when a parenting magazine ran a video about one of their projects – a toy kids can put in their rooms that used our software to make their floors interactive. It got over 26 million views, and I got like over a hundred thousand messages.

The platform we built is currently the most commonly used software for interactive projection displays.

It's not necessarily because it is the most powerful solution; it's because it's the most accessible solution. It's a solution that deeply respects people's ideas, and the main goal should be helping them execute their ideas, not forcing them to learn a bunch of stuff they may never use again.

We have a couple of competitors that sell turnkey systems. We don't sell any of the hardware. We only sell the software, and we designed it to work with any hardware. Because again, it goes back to the fact that that's one of the nice things about running your own company—you can kind of impose your personal ethics on what you do.

One of the things that we believe in is that in the face of things like climate change, it's really important to be respectful of the best solutions when it comes to the supply chain.

So to use our software, you could just go to your local Best Buy and get the equipment you need or find a local supplier for computers, projectors, and stuff. It doesn't make sense for us to ship you something from Canada. Logistically if we ever got big enough to partner with a company that has a global footprint and can manage the supply chain properly, then I would consider making a turnkey system. But the companies that currently make a bunch of their margins reselling other people's hardware, they are, in many cases, shipping systems overseas and adding quite a bit of margin.

Then those systems become very hard to replace, so they become disposable.

We're software developers. We don't want to be part of that.

What we've done instead is we've partnered with companies that have very clever ways of delivering hardware. And in some cases, they have lease programs so that people, schools, in particular, can have an interactive floor in a classroom for a specific period of time, say for a STEM program. Then afterward, they can send it back, and that equipment can continue being used elsewhere. So, instead of shipping out hardware, there's recycling and reuse built into the model that we follow. In some cases, bigger businesses like airports prefer to just buy a bunch of boxes and install them because it is extra work to get the software and then source the hardware. So, there are a bunch of different models in the space.

But as far as software distribution, because our software is actually free, the intro tier doesn't cost anything. So it's just been really easy to get market penetration because anybody with a projector can just download our software and make an interactive app.

Fishponds and Dementia

We're really interested in democratizing the process of creating your own content, especially because a huge part of our demographic is in health care.

People are using the software with patients who have dementia or with kids who have autism. We're not domain experts. We can't make content for those people. So, we've made a patented set of tools so those people can make their own experiences for their patients.

Our most common setup is an interactive floor.

But for dementia patients, because they often also have mobility issues, you would do it on a table instead. They're engaging with their hands instead of walking all over the place. The people who use our software create things like memory games with objects, items, or pictures from the person's past. They'll use photos of people that the person knows and create memory-matching games. The idea is to help keep some of the existing neural connections active because a huge part of dementia is not being able to make connections to memory anymore. The patients have better outcomes when using the neural networks they've already built in their brains.

Having a novel way of doing this where it's low-touch and nothing bad happens if they don't find a memory path match is reinforcement learning. We've been told that it's an excellent way to help dementia patients who have progressed to the point where they're having trouble communicating. It keeps them in a social setting where they can still interact with one another.

One of the other really popular uses of our technology for dementia patients is just for the ambient nature effects. Like, a field of grass that butterflies and flowers bloom out of if the patient puts their hand over it. These patients don't really get that chance to engage with nature in the same way they once did. It's like magic to people who are stuck indoors.

Empowering Others

One of the things that we decided as a company was that we would focus on making it possible for these people to create their own content affordably.

Normally if you were running a network of long-term care homes for dementia patients, you would have to hire an entire software development team if you want to make this content. Same thing with one of my other business partners. Early on, just as friends, we had conversations about how ridiculously expensive some technology can be. A huge driving factor in how we built our company was making sure that the technology is accessible and affordable and easy to use for people that have these . . . I don't want to call it fringe use cases, but there are not enough dementia patient homes to justify a typical business model.

For every dementia patient home, sensory room, and place for medically fragile children, thousands of retail locations want to use this technology for advertising. So, we built our model around helping agencies, event planners, and people that want to do interactive experiences for profit. We take what we are making from these industries to make sure that we can create a low-cost solution for everybody else. It's actually a very viable business model. If you can teach somebody who has never used technology like this, never touched a depth sensor in their lives, never really programmed ever, and you can empower them to create these experiences, there's no reason not to do this for everyone.

The bulk of the people who find us come from one of two sorts of places. Either they belong to organizations like schools, nursing homes, or dental clinics, where they're just looking for a fun, interactive experience, or they are developers. The people have worked with programs like Touch Designer or seen things like the huge installations that Moment Factory or TeamLab did and want to learn how to do that. Or they've got some experience but have worked with tools created for developers versus designers.

But when the end product is a very intuitive and integrated combination of development and design, there are basically only two ways you can come at that, either from the design side or the development side. And most people come at it from the development side because the development part of it is crucial. So, for example, you can't turn a projection on the floor into an interactive fishpond that ripples when you walk across it without code. There's just no way to do that.

Yes, you can project a pond, like a simple linear video on the floor, without the code part. As a designer, you can create that without knowing too much about how cameras work, how to do frame differencing, or what all the different techniques for 3D depth sensing are. But once you start getting into the combination, the interaction, it is not all that different from augmented reality (AR), and you need code.

Usually, when people think of AR, they're thinking about looking *through* a screen *at* something. So, you're holding up your phone or iPad and looking through the camera at the real world, and then something is superimposed on the real world. This is basically that, except instead of looking through a screen, you're *projecting* directly on the real world, and it's reacting to physical objects, like people walking through the space or objects being placed on a table.

There's just so much stuff that you can do with that full integration that I think designers have a clearer picture of it than developers.

In a lot of cases, developers know how to make it happen, but they don't necessarily have a complete vision for what they want it to look like or what that whole experience should be. The design of it all.

I think that's why our software is attractive to people who come in from the first side, who are like, I want a cool dental experience for my business, or I want an interactive table for the patients in my long-term care facility. As soon as they start working with our software, they realize they can make these experiences themselves without learning how to code. A switch flips in their heads, "Oh my gosh, I have all kinds of ideas for how to use this!"

Imagine for a second using projectors or digital displays on literally everything.

I'm not saying we should necessarily do that, but if you went into, say, an Ikea or went into a hospital and graphics were projected on every surface, the amount of information you could convey with that type of a system is enormous. It's basically an actual overlay of the physical and digital worlds. It integrates them both in a way that can't be done in any other way. So, if you're looking at stuff *through* a screen, you're the only one who can see that perspective. But if it's *projected* directly on the floor or the wall or an architectural feature, everyone there can see it, and everyone's experiencing it the same way, which is pretty cool.

For me, the biggest joy in what I do is empowering people to make their own stuff.

At the end of the day, I really love the challenges that I get where people come to me, especially for stuff that has to do with kids, where they want to be able to give kids an intuitive, interactive experience that helps teach them something, because that's where my heart is. My mom was a special needs teacher. The things that really inspire me and where all my ideas coalesce are the challenges around communication with tiny people who don't necessarily have the same life experience as an adult yet. They see things differently. Instead of trying to teach facts to small children, you're trying to teach them how to think about things, which is much more interesting to me.

I prefer that because it has this trickle-down effect of impacting who they become.

Creativity, Culture, and Caring

When we started, we had the technology mastered. We figured out how to do it. We got patents granted. We had a really solid platform. But nobody on our team knew much about marketing. Nobody went to business school. So, very simple day-to-day things like bookkeeping have always been a huge challenge.

We're much better at it now than we once were. But it's been hard to get to this point. And it slows things down when you don't have somebody who understands cash flow forecasting. So we ended up finding technology solutions for that as well. We knew we would never be spreadsheet masters, so now we use technology for that, too.

There will always be parts of the job that are not that interesting.

But for the most part, the main thing with Curt, Keith, and I that we shared was that all of us had had jobs where it was not important to the person who had hired us whether or not we were enjoying ourselves at work. So the biggest thing we have in common culturally is a belief that if you spend eight hours a day, five days a week, working on something, you should enjoy what you're doing.

I've also seen the opposite end of the spectrum where the idea of enjoying yourself at work is, like, there's a foosball table, and everybody gets as much crappy cereal for lunch that they want. We wanted our job to feel like we were hanging out with our friends every day and solving problems together, enjoying our time together, and feeling a sense of accomplishment from doing things together.

I've invested in registering patents for the IP we've developed together. There's something really powerful about acknowledging that the team has invented something together and accomplished something recognized in multiple countries as an innovative technology.

That's the core of it all.

When people join us, we have an employee handbook with the processes we use, but the main thing that is respected is that people really want to work with us. So, once a year, I talk with everyone, and I ask them if there's anything they want to learn in the following year. Sometimes it's completely unrelated, like we had one guy who just wanted to learn how to use a 3D printer. So, we came up with an R&D project that involved 3D printing parts.

We come up with things that we can work on together to help us reach personal goals.

There are definitely people in the world who don't want to invest creatively in their jobs. They would prefer to go to work and have something repetitive that they don't necessarily have to think about too hard. And then their creative energy goes into, like, renovating their houses or doing something else that is not necessarily work-related.

I totally respect people who choose that.

But for us, that's just not a great fit.

We want the jobs we're doing to be a core part of who we are and what we do. We want to be able to support one another. For the people that work at Lumo, there's a very blurry line between their personal interests and what we do for a living. That's intentional. This is part of who we are as people. We want to create experiences and opportunities for ourselves through our work together that allows us to do projects we wouldn't get hired to do.

For example, I got a sponsorship from a projector company and now have an unbelievable number of projectors to do cool, crazy art projects with. I did one art gallery installation with a couple of friends. One of our friends is a glassblower, and he covered a fifty-foot-long wall with thousands of tiny little glass sculptures. We used a number of projectors to map them and make them all interactive and stuff. He's a nice guy and a really good artist, but he doesn't have a lot of money. No one is going to hire us to do that. But because of the work that we do, we are still able to work on these projects with our friends.

Another really awesome project that we got to work on was Burning Man, this huge festival that happens in a desert in Nevada every year.

It was during the year that Google released a neural algorithm called DeepDream. You've probably seen it. The videos are pretty viral.

Basically, it's an image recognition AI algorithm where you give the algorithm thousands and thousands of pictures of dogs. So, if you think about it, looking at four different types of dogs, a cocker spaniel, a German shepherd, a chihuahua, and a goldendoodle, as a human, we'd say, "Oh, all of these things are dogs." But the computer wouldn't know that they were all dogs or even that they were all animals. And so, what DeepDream does is it provides computers with a framework, and then you send a data set in, and the algorithm itself looks for commonalities. So, it teaches itself what a dog is based on the data set you've given it.

There are all kinds of hilarious, bad consequences from this.

If you've never heard of this, I encourage you to Google "DeepDream images." They look exactly like what people see when they're on acid. It totally does have to do with the fact that the computer is putting together commonalities. And in the case of pictures of dogs, for instance, noses all kind of look the same. Eyes all sort of look the same. Certain physical attributes overlap. So, the immediate side effect of training this neural network to recognize pictures of dogs was that it started seeing dogs fucking everywhere. And these images had like dogs poking out of people's hair, and it was very, very cool.

So, we're still in the very early stages of image recognition algorithms. But DeepDream was interesting in that you could see what the computer was looking for.

So, when it came out, we did the first live installation of a Google DeepDream ever at Burning Man.

It was a series of LED panels around the very center of the event. There were two big buttons on either side of the room and no instructions. You just walked in, and there was a giant button you could press if you wanted to. It would take your picture, then it would run it through Google DeepDream and put it on this screen. So, you would see this extremely bizarre picture of yourself with dog heads and stuff coming out of your hair.

It was just a lot of fun, but no one's going to pay us to do that.

It's an art project that we all really wanted to do because it was super cool. So, culturally, that's the kind of thing that drives the people working at Lumo. This idea that your work and your life are not two separate things. If you're gonna spend a good portion of your life working on something, the goals and the things that motivate you to do that work should feel good.

There's nothing worse than feeling like you're not doing a good job at something because you don't care about it. So I think a lot of people suffer from depression because they're in this situation where they feel trapped doing something that they just don't really care about.

A Decent Living

One of the people who ended up using our software was a man named Paul from Ireland.

Back then, it wasn't like we had tons of customers, and I didn't really think about the dire consequences of doing things like putting my personal phone number on our company page. I remember getting this phone call in the middle of the night, which was probably first thing in the morning in Ireland. This guy with an extremely brogue Irish accent was talking about wanting to use our software for his special needs boy.

He started describing the condition that his son, James, was in. He had a rare congenital condition. Nobody knew exactly what was up with him. But, whatever it was, this little boy could not sit up. He was unable to communicate. He was completely nonverbal. When Paul reached out to us, his son was five or six. Paul basically was just trying anything to give his son a better life. He was looking for this solution because somebody had put an interactive display in a mall near his home. When he and James were at the mall, it was the first time he had ever seen his son try to reach for something and engage with it. So, he was like, "I have to get one of these in the treatment clinic. I have to get one of these in my home."

I just really wanted to help this guy.

Immediately, I was like, "Anything we make, you can have it. We'll just give it to you." This happened in 2011, and he had access to every piece of software we'd ever produced. We just put it in his account. So, he took our software and installed it at James's therapy clinic and in his home.

He kept us informed every step of the way. He called me the first time James was able to get to the bathroom by himself in school. He called me when James went to his first sleepover. He still keeps in touch with us a couple of times a year. He's kept the system up to date over the years. We've added support for better cameras because he went and upgraded his camera.

I get teary-eyed just thinking about it.

There are hundreds of stories from families like James's. He just happened to be the first one that reached out to us. There was a little girl named Emily whose grandparents set this up in their kitchen. We heard from these people that they would never have been able to do this for their loved ones or their businesses if we hadn't made something that was affordable and easy for them to use.

This reminder that something we made has had such a profound impact on another human being is another reason we do what we do. That's what makes my team say, "Okay, we're doing something good with our lives."

For us, it's not about how much money we make. It's about how much of a contribution we can make.

Obviously, we want to make a good living, take care of our families, and have benefits and stability. But if the only impact you're having is that you've accrued a bunch of money and stuff, to us, that's not very satisfying. At the end of the day, your work impacts the people around you.

And the only thing we've ever wanted is to make a decent living doing something we care about.

Empowering people to create cool things and help each other is more of a driver for us than making as much money as possible, which means that I've never been able to raise a dime in terms of investment. But that's okay.

I think that's the thing that sets stories like mine apart.

Meghan's Reflections

On Sharing Your Child's Interests

If your child is super interested in something, the best gift you can give them is to share their interests. Spend time with them. Figure out what it is.

I follow a woman in her late sixties on YouTube called Lady Gray. She makes arts and crafts. She laser cuts. She 3D prints. And she puts together these tutorials on making World of Warcraft–themed gear for your house and stuff. Really amazing woman. One of the things that she said in an interview was that she got into video games because she wanted to spend time with her son.

She said it was a huge learning curve. It wasn't easy to understand how to use a console for the first time at sixty. But she got into it and started playing Fortnite with complete strangers. I think that's something that many parents don't do, maybe because their parents didn't do that for them. But you have to assume that your kid lives in a different world than you. And if you don't take the time and effort to step into their world and see it through their eyes, you're losing a huge opportunity.

The coolest part of being a parent is seeing the world from a completely different perspective.

That was what I tried to do differently when I was raising my son.

When he got really into Minecraft, we started a Minecraft server together. When he got really into *Doctor Who*, I taught him how to do *Doctor Who* review videos on YouTube. For every opportunity he had an interest, I was like, let's go follow this thread. This thing is shiny to you right now, so let's go follow it, and you'll learn something.

The most important thing you can teach anybody is how to continue learning. These learning opportunities are how humans evolved. And when you think about how human civilization has existed for a good chunk of the twenty thousand years that we've been around, most of it was generalist learning.

You just learned by doing things with your family.

Today, we have this formal education system that takes a lot of time away from being able to do that.

I don't want to say this relieves the responsibility from parents, but it definitely puts parents in a position to not be as involved. And now the pandemic has freed people to be at home with their kids much more. They're starting to realize this is an opportunity and that it should be more of a priority. Unfortunately, we've created a system where parents don't recognize themselves as being good enough teachers. They think they have to send their kids to someone else to learn. I'm not saying school is bad. There are a lot of really good things about formal education.

But I don't think formal education is the best way to teach all kids.

And so, if I could go back in time and give my parents advice, it would be, "Hey, this is a very strict sort of formal education that doesn't have a lot of diversity." Again, we were in a very small town. It might not have been the best environment, but maybe just allow your child to learn in their own way. You have to assume that kids want to learn; it's ingrained in them. And the best you can do is guide what they get out of this thing they are interested in.

And *you* are learning stuff too.

For most parents, all they really want is for their kids to be better than they were.

I have no empirical evidence for this, but I don't think every person on the planet has a thing they get really excited about and want to do. But if you have a kid who is extremely into furry culture and wants to learn to make their own fur suit, all of those skills you have to learn to be able to do that are transferable. They're all things you can build on and later in life use to drive the direction of your career.

To me, anything a child can spend a lot of time dedicated to and get better at, even things like video games, has a benefit. There's a reason that we're kind of wired to focus on and become really good at stuff. That's kind of what separates us from every other animal on the planet.

I think, too, that passion and what you're interested in are liable to change throughout your life. Embracing what you're passionate about now will lead you to what you're going to be passionate about in the future. For example, the thing that I was really passionate about as a kid was drawing and making stuff, and that led to learning how to use computers and create technology that other people can use.

I think that's what puzzles me the most about people who are like, "Oh, I'm not interested in that because it's for kids." I totally understand why somebody might not want to play Fortnite. It's not for everybody. But if you don't take the time to understand what your child is enjoying, you're gonna assume the worst. You're gonna assume, like, "This game is about killing as many people as possible. Maybe my kid's a sociopath." And it's easy to go down conspiracy rabbit holes when you don't know what is actually happening because you've already told yourself a story about it.

This is what can drive a wedge between different generations because people choose not to take the time to understand the next generation's interests. They prefer to write things like TikTok off as stupid because they don't understand it. Not only is it unfortunate because you're not going to understand your child nearly as well, but it's also unfortunate for all of society because we're not all growing at the same rate around the same technologies anymore. It creates everything from the inconvenience of your parents calling you to ask you how to fix the printer to people in the highest courts asking what Facebook's revenue model is because they don't understand ad bidding.

It's embarrassing to see an older generation with a significant amount of power who doesn't understand what TikTok is, even though their kids are definitely using it. You could sit down with your kids for fifteen minutes and look at videos together.

I feel like this was something that drove a bit of a rift between my parents and me.

I had websites; I had a Myspace account. I was very much on the internet. It was a way of putting yourself out there and saying, "Hey, here's what I'm good at. Here's what I'm interested in. And this is me as a person." It's all curated. You're presenting yourself through a filter, and the people responding to you are presenting themselves through filters.

It is this imaginary world where everybody's making stuff up as they go. So, there's a dopamine rush. But it really impacts your sense of self-worth, and somebody you don't even know saying things about your physical appearance can be pretty devastating. And that's made ten times, maybe a hundred times, worse when you're a teenager.

I think this is also really important for parents to help kids understand the impact these technologies have on their mental health.

That's where really good role models are super important, too.

One of the things I did with my son when he was growing up was spend a lot of time looking at other creators together: "Here are some people, good and bad. Here's somebody who gets a lot of attention by tearing into what other people create." Like their entire deal, every single video is just about making fun of somebody. Then on the other end of the spectrum, there are people who run massive social media collections of channels where everything is focused on science communication, with content designed to help educate people in an entertaining way.

And so, if you get into the dirt with your kids, you can point out which part of the sandbox people are using as a kitty litter box.

If all you're hearing about is the kitty litter part of the sandbox, go find out where it is. So, you can tell your kids, "Hey, that part is not great. Don't hang out there." And explain why and have these open conversations about the social impact of unregulated pornography on the internet, how people are being exploited, and talk about some of the things that could make it better.

There are all these really interesting conversations that you can have if you get into the sandbox and you look at what's in there. It's about not being intimidated by technology.

We know that there will be problems with technologies that need to be solved. So, teach kids to solve problems. That's the biggest thing you can do. If my dad or mom had gotten into the dirt and sat there while I was BBS'ing and engaged with people, they would have seen that I wasn't online sexting or flirting with boys or worse. I was making art and trying to get people to pay attention to the things I was making rather than to me.

That one nugget of information would have changed their perspective on whether or not they should take the computer away as punishment.

On Female Leadership

We work on stuff that we believe in. That's the core of our culture.

If it ever gets to the point where that is no longer the case, then we won't do it anymore. This happened to one of the founding members. They were like, "Yeah, this isn't what I really want to do anymore." She started with us when she was nineteen. So, it was completely understandable for her to want to do the next thing.

The other three founding members are very honest and open with one another about the decisions we make and what we do with the company. Bottom line, I make decisions based on whether or not it's going to continue meeting that need for the team. That's an important criterion in what we do as a company. If we turn into something or focus on something that will not give us the sense of satisfaction that we're spending our time in a way that we want to, then we won't do it.

That's one of the diverse attitudes I bring to management that may not have been a particularly male way of approaching leadership. It's about whether the team feels fulfilled by their jobs. I haven't met a lot of male leaders who even consider this a part of things.

I've worked as a consultant in other organizations where the team members express interest, for instance, in learning how to do paid placement marketing or they want to learn how to do live streaming. And they'll be given responsibility on a volunteer basis, where the leadership will say, "Yeah, okay, you're in charge of this now," but they won't pay for training. They won't check in with the person and say, "Hey, have you learned how to do this?" And then there's all this scapegoating when it doesn't work out well.

You can't suddenly say, "Okay, this is your job now." You have to give them the tools to find out whether or not they can do that job, whether they're going to be good at it, and whether or not it's something somebody else should do.

One of the things that I see more in female leaders than in male leaders is that level of communication and insight into the inner workings of the psyche of their team. It is entirely possible—and I've done it—to take a group of people who don't know exactly what they want to do or what they're good at, or what makes them happy and figure out where those pieces can fit together to make something bigger than the sum of its parts.

On Women in STEM

I think it's always the outliers that forge the way. But it's really encouraging to see more women getting into STEM who are not outliers. They're just in a position where they can take advantage of a good education and really wonderful family support. Like, that's how it should be.

We want those people.

But we can also help more people recognize that they can make that choice too. And that it is a choice. That you aren't locked into the roles that your family or your society decided to impose on you. Knowing that you are an autonomous human being is a really powerful tool.

I think when it comes to trying to inspire more women to get into STEM, one of the things that for me was really powerful was realizing that, yeah, understanding how the technology works and what technology is available and how different components talk to one another and what the standards are—all of that is important, *but* the really hard thing is having good ideas and bringing your experience and your passion to the actual execution of *how* this technology is used.

I will never have all the good ideas. No one person will.

I have very specific things that I'm good at, and they all tend to have to do with communicating ideas to kids under six. For whatever reason, that's where my brain is at. I can watch a small child play and understand what they're thinking and feeling. I definitely don't feel that way about people dealing with early-onset Alzheimer's, but somebody else understands that. Other people have these interesting ideas about how to communicate information to different people at different points in their lives that I probably have no concept of whatsoever. All they need are the tools, the understanding that it's possible, and the abstraction layers removed. So, if somebody wants to make something, like a real-life AR experience, they don't have to go through all the things that our team had to learn how 3D cameras work or how to make all of these different systems speak to one another.

The reason that I got into STEM wasn't because I was interested in computers. I didn't want to learn how to code. Instead, I wanted to make stuff that had code in it.

I kind of regret that I have to go back and actually take pure coding classes.

When I was traveling in China for a little while, I picked up a bunch of phrases and words in Mandarin. But it was completely contextual. I didn't *feel* the language. I just knew how to ask for a beer. And that's the way I am with code. I don't know it well enough to look at code and think of different ways to do things because I'm just not as immersed in the syntaxes of the different languages. Part of that is because I came at it through action script, which at the time was really nice. Now, I recommend that people learn Python if they want to get into doing interactive visuals. It's the simplest door. There are a lot of code examples out there. You don't have to really understand what you're doing. I'd like to learn C+ and Java. I'd like to learn .NET and the languages that are actually core to our software platform.

When I talk to people who are like, "Oh no, I could never learn how to do that. I don't understand it. It's really confusing." A lot of times, it's confusing to them because they've had bad experiences with terrible UI or they're just too hard on themselves. It's not right to compare your comfort level and ability level to somebody who's grown up in the digital world. I find, especially with older women my age that I talk to, that they think it's some kind of magic to understand how computers work. In many cases, it's because they're comparing themselves to people who spend a lot more time in it. Like, you would never go to a concert and then come out and go, "I'll never learn how to play the violin like that." Chances are you're just not going to dedicate the same amount of time to it as the person that you just saw playing.

Computers are the same way.

If you spend a lot of time learning how to do something, you'll get better at it. And the thing that drives you to get better is because there's something specific you want to do or make or a problem you want to solve.

For instance, I can't cook at all. I'm terrible at cooking. But my boyfriend is really into cooking and baking and stuff like that. I've met people who are extremely good at dealing with food and making amazing meals. They understand how different tastes go together, the cultural implications, and the evolution of different types of recipes and tastes. I've just never been super interested in that. But if you are really interested in food and making a really good meal is something that you would like to be able to produce, you take the time to learn it. People spend years learning how to make amazing cakes, create their own recipes, or properly plate a five-course meal.

It takes a long time to get good at something, and computers are no different.

It has nothing to do with gender.

I don't think this is true of younger generations, but in my day and age, computers were not marketed to women. There weren't a lot of experiences on them that were designed for or by women. The available video games were from dudes making games for other dudes. And so, women didn't see a place for themselves there. So, it was really hard for me to imagine a career in technology because you're looking at it, and 75 percent of it was porn, and the other 25 percent of it was productivity tools for middle management.

That's changed dramatically now because technology is in everything.

Now, no matter what you do, you can make it better with technology. Even if your thing is cultivating Bonsai trees, you can use computers to research so that you can choose the proper kind of plant, connect with people who know more about the art than you do, and trade seedlings with people. All of that is worth learning about because it will make you better at the thing you're passionate about.

I don't understand why anyone would put more value on one activity over another because it is super arbitrary. There are definitely things that people do now regularly that are considered really important but that people would have made fun of a hundred years earlier or even twenty years earlier. Then when you consider this along racial and gender lines, it's even more extreme.

There are tons of things that women do now that are a critical part of how societies work, but they weren't allowed to do those things a hundred years ago. It was a boys' club for a long time, and it's taken a long time for women to step in and say, "No, we're going to use this, too. We're going to make a place for ourselves here."

On Just Doing Stuff Together

My son was eleven when I started the company and was already quite used to coming to work with me. I was in school when I was pregnant with him. He was born halfway through my college course. I was bringing him to school and breastfeeding him there. And I started bringing him to work with me when he was just an infant.

He's just always came to work with me. I think because I had him super young, I decided that he would just be part of whatever I was doing. I wasn't ever going to be one of those parents who said, "If it wasn't for you, I would have done these awesome things."

I hate that. Don't blame your kids for things.

I did whatever I wanted, and I brought him with me. When I went through my phase of doing club visuals in nightclubs, he was there helping me. He grew up watching me work. Having said that, he was an awesome kid. It was really easy to take him places. I don't think that every kid would be that easy.

And we're very similar.

I remember distinctly when he was about twelve or thirteen, I got a couple of gigs in Toronto. I threw a projector in my backpack, and I had these all-night parties, these crazy raves. He came with me. There are pictures of both of us just covered in black light paint and doing visuals. Eventually, four or five in the morning would roll around, and he'd curl up into a little ball underneath the computer stand and take a nap. We just did stuff together in the same way that during the pre– Industrial Revolution, you brought your kids onto the farm and harvested crops all day.

Part of our relationship was just doing stuff together.

I never really worried too much about how age-appropriate it was. As long as he had my attention and felt like I wanted him to be there and we were doing stuff together, it was all good. I wasn't like, "Here, sit in the corner and wait for me to finish."

My family was supportive and took him on trips and stuff like that. I got to enjoy being a mom and spending time with my son as he grew up, as well as doing art projects, traveling, and seeing the world. I was really lucky that way.

I never felt like I had to choose between being a parent and being very active in my career.

On Making Time

When the company started, it took a long time for all of us to figure out what we were doing.

During that process, my dad had a heart attack. I had been scheduled to participate in an incubator in San Francisco for about a year. So, there were times when I had to make those hard decisions—do I go, or do I go back home and help take care of my dad? But, for the most part, I've had a really supportive family. So, in situations like that, I would find a compromise.

The company is still based in Winnipeg. All of the teammates have families there. Some of them have kids. They want to stay in the town where their families are, where they grew up.

I never wanted that.

I always wanted to live in different places and see as much of the world as possible. So, we found a compromise and figured out how to work remotely years ago. I've been running the company remotely now for about five years. I lived in four different cities during that time. So, the challenge comes down to what is important to me and how I will ensure that I keep all of the important things in my life.

I always have to reevaluate.

Pets are a big part of my life. I've always had cats. For several years I fostered dogs. I've had birds. I had a really amazing iguana named Pickles for a long time. But when I started traveling, I realized it wasn't fair to drag an animal along with me. So, I didn't get a pet again until we moved to Montreal, where I knew I would be for a while.

I'm now in a relationship with somebody who has a young child. When we started our relationship, I didn't want to move in right away because it's a big deal to commit to somebody with a young kid. So, there was a year when he would just visit me part-time.

I spend a lot of time trying to be as self-aware as possible.

Trying to be aware of the people I care about, those around me, and their needs. It's not always perfect. I am definitely an overachiever. I tend to overcommit and try to do more things than one human can reasonably accomplish. Sometimes I work for sixteen hours, sleep, and I don't actually talk to anybody else for a couple of days. But for the most part, I think the trick to balancing that stuff is just to make sure that you're always thinking about it. I try not to make excuses and say, "I would have a better relationship with my boyfriend if I didn't have to work so much." Because it's up to me how much I work.

So, if I want a good relationship with people I care about, then it's on me to make the time for that. That's something that I think I've made an effort to get better at over the years.

On Being Upfront

I've been in serious relationships since starting the company. My first relationship was with somebody who definitely didn't value cleaning up after themselves as much as I expected. Plus, I also had a preteen child. And because Dylan and I are so similar, we've always kind of been the same when it comes to keeping things fairly tidy.

Cleaning is how I procrastinate. I can't work in a messy environment. I can't function. In the space where I'm working, if dishes need to be done or if the floor needs to be swept, I'll always do that first before I start working. I like cleaning; I find it cathartic.

I don't put that on other people.

I'm not resentful towards somebody else for not sweeping the floor just because I get distracted and can't work until the floor is swept. I got a Roomba, it's fine. But in my earlier relationship, it was a problem. In that case, part of the issue was that he was quite a bit younger than me. He would leave empty beer bottles and pizza boxes around the house and didn't do the dishes. It got worse when I started traveling. When I was at the incubator, I would come back after being away for a month or two, and the house would just be an absolute disaster.

In that case, it was very bad for our relationship.

In the relationship I'm in now, as far as the division of labor goes in our household, I made it very clear upfront that I would do the bulk of the cleaning. I have no problem with it, and I'm a perfectionist. I want to mop the floors once a week. Same thing with pet care. The cat is mine, so I take care of the cat. My partner does all the grocery shopping and all the cooking. He handles all of the other household tasks and chores and stuff.

I'm also, like, a chronic organizer. I label things. I like to make sure that everything has a place that it gets put back into. My partner now is nowhere near as organized or as much of a neat freak as me. But if I ask for his help doing something, he helps. I think he understands that I don't mind doing the bulk of the work, but I need him to respect the fact that if he takes something out of the toolbox, he has to put it back in the toolbox and not let things pile up all over the house so that we can't find them. For me, the biggest thing is I don't like spending a ton of time looking for stuff when I need it. I want to use my time wisely on this planet.

I only get to live once, as far as I know.

When I first started dating the guy I'm in a relationship with now, we definitely had that conversation. "There are two things about me that are deal breakers if you can't live with them. One of them is that I need to be in a clean place. I can't handle clutter. I can't handle mess. I can't handle disorganization. And the other is I don't care about TV. I don't want to care about the show you're into right now. I'm not going to watch Netflix every night." The closest thing to TV I watch is a lot of tutorials, and I do a lot of science documentaries. That's basically it. I'm not going to watch *Survivor* with you. That's not how I want to spend my time."

I've been in relationships where that have led to major problems. It's made the other person feel super isolated because, for them, popular culture and watching TV shows and stuff is such a huge part of their lifestyle that not being able to share that with their partner is upsetting.

I respect that, but if that's the kind of person you are, I'm not a good person for you to be in a relationship with.

On Digital Literacy

I think it's crucial for humans, no matter how old they are, what gender they are, or how they identify, to spend more time understanding how the technology that drives our culture works.

It terrifies me that so many people on the planet don't understand how the internet works. Because if you don't understand the systems that are giving you information about society and your place in it, it's very easy to be manipulated.

Digital literacy is one of the most important things the government should invest in for its citizens. It doesn't necessarily relate directly to STEM training, but I think the aversion to learning technology is a real problem for society. It's not just an inconvenience. We don't have the luxury of half of our population being digitally illiterate. Whether gender, race, access to equipment, or income class, if a huge chunk of the population does not understand how these systems work or, for whatever reason, believes that it's too hard for them, it will end badly.

People will be exploited.

When I watched the review of Facebook's policies when they were investigating the Cambridge Analytica stuff, it terrified me how many members of Congress, the people who make policy for entire countries, didn't understand that Facebook was an ad revenue platform. They didn't understand the whole financial model of the system that billions of people are investing hours of their day in and that the entire model is based on selling those people's data. That's an essential thing to understand. I think that in terms of a lot of the problems we're facing around things like climate change and income inequality, and access to education in general, there are compelling ways to address them with technology.

But over and above that, I don't think it should be an option whether or not you understand how technology works. I don't believe we have the luxury as a society of people going, "Yeah, that's just too hard for me." We can't do that anymore. So if you use a computer for anything, you should understand the basics of how it works and where the software comes from.

If it feels like magic, that's a bad thing. That's like snake oil.

My dad is in his seventies. He ordered a couple of things that I think he saw on Instagram. They didn't show up, and he started to panic. It wasn't a lot of money. It was more that he realized he had just given his money to a business he didn't know anything about. He felt scammed. It was a really bad feeling. I think that kind of thing where you feel like you're powerless in the online world is really dangerous.

Systems that you don't control are learning things about you.

Those systems can be used to make your life way better, or they can be used to manipulate people at scale. Technology in and of itself is not good or bad, but it can be used in really terrible ways. The thing that it does best of all, the thing that makes it different from any other innovation we've ever had, is just the scale of it. The Industrial Revolution greatly impacted how human societies started engaging with one another, and now with technology and innovation that is basically all digital, the complexity is much greater, and so is the potential for harm.

Facebook is a good example of a technology that reached many people faster than anything else in the world. And it had a very measurable impact on our geopolitical relationships within a very short span of time. The Cambridge Analytica thing that happened in the US has already happened in other countries. It isn't something that just affects Americans. To a certain extent, as we move further towards globalization, things will happen that will affect people around the world unequally, and legislation just hasn't kept up.

There's no global legislation for things like social media data protection because it's different everywhere.

Going back to what we do, which is obviously not nearly as widespread, we make a very niche product. But in terms of the ethical responsibility that we feel for what we make and what we're putting into the world, we are heavily influenced by the things that we see other companies doing that we disagree with.

The entire open-source movement is grounded in the idea that transparency is better. It's better to open up the hood. It's better to let people put their own spark plugs in, and it's better to support the community development of solutions. So we're encouraging people to go from, "I'm going to use a computer that I don't really understand to try and solve my problems," to, "You can learn how to create your system yourself."

Again, it's about ethics and how much of a contribution we can make. Digital literacy is part of that.

On Making the Life You Want

What we work on is very much based on feeling that our priorities are balanced across the board.

One of the big priorities in human existence is your personal relationships. I think when people think about work-life balance, that's what they're actually talking about. They're not talking about, like, working and life being two different things. They're talking about maintaining healthy relationships and physically taking good care of themselves.

Your priorities make you a healthy and happy human being and ensure you have time for all those things.

When somebody suggests that you have a bad work-life balance, they're just saying you spend too much time doing one thing and not enough time doing the other important things.

I think the solution is that you have to understand what's important and live in a society where we assign values and define success in ways that are conducive to being a happy and healthy person.

Different classes deal with that differently.

I came from a lower-middle-class family. My parents struggled to be able to buy a house. That was their big priority, being able to own their own home. For a good chunk of my early childhood, my brother and I shared a room in a two-bedroom apartment that was pretty low rent in a small mining community in the middle of nowhere. We didn't live in a city. My parents worked up north, and I only saw my mom on weekends. We definitely grew up in an income bracket where many sacrifices were made for the future to save money and buy better lives for ourselves. When you're in a situation like that, it's really easy to have a very poor work-life balance because you're not thinking about what's happening around you now.

I don't necessarily think that it's bad to have goals or it's bad to sacrifice things in the short term for something that you really want in the long term. But I think there are people who never get to that point where they feel like they have enough. So ,they are always deferring their own happiness.

I don't want to live like that.

That's not necessarily the best way to run a business, either.

People would look at our company and say, "Oh, you guys could be making so much more money if you just did these five things." But we look at that and go, "We started a company so we wouldn't have to do those things. We started a company so that we could be happy every day working on something that we care about," which is very different from starting a company because you want to be the biggest or the richest or the most powerful.

You don't have to get into technology because you want to be the next Bill Gates. That's not really what it's about. Technology is a tool like anything else. You can use that tool to make the life you want for yourself.

I don't want to call it a work-life balance. It's just your life. And I feel like my life is pretty balanced.

On Living What You Love

The main takeaway that I would want somebody reading my story to leave with is that it's possible to make a really good life for yourself while focusing on something you care about.

Technology is a very important part of making that happen, whether your passion is making stained glass pieces, cooking amazing meals for people, tinkering with electronics, or creating weird art. No matter what you consider your hobby or your thing to enjoy yourself, technology can help you reach a wide enough audience that you can make a living doing that thing.

You just have to put some thought into how you're going to frame what you do, how you're going to test what you do, and how you're going to monetize what you do.

There are so many cool examples now, too. Lindsay Ellis is one of my heroes. She does video reviews. She started by just reviewing Disney movies; that was her whole deal. You can do something like that, too. You can build an audience for the thing you enjoy doing. And if doing things in front of an audience is not your thing, there are other ways, like Etsy. There's a woman, a renowned animal behaviorist who has severe autism, Temple Grandin. She consults with industrial farmers on how to set up their factories. Those types of examples are what you should set for yourself. Like, "What is the thing that I want to get up and do in the morning, and how am I going to make that my contribution to society?"

There are a million ways now to build a career doing the thing that you enjoy. I want people to look at my story as an example of building a career like that.

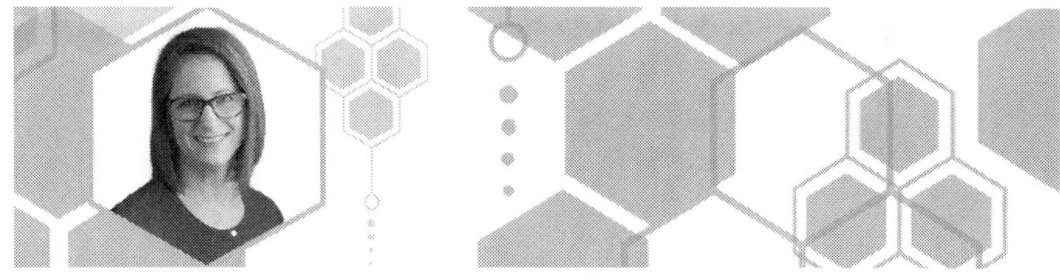

Juliana Vida

GVP and Chief Strategy Advisor at Splunk

I am the Chief Technical Advisor and GVP, Chief Strategic Advisor for the public sector at Splunk, a software data and analytics company. I talk with customers and the public about how technology can help them improve their business, and I lead a team of vertical advisors who do similar work on a more tactical level.

I paint an "art of the possible" picture of how the government can deliver better services to citizens. How the Department of Defense (DoD) can be more effective in its various warfighting missions. How state and local governments can better serve constituents. And how higher education can improve student outcomes.

A Fluke Career

I was born in New Jersey, but we moved pretty early on to Reading, Pennsylvania, about an hour southwest of Philadelphia. I'm the older of identical twins. We have a younger sister and a younger brother who sadly and unexpectedly passed at age forty-three.

We had a pretty normal childhood until my parents divorced when I was ten.

At that point, life changed, but it wasn't horrible. Our parents still seemingly got along or at least made it seem that way to us kids. We moved with my mom, but we were only about an hour away from my dad. It was very congenial. I don't ever remember there being huge fights or unusual drama. I feel I'm very fortunate in that regard now that I've met so many people in my life whose experience was wildly different. Some of their stories break my heart.

I would say we were lower-middle class. We bought our clothes at Kmart and wore hand-me-downs. We didn't go out to eat. It all felt very normal to me. It was just a very different world than it is today.

In high school, I was a better-than-average student, though not in the top 10 or a member of the National Honor Society or anything. I planned to attend a state university in Pennsylvania because that's where my friends and high school sweetheart at the time were going. Fortunately, PA has some pretty good public universities.

I didn't really have anyone driving me to think bigger.

Then by a fluke, one day, my twin sister was walking downtown in Lancaster, Pennsylvania, which is not a metropolis. It's a suburban town in the heart of PA, Dutch county. She walked into a Navy recruiting office—I don't know why; maybe there was a cute guy recruiter. We were seniors in high school, and I was already applying to schools and waiting to get in. She came home that day and said, "I just signed up to join the Navy." I was like, "Are you out of your mind? Only criminals go to the Navy."

I am mortified now that I had been so naïve and uninformed about the military back then. My uncles had been in the Navy. My dad had been in the Marines, but for only two years. Aside from that, I knew very little about military history or career paths. Though my dad remains a proud Marine, his service was not a centerpiece of discussion in our family. We were not raised to go into the military.

Marie said, "No, no. They have this program where you can enter the military and be a linguist."

I have always loved languages. I was very good at Spanish in high school, and so was she. I was curious, so she shared more. She explained, "Yeah, they teach you a language, and then you get to be an interpreter or, like a spy or something. And you only have to do it for two years, and you get all this money to go to college." Well, that sounded pretty cool to me. So that's the path we took that changed the first major trajectory of our lives.

I signed up with her at the recruiting station, and we enlisted in the Navy together.

In the Company of Women

I'm so grateful to have a twin sister that I love and who loves me, and we've gotten closer over our lives. Of course, I didn't orchestrate having a twin in my life, but I was fortunate to have one. It was an advantage having each other, along with all these other strangers in the Navy. We were assigned to the same Company (training unit) in boot camp.

I don't remember everything we did in boot camp, of course. But, I recall we marched a lot and learned how to fold and stow our clothes in our lockers. The point was to prepare us for serving on ships at sea, where you had to be able to pack a lot of stuff in a small space and live in tight quarters with lots of people.

We did a lot of physical training that I wasn't used to. It was hard for me because I was not a competitive athlete in high school. I remember being exhausted much of the time and struggling with push-ups and running. But overall, the feeling that sticks with me is that I loved the structure! I enjoyed wearing the uniform, marching, knowing the rules, and following them. I'm a hopeless rule follower to this day. I often drive people nuts; I only cross at the crosswalk, drive the speed limit, and obey posted signs.

Yeah, I'm that guy.

I didn't necessarily love being yelled at in my face, but I could get by because I was good at following rules. So, they trusted me with a little bit more leadership and responsibility than the rest of the girls.

There were specific things in boot camp that were kind of crazy. They actually made us experience a tear gas chamber. Since at the end of the 1980s, there was still a very real threat of World War Three against the Soviets, the training was intended to prepare us for the potential use of chemical weapons against us.

Wearing gas masks, we marched into a large metal box-like structure.

This was my first experience with a "connex box," which I didn't know at the time would become a hallmark of my military training in various iterations over the next two decades. Once inside the box, we were ordered to remove the masks as the instructors turned on the gas. We had to stand there and breathe it in for ten to fifteen seconds, which felt like a lifetime. It was miserable. Then the order came to leave the chamber, masks in hand. We marched outside into the glorious fresh air but weren't permitted to touch our faces, rub our eyes, or do anything to relieve the miserable burning. Snot, tears, coughing, goop coming out of my face . . . it was awful.

I realized nobody cared what I looked like; they were all managing their own issues. It was a lesson in resilience and humility. And a determination to avoid a chemical attack at all costs.

It's one of those memories that's seared into my brain.

The whole boot camp experience was very challenging and so new in many ways. But honestly, facing something difficult and performing well beyond others was another first for me, and it felt good. These were my first experiences where I recall feeling proud and confident; I realized, "I can do this shit! It's hard, and it sucks, but I can do it." Those weeks of training and doing uncomfortable things left me feeling "It's going to suck, but it's not going to kill me." The training also forced us to bond with other people, struggling through the same really sucky training scenarios and living conditions. We were in it together. We learned to trust and appreciate each other more.

I'm glad that I was able to learn those lessons in my early adult life. They repeated themselves over and over throughout my military career and into my post-Navy civilian life. Building the muscles of persistence, confidence and tenacity served me well through many struggles over the decades.

Luck of the Draw

And so, Marie and I finished boot camp together. We not only survived but finished at the top of our training group in leadership roles. In fact, she graduated as the Honor Graduate, the top performing Sailor of all women in our Company! We subsequently moved on to language school together in Monterey, CA, which was another awesome experience.

This was at the end of the 1980s. The Cold War raged, and the Berlin Wall hadn't come down yet. The USSR was still our big enemy.

Marie and I had tested high enough to learn Russian in language school, with the goal of becoming Russian linguists and potentially one day attaches or spies! The training began on day one as we stepped into our WWII-era wooden classrooms, adorned with very simple graphics depicting the letters of the Cyrillic alphabet like you would see in a kindergarten class. "A" for Apple, "K" for Kite, that kind of thing. But in Russian – it was really cool. Instructors spoke to us only in Russian from day one; we had to pick up their patterns and repetitions in order to catch on. There were hours of study every evening, including audio and video tapes to enhance our learning of all the language forms. I loved the immersive training and was good at it. I graduated first in my class and got accepted into a follow-on intermediate program, another full year of instruction at a higher, more difficult level.

The military has the enlisted forces, that's where I started, and the Officer ranks. The enlisted force are the ones who generally do the technical jobs. They are the engine repair people, the linguists, the journalists, and the hands-on keyboard IT folks. Officers typically have different roles as managers and leaders. In the Navy, officers are pilots. They drive submarines. A good way to think of it loosely is blue-collar vs. white-collar, though lines are blurring more and more these days.

You have to get in through a military recruiter on the enlisted side. They have a quota, just like they do at companies. Their job is to fill that quota. So, if they have ten warm bodies walking in the door and ten quotas to fill, they may or may not tell you what you want to hear to convince you to sign up. They'll tell you what they need.

The bottom line was I was very fortunate that my sister had talked to a recruiter who mentioned this whole linguist thing.

Most young high school kids, men, and women recruited to go in the enlisted force do not hear of those opportunities. They get sold on the adventure, the independence, getting away from home, getting a paycheck, and seeing the world. They go in a little bit blind regarding what their job will be coming out. More than anything, the Navy needs people called deck seamen to just be there. In the Navy, deckhands paint and maintain the outer parts of the ship, including refueling rigs and the flight deck, and they tie ropes. All of this is vital work, but it kind of sucks. So, most young recruits do not get to choose their job. Sometimes someone says, "Hey, the Navy needs a lot of electricians right now. You ten people, you have the aptitude to be electricians. So, you're going to go be electricians." Sometimes it works like that.

I was lucky.

In my contract, before I went to the Navy, I had signed up to be a linguist. So, the point is you can actually look into what jobs are available and put that into your contract before you join the military as an enlisted, but young kids often don't know to ask.

So, during my language training, where I was doing very well, I got my next big opportunity to do something new, different, and unplanned. In the military, professional career counselors help sailors find other opportunities for higher education. So, my career counselor came to me and said, "Hey, did you ever think about going to the Naval Academy?"

And I'm like, "What's that?" She says, "Have you heard of West Point?" I go, "Yeah." She's like, "It's like that, but that's for the Army; this is for the Navy." My only knowledge of the Naval Academy was from a high school friend whose dad is an alumnus; she used to wear the iconic gray sweatshirt with NAVY and the academy crest in navy blue. That's literally how I made the connection in my mind. I seriously knew nothing.

I feel so embarrassed about that now.

I said, "I'll never get in." She said, "Why do you say that?" Once I realized it was the West Point equivalent, I remember our mom mentioning West Point from time to time (no idea why – her brothers had been Navy), and thinking you had to have perfect test scores, be at the top of your high school class, that kind of thing. And remember, I wasn't an athlete.

I learned later that this lack of confidence is very common among women and girls. We downplay our strengths. We give ourselves a lot of negative talk, and I was doing that. I said, "I only got 1200 on my SATs. You have to have 1600. Don't you have to be a varsity athlete? I didn't graduate first in my class. And don't you have to . . ." She was like, "No, all of that stuff might help, but you don't have to have it. Trust me—you have what they're looking for at the Academy."

So, I said, "Fine." So, I applied, and I got in. First try!

Fortunately, I had some help from some recently commissioned USNA Ensigns at DLI, who guided me through the application process. They remain friends today. [Thank you, Larry Gloss and Dave Bondura].

I didn't have to go to the prep school. Some kids that either came from disadvantaged areas or were varsity athletes being recruited needed to get their scores up and they had to take a yearlong detour at prep school. I didn't have to do that.

So, off I went to the Naval Academy to join the Midshipmen ranks on the path to becoming an Officer. I had to leave linguistics behind because that was an enlisted job.

I loved it in Annapolis, too.

From day one, though, if I thought boot camp sucked, this SUPER sucked. I loved the structure. But it was hard! Again, I had never been a great athlete or runner, and there's a large physical component to the military. In fact, I will write my next book titled, "Good Leaders Run Fast, and Other Lies They Tell You in the Military." It is very highly regarded when you're in shape, and I get it. You have to look good in uniform. You have to be ready for arduous work and all of that. But I think there's a little bit too much emphasis on how fast you can run when the job is really about leadership.

Anyway, that was a big struggle for me, but I also have charisma. So I can generally get along pretty well with people.

Charisma saved me in a lot of ways at the Academy, especially as a woman. I started at the Academy in 1990. Women had been going there for fourteen years, but it was still very much a boys' club. It was very male-centered, very male-dominated, and remains so today. Luckily for a woman, I was very well suited to fit in because I just get along with people.

First Class in Combat

When you come out of the Naval Academy, most graduates go into warfighting communities. They want you to go on the ships, fly aircraft, be on submarines, or be in special forces, like the SEALs.

Then there are a handful of jobs selected for the midshipmen who graduate and have some kind of physical disability. For example, being disabled could mean you're color blind or have serious seasickness. If you're color blind, you can't be a pilot, and you can't go to sea. So maybe you get to go be a cryptologist, which is like a linguist. Or you get to be an intelligence officer. But that's for a tiny percentage of graduates. They really want most of the Naval Academy graduates to do warfighting.

However, at the time, only men could go into warfighting.

Up until 1994, Congress had prohibited women from going into any combat-related role in the military. So, up until then, all the women who had gone to the Naval Academy, West Point, and the Air Force Academy were learning in this leadership laboratory how to be leaders of men and warfighters—oh, but then you graduate, and you can't actually go do that.

How's that for some shit? Women did the same exact things men did for our four years but then couldn't join the Navy in the same jobs our male counterparts did. Like they say...life isn't fair. Suck it up, buttercup.

Women had to go to the Supply Corps (supply, logistics, combat support, readiness, contracting, and fiscal matters) or other support-type jobs. That's fine if it's your choice. We had no other choices, though. Women's options were limited until 1994 when Congress lifted the ban on combat exclusion right before my class graduated.

That was another stroke of luck.

Now women could go into combat-related roles! We, too, could finally be warfighters. And by warfighters, I don't mean carrying a gun in the infantry. Warfighting means any class of ship or aircraft with weapons on it (cruisers, destroyers, aircraft carriers, fighter jets, helicopters, etc.). My class at the Naval Academy was the first class of women to have those options. Totally the best thing that could've ever happened to many women and to me. I was able to select the specific ship that I would be on after graduation. It was a destroyer, a warfighting ship.

It was great and fated that it happened that way.

When I got to my ship, USS BARRY (DDG-52), in 1995, there wasn't really a whole lot going on in the world. This was pre-9/11, so the world was at relative peace.

When we went on deployment, BARRY went out to the Mediterranean. (Deployment is when a ship goes away from its home port for six months.) We went from port to port. We did some exercises with other foreign navies and stuff. Over a six-month period, we were in different ports like every other week. We went to places like Palma de Mallorca, Spain; Slovenia; Nice, France. It was a European vacation. In fact, I remember being so sick of being in port and spending money we secretly hoped the leadership would leave us alone at sea for a while and not direct us to another port. Ha! It was a nice problem to have.

The world's different now, but I got to live that experience and be a warfighter.

Anti-Submarine Warfare Officer

On the ship, officers have a professional role. I was the anti-submarine warfare officer. I managed the men who operated the sonar that looked for submarines and torpedoes and the men who shot at the submarines and anti-submarine rockets.

So, I was their leader and division officer for all of those guys.

This was the first time any of them had worked with women, which brought its own challenges. But I was fortunate. I had good support and a great commanding officer who lifted everybody up.

In addition to their specific officer job, all officers also have to learn how to drive and direct the ship's operations. Now, Officers don't really *drive* the ship; you give the orders to direct where the ship is going to go. Officers are generally the ones standing there with the binoculars, looking at the compass and saying, "Come to course one-eight-zero," or whatever. Then the enlisted team are the ones actually looking at the radars, making sure it's safe, operating the engine— How fast do you want to go? Do you want to turn starboard or port? So, it's a team: you have officers and enlisted sailors on the bridge working together.

Tied up to the pier in port, the ship doesn't just shut down. You don't just turn the key, and people go off for three days. There are always people who have to stay on the ship. They're called the watch team, and everybody is assigned a watch section. Let's say the ship is in port for three days. If that ship has a three-section duty rotation (1/3 of the crew on board at all times), then one of those three days, you'll be on the ship, just making sure there are no fires or that things stay clean, and taking the trash out, that kind of stuff. Oh, and giving tours because tourists will always come on board. The tours were always fun and exciting.

At least it used to be before things changed after 9/11.

So, I learned about anti-submarine warfare. I learned about how to drive the ship. I learned how to respond to an emergency in the engine room or any other kind of emergency. It was great. Seeing it all on a warship is what the real Navy is all about.

Fantail Workouts

Not everything about the military is lockstep; let's go shoot things. Ninety-five percent of the time, it's just normal people being professional patriots who want to do good work for the Navy and have fun along the way.

On a destroyer, there are only like twenty-five officers and about two hundred enlisted people. Of the twenty-five officers, four of us were women. Three of us were classmates from the Naval Academy. It was wonderful! Though not super close at the Academy, on board Lori (Rickert) Dague, Shannon (Guthrie) Perrin, and I were roommates. We had common experiences, too. We were all newly married to Academy classmates. So, we had a lot of common bonds. When we went to port, we'd have dinner together and happy hours and stuff.

We took care of each other.

One of the young woman officers had been a varsity cheerleader at the Academy. So, she and I decided we would hold aerobics classes for the ship. They let us do them on the back of the ship called the *fantail.* There's a nice, big flat area, and we put a boom box out there.

It was a pretty popular class. A lot of the sailors would come out. We were so naive. We thought, "Oh, they just want to come out and get exercise." That wasn't really what it was about.

We found out later that the guys who worked the cameras to make sure the fantail was safe were doing close-ups of us. It's kind of funny now that I look back at it how dumb and naive we were. We were actually having a good workout, so I felt good about that part.

But I'm also like, "What were we thinking?!"

Earning My Wings

I deployed once on that destroyer. Then I went to another ship because, as an officer, you only do a tour for two and a half or three years, and then you go do something else.

I went to an aircraft carrier the second time. At that time, I was married to a USNA classmate who had always wanted to be a pilot. So, he said, "Hey, why don't we ask the Navy if we can go from being surface warfare officers [which is what they call ship drivers] to pilots?"

The Navy goes in cycles with their manning. Like, sometimes there are way too many people, and they're encouraging people to get out, and then they let too many people get out, and they're like, "Oh crap, we don't have enough people," and then they're begging people to stay in.

We were at the bottom of the cycle, and they were doing anything they could to keep people in. So, we said, "Hey, Navy, if you let us go to flight school and become pilots, we'll stay in. If not, you're going to lose two officers."

They let us transition to Naval Aviation and go to flight school. Sometimes the "needs of the Navy" work in your favor.

I ended up becoming a helicopter pilot. I had never had any inkling about being a pilot. I didn't grow up wanting to be a pilot. I had never flown a flight simulator game or anything. I started from zero in our training. That was another confidence builder for me because not everyone makes it through flight school. Not everyone even makes it through ground school, where we learn about aeronautics, weather, water survival, that kind of thing.

I got my wings. I made it. I graduated. I didn't die. Yay!

I didn't love flying, but I liked it enough. It was fun during the day. I hated it at night. While I was a helicopter pilot, my then-husband went jets. Helicopter pilots trained in one area—I was in Florida. Jet training was in Mississippi, so he went there. That was the first moment our careers started to diverge, which can be a problem for dual military couples.

The first two times I deployed, I was an SWO, a surface warfare officer, on USS BARRY and USS THEODORE ROOSEVELT (CVN-71). Once I became a pilot, I deployed three more times, once on an amphibious assault ship, USS PELELIU (LHA-5), and twice on an aircraft carrier, USS NIMITZ (CVN-68).

When 9/11 happened, everything changed. Going into port was not so much fun anymore. There were really dangerous scenarios. But I still got to do some really cool things.

I Heard You

My first deployment as a pilot was supposed to be just a regular deployment. The ships go out; they stay out for six months. Then they come back, stay home for eighteen months, and go back out. So, it's a fairly well-planned cycle of training, deploying, training, deploying. Well, during my six months out on PELELIU, we had been gone from home port for about a month when we stopped in Australia to have R&R—rest and relaxation. The Navy calls it liberty.

Then 9/11 happened while we were in port in Darwin, Australia. Middle of the night.

PELELIU was an amphibious assault ship. It was for US Marines to go overseas to fight. They had a landing craft that could come out of the back of it, and it transported gear. On an amphibious assault ship, a few pilots were Navy helicopter pilots, but the rest were mostly Marines—Marine jet pilots, Marine attack pilots, and Marine tactical pilots. About sixty Marine Corps pilots and six Navy pilots, including me.

Every single pilot on the ship was a man but me. No female Marine pilots. No other female Navy pilots. That was just really hard. I was a brand-new pilot, too. So, I wasn't a star player; I was new and learning, making mistakes and finding my way, just like my male counterparts. But everyone knew when I talked on the radio. They all knew it was me when I got out of the helicopter with my ponytail sticking out of my helmet.

I could not hide.

That's a hard position to be in when everybody is looking at you. Women in any industry or business, when you're the only one, you can't escape people paying attention to you. You stick out. That can be good, but that can also be unfair pressure. I wasn't the best pilot, and I wasn't the worst, but I felt like I had to be the best at everything, which sucked. I made two good female friends who were not pilots, which helped. But overall, it was a very lonely time for me.

But one good thing came out of it.

One time, we were flying at night. Nighttime flying is always more stressful than daytime flying. Night vision goggles, all of that.

The tower is high up on the ship, just like an airport tower. They watch everything that's going on for safety. There's a guy in the tower (they were all men at that time) called the Air Boss. He's the most senior officer there and is responsible for everything happening. Generally, he's the one who talks on the radio. There are two pilots in a helicopter, and I was the one flying that night. I was the one who was actually doing the controls. I was the one landing on the ship.

When you land on the ship, there's an exact landing spot. There's paint on the flight deck that says your main landing gear wheels go here, and your tail wheel goes there. It's for safety. If you land on the box, you're good. If you land a little bit on the box, you're still good, but people make fun of you. If you land too far out of the blocks, you could actually hit something, and it could be disastrous. So, I landed. I nailed it. Perfect landing, dark as crap outside. And the air boss's voice comes over on the radio and says, "Nice landing." I should have said nothing, but I said, "Thank you, sir."

Now, back to how everyone knows it's me. So, of course, people were making fun of me. They were saying I was kissing his ass— "Oh, you're such a suck-up," and all that stuff. But two months later, I'm somewhere on the ship, and this young female Marine comes up to me. She wasn't a pilot. Remember, there were no female pilots, but there were a few, very few, female Marines. So she came up to me and said, "I just want you to know I was in the tower that night."

And she says, "I heard you on the radio. I've never heard a female pilot's voice before. I never knew I could do that, too. But I've been talking to my career counselor, and I'm going to put in for an officer program. And I'm going to be just like you."

This was twenty years ago, and I'm still so emotional about this.

I couldn't believe it. I was like, "Me? I'm not even a good pilot." But it made me feel so good. Then I realized we in the minority have a lot of opportunities to give other people a view of what they can be. I don't know if she ever went to flight school; I lost touch with her. But just the fact that she had said that to me, I was just like, "Oh my god, I never saw myself as a role model. But I am."

I needed her to tell me that. Not just that she needed to hear me or to stroke my ego, but that I needed to hear her, too. Because all the other times, I had guys talking to me about how I didn't belong here. Their words were spoken and unspoken but very, very clear. Of course, not everybody said this; I had a great squadron and a few male pilots who were true friends and supported me in every way. But there were some assholes using really bad language. Telling me, I didn't belong in *their* Navy. I didn't belong on *their* ship.

When she said that to me, I was like, "Screw you guys!"

But say that even if none of that bad shit happened, the fact that she said she'd never known she could do that, be a pilot, until she freaking heard my voice . . . that's why, twenty years later, it's so impactful to me.

That's why all women need to surround themselves with people to support them and who will boost them up because you will have many people around you who do not want you to be successful. It is exhausting. Sad as it is, it's true. I hope she went to flight school and powered through it because she had a lot of pressure on her shoulders.

This is why women get out of STEM. It's why women get out of the military. You just get tired of bearing the burden. Tired of fighting the fight. You just say, "You know what, I'm going to go over here and do something where they appreciate me."

The Pentagon

The military kind of has a plan for you.

You have some input, but they'll put you where you need to go. So, that burden of career development is somewhat taken off your shoulders, at least for junior officers. For the first ten years, it's pretty scripted. You'll do this, then you'll do that, then you'll do this, and maybe you'll get grad school in there. If you're staying in uniform and as you get more senior, though, there aren't as many roles available. So, the path isn't as clear or pre-determined. But maybe there's an opportunity to cross over to a different specialty within the military.

I went from driving ships to flying helicopters early in my military career. That's quite unusual to switch from one warfighting community to another. I've known people who have switched to become lawyers or IT people or that kind of thing–all within the military. Some people, for example, start out as a pilot, but then the Navy doesn't need pilots at that senior level as much as they do earlier. It's a pyramid. There's only so much room at the top.

For many military officers, if you stay around long enough and get to that senior level, you kind of have to do your Pentagon tour. Not everyone does, but most people do because they need people there to help write policy, help manage the budget, and work with Congress to push legislation. Some roles in the Pentagon are for uniformed military people, and some are for senior civilian folks. If you're in uniform, you may not be able to be the CIO, for example, because that person is a civilian. So, it gets a little bit tricky and a little more difficult to maneuver when you're going for those senior roles. I was not thinking in those terms when I was in the first few years of my military career.

It just wasn't in my view.

By 2008 I was a lieutenant commander, a fairly mid-grade officer when I was promoted to commander, considered a senior officer in the Navy. So as a senior officer, it was my turn in the barrel to go to the Pentagon.

Learning IT

By luck, the job I was assigned to at the Pentagon was to be the executive assistant secretary to the senior executive, who was the Navy's chief information officer (CIO). I didn't know I was lucky at the time; I didn't even know the Navy had a CIO, let alone what that person did or who it was.

I didn't know anything about IT at that time. I struggled at first— "Oh my gosh, how am I going to help this guy? How am I going to put a good product through when I don't even understand what anybody's talking about?" There were all these reports and policies that came across our desk. I was expected to ensure they were formatted correctly and that the right content was in there.

So, with no real clue or other options, I started doing what I advise other people to do: show humility and curiosity.

I basically went to people I knew and trusted who were already in the Pentagon because, remember, everyone eventually goes to the Pentagon. There were people there that I hadn't seen for years. I asked them to explain stuff to me. If there was an acronym I didn't understand, I would ask. The list of acronyms for the Department of Defense is a mile long.

I did not pretend I knew about stuff I did not know. Instead, I would say, "I'm not really sure what this means. Who can I go to?" My boss or someone else would point me to the right person. Then I'd make a connection, build a relationship, and learn something. My charisma came in handy again; people liked me and wanted to help me. I thanked them for their time.

You know, basic courtesy and manners.

And I also took classes. I learned that the military and the federal government provide free education on a lot of these topics. I started taking advantage of that at the Pentagon. My boss would let me go for a week to take a class, or I would do it during my off time. I needed to ramp up quickly and not be another barrier for people to get stuff done in the Pentagon. Lord knows there are already enough barriers with bureaucracy and all that.

I found out that I'm a pretty quick learner. (it took me four decades to clue in, but I finally got it.)

I accelerated my learning like wildfire by opening myself up to learn from other people. It made me successful quickly. People knew they could trust me. They knew I wasn't the one in the room saying that I knew everything and was smarter than everybody. I was the opposite of that person. As a result, I built really important relationships in The Building, which is critical.

That's how I made my pivot into IT.

I didn't have any formal education in technology or coding or anything like that. Once I started attending those classes, the CIO moved me from that executive assistant role into different roles. He made me the branch head in charge of enterprise architecture, then the branch head in charge of information assurance.

I gained good experience in several different IT roles by the time I retired from the Navy.

Fake It 'til You Make It

Nothing too interesting happened at the Pentagon. It's policy work.

This is kind of funny, though. I remember I was new, learning and trying to figure out how to fit in around this place. There were far fewer women than men, naturally. I was in uniform then and knew I needed to present myself as a professional.

So, I would sit with my notepad and my pen along the back of the room. Only the important people sit at the conference table in the Pentagon. So, I would be in the back, taking notes and nodding my head. I'd write stuff down and pretend I knew what I was doing.

It was about totally going along with it. Fake it 'til you make it. So I did that all day, every day.

Then I literally took my notepad to other people in the meeting, who I knew, and I would say, "Can you explain this?" Some of them really laughed at me. I was asking some really basic shit. They were like, "Are you kidding me? Why did they put you in this job?" I'm like, "I don't know, but I'm here now."

I quickly learned that most other people in the Pentagon are also not experts in what they're there for, especially the military people. They only come in for two or three years and then leave. How can they possibly be an expert on something in two years? So, they probably do exactly what I did: fake it 'til you make it and hold your breath until you leave the Pentagon. I actually thrive in that kind of fast-paced, learn-it-as-you-go environment.

I stuck around. I finally felt confident, like I got this Pentagon policy stuff!

I was in the Pentagon for four years until I retired from the military.

My Champion

By the time I retired, the civilian CIO was a woman. She was a champion for me. She got the headcount to have a deputy, a new role on the Navy staff.

When she opened the role, I competed for it and got it as a civilian. It was a senior-level GS-15 job– the highest rank of the General Schedule, the civil service pay scale. I became the deputy CIO for the Navy. By this time, I knew I had built relationships with people I could trust and lean on.

I figured I knew what I was doing.

She really appreciated my military service. Her father had been retired Air Force. She was not military herself; she was a career civilian. But she had grown up around military. So she respected the fact that I was in uniform and that I was a pilot.

I helped her get her job done because I built coalitions of people that could work together. I had skills and talents that she didn't have. We were a very good team. Even before I was her deputy, even when I was just another leader on her staff, she knew she could rely on me. She knew I would tell her the truth but be professional about it. We had built that kind of rapport.

She did a lot for me.

She would push me into situations that I felt I wasn't ready for but that she knew I was ready for. For example, there were senior-level staff meetings with CIOs of the Army, the Navy, the Air Force, and the Marines, 2 and 3-star Admirals and Generals, who would be sitting around the table (the power seats). And there would be a representative from the Joint Staff and somebody from the acquisition community, all very senior people. One day, as we were walking to this meeting together—I was going to be taking my notes—she was like, "Oh, I just forgot. I have another meeting to go to. You'll have to represent the Navy's position at this meeting today." And I was like, "Wait, no." I had done no preparation. I didn't really know what I was supposed to do. I was like, "No, you can't do that to me. I can't do that." She was like, "You are ready for this. You can do this. All this stuff you already know, and you have to do it."

She turned around and walked away.

I was like, "Well, shit."

I went in. I sat at the table confidently, even though they were like, "What's she doing at the table? She's a 15." But I sat there, and I added value to the meeting. I had people nodding when I made comments. Afterward, I had a couple of them say, "We really appreciated your input." That was a great day for me, so important in my professional growth!

I built relationships in that meeting. It was only one meeting, but it was a big deal for me. The Pentagon has a lot of structure about who sits at the table, where they sit, and who is at the head. So to have literally had a seat at the table, like from the *Lean In* book, was one of the biggest career moments of my life. I realized I knew what I was talking about. I could speak in a language that other people could understand and that they appreciated it.

I've never asked her why she did that, but I think the point was there's just never enough time to prepare. So, we would have gotten stuck in what we called in the Pentagon "analysis paralysis," where you get yourself caught up in "How much preparation is enough?" So, she was just like, go do it.

She did those kinds of things for me. She pushed me. We remained friends over the years, and I am eternally grateful.

Breaking Into the Tech Industry

I was the deputy CIO for the Navy at the Pentagon from 2012 to 2016, about three and a half years. At the time, my CIO was a Gartner Executive Programs client—a product for C-level technology executives. She would bring me with her to Gartner events to the extent that she could. She exposed me to the benefits of being one of Gartner's clients.

That helped me build relationships with Gartner when I was looking for a job change.

At the Department of Defense, I had been the last candidate for two jobs that would've made me a Senior Executive. The Senior Executive Service is the military's civilian equivalent of Flag and General Officers. In both cases, they picked the white guy over me. So that happened to me twice. I was angry; I was so mad. I truly deserved those jobs. I was gonna talk to HR about it— "I think I'm being discriminated against." But then I also was like, "Maybe I should read the handwriting on the wall. They're just not that into me."

The Gartner team had been helping me to prepare for those interviews. They knew I was looking for another job. So, they came to me and said, "What would you think about applying for a job at Gartner?"

And that's how I got out of the government and into the technology industry.

If I had gotten one of those jobs, I would probably still be in the Pentagon doing the same thing. Not that there's anything wrong with that. I probably would've just stayed on that trajectory for the rest of my career, being a senior executive in the government. Again, not a horrible thing, but for me, it would have really limited me because I would have never gotten this great industry experience and been able to be my authentic self, which my current job lets me do. I look back now, and there's that country and western song that goes, "Some of God's greatest gifts are unanswered prayers." Amen to that.

I was with Gartner for three years.

The Executive Partner role in Gartner Executive Programs is being kind of an executive coach and strategic advisor to chief information officers and senior IT leaders in all industries, both public sector and commercial. My clients were across the whole federal government. My experience up to then had been only in the Department of Defense but being an Executive Partner at Gartner expanded my reach across all the federal agencies, which was awesome.

Through my role at Gartner, I helped CIOs and IT leaders, about fifteen to twenty at a time. I loved having one-on-one relationships with them and working with all the different agencies. I also learned from my clients—how the other agencies and subagencies work, how they work with Congress, and how the government works overall.

What an education!

While at Gartner, I went from being an individual contributor to being promoted to a management role, which I didn't want. I think this is important for women. I really didn't want the management role because I knew I would have little to no one-on-one client engagement. And I really enjoyed that. But I was approached with the opportunity to compete for this management job, and I felt like, as a woman who's always talking about the glass ceiling, about women not being able to move up, and about not enough opportunities, that when an opportunity came my way, I couldn't say no. Like, I had to say yes even if I didn't want to, which is unfair, but that's how it is.

So, I chose to pursue this management job, and I got it.

I didn't like it because it was less client-focused and more about metrics, spreadsheets, and analysis, and that's not me. I am a humanities-focused people person. The job was not a people job anymore. I wasn't enjoying it, and I started looking around at other roles.

The Software Side

I found the job that I'm in now through LinkedIn.

I didn't know anybody at Splunk. They didn't know me, but I saw the job description. It was all about outreach and executive engagement, being a technology evangelist, and talking in public about the mission value of technology. I was like, I can do that. So I applied for the job, and I got it.

I've been at Splunk for a year and a half. Gartner was my first industry company, and Splunk was my first software company. I'm learning so much about the difference between a tangible product, like a piece of software, and a product that's not so tangible, like knowledge.

I loved the military. I was very good at it and operated well in that environment of structure and regulation and all that. Splunk is the exact opposite of that, and I love it, too.

Splunk allows people to be creative.

They really like people to be authentic and open and transparent.

It is a very good feeling to not feel like you're being held down and have to be all buttoned up and wear a suit all day. Even before the pandemic, we were a hoodie-wearing software company, but it's a serious business, too. I'm learning that there's beauty in the balance of both. Maybe five years ago, my old government self might've thought, "Splunk? Oh, that's one of those crazy companies out in Silicon Valley, and they all have blue hair and stuff." But, no, there's serious business going on in software companies. I have enjoyed learning more about business and the product development life cycle and how hard it is.

Here's another thing. I've learned how much money, time, and effort it takes for the commercial industry to keep up with all the requirements that the government continues to place on the private sector. When I was on the government side, I had no idea how hard it is for companies to meet all the different requirements just to do business with the government.

Not only did I not have an appreciation, not only was I not aware, but I also didn't care. "I was like, they all make a lot of money. They're selling their product and making a lot of profit, so put more requirements on them, make them be more cyber secure."

I'm simplifying it. But the government lacks awareness and appreciation for the burden it places on industry, which just turns around as higher prices for the government. So, seeing that from both sides is eye-opening. Seeing how the government buys things, operates, and puts all these requirements in place. And then how industry responds and what that means for pricing and products.

It's About Data

Splunk has been around since 2003; it went public in 2012. It has matured exponentially over the last two or three years through acquisitions of other companies and capabilities. It's an end-to-end data platform that can do all the advanced analytics with data that you hear about.

Think about twenty years ago when Google came out, and everyone was like, "What's Google? What's a search engine?" Now, Splunk is like that with data. Google is about search, and Splunk is about data. So, you can bring data in, do analytics on it, do predictions on it. You can automate tasks that help your workforce be more efficient. You can predict when things will happen in your environment and your network so that you can be proactive, not just reactive. It has inherent artificial intelligence and machine learning that helps the data platform learn and be more efficient as it goes.

Anything that you can think of related to the cool things that data does, Splunk does all that and makes it easier for people to manage all the data they have in their lives. Just think about your mobile phone alone. How much capability does that device have that most of us don't even use? How much data is moving through that phone that you don't think about?

You don't know where it's going. You don't know who owns it.

With a platform like Splunk, imagine knowing where all that data is going, and how you can use it to your best advantage. How you can interact more efficiently with your banking app, your calendar app, your collaboration on Zoom, your Trello project application, or whatever it is. Imagine how much better your life would be if you could harness all of that capability.

That's what Splunk does.

It's a great job.

It's also very much a people job. I'm essentially the public face of Splunk for the whole public sector. I'm the one who speaks on panel events, and I'm the one who talks at executive round tables.

I don't get into the nitty-gritty details about how the products work, how the data is captured, and where it is in the stream. Instead, I talk about the "so what" factor. Yeah, data is important, but so what? I talk in terms that executives and people who aren't technology people can understand. We all know what a smartphone does, but you don't need to know the details about the ones and zeros in the code.

You need to know how to use it more efficiently and effectively.

I love that I get to build trusted relationships with people because, in general, especially in the public sector, it's hard to get a meeting with executives in the federal government when you're from industry because they try to be very agnostic. They want to be fair when issuing contracts and spending the government's money. That's good, but when you build a trusting relationship with someone, and you show them that you really care about their mission and not just your bottom line, they're more inclined to talk to you.

I have credibility because of my background, coming from a full military career and being a government civil servant myself. They're like, "Oh, you used to be one of us. You're like me. I trust you more than somebody else who's only sold stuff for their whole life." So, it's a great job for me.

I can't believe how my life has turned out, honestly. Twelve years ago, when I was getting divorced and losing custody of my son, shit wasn't going well. Now I'm happy. I have a supportive husband who loves me and trusts me. I have a great relationship with my son. I have resources. I can help people. I can give to charity.

Life is about meaning and fulfillment and being a good person, whatever that looks like.

Juliana's Reflections

On Partners in STEM

I'm not telling you everything.

Like, I got divorced, and I'm not going to talk about that. But I still want you to know that I'm not really telling the whole story. Everybody has stuff about their life that they don't want to dwell on or wish they had done differently.

Some part of me does feel like saying, "Juliana, if you're going to tell the story, tell the whole story. Don't leave that out." But no. Men don't do that. Men aren't talking about all the shit that they did wrong. They're talking about all the things that they did and all the ways that they've helped people.

I'm divorced, and my son lives with my ex.

Biggest heartbreak of my life. I fought through the courts and all that. But in the end, the court decided the young man should be with his father. Thank God I have the money and resources to fly to Florida and see my son. But I didn't do the majority of raising him, to my great sadness. I've come to peace with that. We have a great relationship; it's fine.

In the meantime, my second husband is an angel. He doesn't begrudge me.

I always tell my husband, "We could not have all of this without you." 'Cause he always puts it on me—he's like, "You are the brains. You're so successful. You're doing so great at Splunk. I'm so proud of you." And I'm like, "Make no mistake, I wouldn't be me today if it wasn't for you. If it wasn't for you supporting me and not rolling your eyes every time I have to do something after hours or have to travel or whatever, we wouldn't have this life."

It makes all the difference in the world to have somebody who trusts you to travel with other people, go to happy hours, and come home and still be a loving spouse.

He gets up at 5 a.m. He stays up late. He is OCD with cleaning, so he cleans everything. He makes coffee in the morning for me every day. I grocery shop, and I cook when we eat at home. But he cleans it up. He takes care of everything. He's like, "You love your job. You have a great job. You're good at it. You do that; I'll take care of all of this." I'm very fortunate. I have to tell you. I almost feel guilty that I don't fall into the category of most women who bear the brunt of household work. But I'm so grateful. I don't know how to say that any other way.

My husband has a very satisfying job for him. He's a fitness guy, a marathoner, a triathlete. His job is in Fairfax County, Virginia, where we live. This group of community rec centers, like YMCAs, is peppered throughout the county. He is the fitness director at one of them. He manages the group exercise classes, yoga, strength, and weight room—that's his job. It pays crap;

it's for the county. But it is satisfying to him because he wants to help others be their best selves. He's healthy, and he wants a high quality of life. He enjoys helping other people achieve those goals, too. So, it's perfect for him. We're so fortunate. We're so blessed.

Part of being successful and staying in STEM is having a supportive partner. If you don't have that, or you're still living with the spouse you hate, or the one who abuses you, or whatever, it's harder to succeed in a predominantly male environment.

On the Power of Being Included

For most of the rest of the world, the man makes the money, the woman does the housework, or the woman also works but still takes care of the kids and the house. It's stressful for men who aren't the primary breadwinner, too. It's a lot of pressure for them. So if we want to talk about being equal at work, we need to talk about being equal in every aspect of life.

The one thing that I keep coming back to, which might be a thread in whatever book I write someday, is the power of feeling included.

The burden can be so heavy. Why? Because the feeling of being included or being excluded is so strong. I try to remind people, "Remember how much it sucks being excluded from something?" I'm an over-fifty-year-old woman now. I can still remember how much it sucked being ten years old and not being picked for the kickball team, or not being asked to the prom, or not making the cheerleading team, or not being invited to the after-work happy hour or the golf outing that all the men were going on. Or "Hey, we're all going to go smoke cigars," and I'm not included because I think cigars are gross, and you get the sense that though you were asked, you were not meant to be included anyway.

Exclusion and inclusion are such strong feelings. Those feelings stay with us forever. So when you keep getting reminded every day that you're not one of them, after forty years, you're like, "Fuck this."

So when I look at the military, the women who make Admiral and General level, I think of all the years when they had to put up with all that crap to make it to that level. That is why I think the situation is not because women aren't capable of being CEO at a company. There are so few women in STEM, and fewer of us as you go up because we have to shoulder that feeling, "Hey, why are all the guys going out to lunch? Nobody asked me." That hurts. And you miss all those opportunities to build the important relationships they're all building. Just to put up with that, it beats you down.

Inclusion is something I like to talk about, not inclusion in terms of diversity, but just being human. Feeling wanted by someone or being needed by someone.

On Sexual Assault in the Military

Last year, the Academy got a new superintendent, a three-star admiral. They've only ever been men. In fairness, it takes about twenty-five years to grow a 3-star Admiral. Women haven't had opportunities for long enough yet to develop a deep bench of talent. This one is a good guy by all accounts from the women who have known him. He is an Academy grad himself. Women in his class way back when over the years have all said that he totally gets it about diversity and the importance of women and all of that.

When he took office last summer, in 2019, they did a feature on him in the local Maryland and Annapolis papers and also in the *Washington Post.* The story was about his top two priorities as a superintendent. One was to fight the flooding problem that the Academy has. It's surrounded by the Severn River and the Chesapeake Bay, and it's basically falling into the water. His number-two priority was fighting this sexual assault problem that the military and the Academy have. In my jaded fifty-year-old mind, I was like, "Oh, great, another one who talks about trying to get at this. Let's see if he will put his money where his mouth is."

I made a comment on LinkedIn.

In my old age, I've learned to speak truth to power in a way that doesn't piss people off. So, I just commented, "Admiral Buck, I'm so glad to hear that this is a priority for you. Many of us have some creative ideas to help you address this problem. I'd be happy to share some of them with you." And I just kind of wrote it off. I was like, eh, whatever, it's LinkedIn; he's not going to listen.

But he responded to my comment on LinkedIn with his phone number and said, "Thank you for your comment. Here's my phone number? Call my staff. I'd love to meet with you."

I was like, "What?!" So now I have to think of something witty and smart to say.

He did what he said. I went to the Academy. He made time for me. We had a conversation. And they weren't just my own suggestions. I have this whole community of women graduates and women Naval officers who have also given me ideas. And so I gave him ideas that were very simple things he could do. And he listened very respectfully. I don't really know if he took any of my suggestions.

Then the world turned upside down.

That was the fall of 2019. They had a couple of midshipman deaths at the Academy that he was dealing with. Then COVID happened. I imagine he has different priorities now, but at least he is trying to come at this. Yes, harassment and assault are still problems in the military.

Unfortunately, there's still harassment and assault at colleges, at work, and anywhere.

On Reinventing Yourself

I tell people all the time, "I have a degree in history, a master's in leadership." I spent twenty years driving ships and flying helicopters in the Navy. Now I'm at Splunk, a software data and analytics company. People are like, "What?" I tell people you don't have to have been a coder your whole life to end up in a cool tech company.

It's all about reinventing yourself.

I was in my forties when I joined Gartner. I had never worked for a private company before, so I was learning about interacting with sales, quarterly goals, and how a business runs. I didn't know anything about business, so I used that opportunity to learn as much as possible.

The networks and relationships I built have always been important, too. It's the people you know. I was building a brand as someone who is trusted and shows up. Someone who is not trying to sell something every time they turn around. Someone people can rely on.

The learning and doing, plus the expansion of my network, have all been very helpful and very satisfying.

So, the role that I'm in now with Splunk as the Chief Technical Advisor, I got it without coming from a technical background. I don't have a bachelor's or master's degree in information technology or computer science.

When I applied for this role, I was very clear about that. You don't tell your whole story through your résumé. You tell your story when you actually talk to people. I said, "If you are looking for someone to be a product developer or to talk about how software is built, I am not your person." I think they really appreciated the fact that I was upfront about that.

By the time I applied for this job, I had built enough confidence in myself to not feel that I had to have the technical skills. Other people can do that work. I bring a really unique set of skills and my own personality that nobody else has. I love engaging with people. I can speak publicly because I have a theater background. I love being on stage. I was very honest about myself and what my strengths are and what they aren't. I had gotten comfortable enough in my own skin to be proud of that and to talk to Splunk about it.

I thought, "I'll take some risk and apply for this cool job at a software company, though I don't even know what they do." I just felt like, yeah, I can do that comfortably as opposed to biting my nails every night, thinking, "Oh god, if I get this job, what the hell am I going to do?" I didn't ever want to feel that way. Some people go after jobs they know they're not qualified for, but I don't ever want to feel unqualified.

I also relied on the fact that I learn quickly. When I go over my life story, I can see that I have done many different things, and I've been successful, which means I can pick up on stuff pretty quickly and be good at it. For example, when I came out of high school, I knew nothing about the Russian language. Yet, I graduated first in my class at DLI. Then I went to the Naval Academy, questioned my ability to be a good student, and graduated with merit. And then there was flight school. I had never sat in a cockpit or played a flight simulator game, nothing. Yet I beat the odds and graduated from flight school, and on and on.

I'm a pretty quick learner. I've proven that. I use that as a plus in my interviews— "By the way, Mr. or Ms. Interviewer, you might notice over my life, I've done a bunch of different things and been successful. I may have gaps in my technical knowledge, but trust me, I can learn it if I need to."

It's about your character and personality. Your unique style. You are who you are when you're in your forties or fifties or whatever, but skills and knowledge you can always learn and change. You can reinvent yourself.

On Building Your Network

We now have access to people we wouldn't have had access to five or ten years ago through social media. Use it.

For example, if I see a senior person, like the CEO of a major corporation or from the government, posting something on LinkedIn or speaking at an event, I reach out and send a note. I just say, "Hi."

But I don't just blindly connect. I say, "Hi, so-and-so. I saw you speak at this event. I love what you had to say." So, I make a personal connection. I tell them what I appreciated about what they said or what I learned from them. And it's always genuine. I don't make it up. I add, "I would love to invite you to my network," or, "Would you invite me to yours?" Something like that is so easy to do.

Most people are afraid to do it. So I encourage people looking for mentors but who don't know how to get them to do what I just said. When you see somebody who says something really cool—I don't care if they're a professional athlete or famous actor or actress—they're human beings, and human beings like to be wanted, and they like to be liked, so reach out.

And if they don't, if they say, "No thanks, too busy," or they don't respond to you, at least you tried. Like, who cares; what's to be lost? So, leverage social media.

Also, a lot of organizations have mentorship mechanisms, whether it's an employee resource group (ERG), or it's through human resources, or alumni networks from your college or your high school, or whatever. Use them. I got involved with formal mentoring through the Naval Academy. I said,

"Sure, I'll be a mentor for women in technology, women in defense, and women in aviation."

Other people aren't going to do the mentoring and championing for you. You have to look out for yourself. Being proactive is important. You need to take ownership of that and at least tap into available resources.

I was speaking with a group of girls who code just last week. There's a chapter at a high school here, and they asked me to speak to them virtually. They asked, "We hear all these bad stories about women in STEM and how they don't treat other women so well. Do you have any examples of when that happened to you?" And I said, "Actually, no, because women in STEM today are much different than they were ten years ago. It used to be that often women didn't want to help other women. Like they felt as if, 'I had to work hard to get here, and you're going to have to work hard to get here, and I'm not going to help you because if there's only one, it's going to be me.' But that is not the world today. I don't ever see that anymore. Yes, there are still fewer women than men. But I see women tripping over themselves, looking for ways to help other women like you."

On Confidence

My advice for overcoming your lack of confidence is to take more risks earlier.

Don't wait until you meet a hundred percent of the job requirements to apply for the job, because you will never apply. People spend way too much time criticizing themselves about what they don't know or how hard something is for them, and the years go by. Missed opportunities pile up. When you do that, you miss the opportunity to build confidence in yourself.

My advice to myself would have been to take more risks sooner. It's kind of weird because I did take a lot of risks. Yes, I went into the military, but then I still shied away from things I didn't think I was qualified to do. And now it turns out I could have done all of it.

I didn't open my mind enough.

I wish I had done that when I was younger. I could have talked to more people before making decisions about what I was not going to do. Instead of saying, "Nope, too hard," I could have talked to four other people who might have done that thing and asked, "Hey, is this hard?" An example is staying on the women's crew team in Annapolis. The introduction to crew included lots of running. I hated running. So, I quit instead of talking to more experienced crew women who could have taught me about all the benefits of crew, of being a Navy varsity athlete, and building those strong bonds that last a lifetime. Instead, I made too many decisions on my own, listening to my own negative self-talk.

I self-filtered. I self-limited.

All you have to do is make an effort. Ask more questions. Take one more step down the road.

On Practicing Failure

As a pilot, you practice emergency procedures all the time in case something goes wrong. You have to build your muscle memory to go to step one, step two, step three, so you're not thinking in the moment of crisis.

We used to practice engine failures. When you're flying in a dual-engine aircraft, that's fine. If the conditions are right, you can take one engine offline and still fly safely, though it's not all that comfortable because now you're flying with half of the engine power.

Once, I was being tested to do that. You're not supposed to actually turn the engine all the way off. You're supposed to bring it to idle so that if the other engine isn't strong enough, you can bring it back on quickly without having to refire it up. But I turned the engine all the way off. So now we had an emergency. We were heading toward the ground very quickly. I can laugh about it now, but I was like, "Oh my god! Holy shit!"

It was almost really bad.

Fortunately, my instructor pilot took over and landed us safely. I really thought my flying days were going to be over. I thought I was going to be grounded. I worried about this for a few days. Of course, I didn't talk to anybody. I didn't ask the commanding officer, "Is this a groundable offense? Am I going to lose my wings over this?" I just mulled over it and worried about it. Every time somebody gave me a crosswise glance, I was like, "Great, they think I'm a horrible pilot." I was making up all these stories in my head. As it turned out, yes, it was bad. Yes, it went in my record, but it wasn't going to ruin my life as a pilot.

I learned a lot of things from that. First, just being smarter about my procedures was one of them. I wasn't ready for the emergency. I had to study more. It was on me. Second, I have to talk to other people. After I landed right away, I should have asked, "What does this mean for my career?" But I didn't. I let all that fear kind of build up, and it consumed me for a few days.

That was a pretty big failure. But yeah, it happens. Not everyone is perfect all the time. In fact, nobody's perfect all the time. Don't assume that other people, because they're successful, have never failed at something before.

Picture an iceberg with success at the top above the waterline, and then under the waterline is failure, resentment, disappointment, heartbreak, bankruptcy, all these things. When we look at others and say, "Oh my gosh, she's so rich and famous," we don't know what she had to do to get there. We don't see below her waterline.

My mom used to say, "All that glitters is not gold." Everything that looks awesome isn't always awesome. But I blew it off because I thought, "What did my mom know?" Turns out she was on to something.

I wish I had had that in my mind earlier in my life because I would have stopped questioning myself, like, "I failed that one time. I guess I'm never gonna be good at that." When I was growing up, nobody talked about failure as a way to learn. They were talking about failures as "You failed. You are a failure."

No, you have to fail at stuff to learn. It's what we learn from our failures that matters.

The key takeaway from my story is that you have many opportunities to reinvent yourself if you want to, so don't let fear of failure in your past limit your future.

Epilog

Life goes on...my son is now off to freshman year in college, and I've shared in the majority of the decisions leading to his choice of school and major. He's studying Industrial Systems Engineering and frequently mentions his growing interest in data and analytics, much to my delight. As the pandemic winds down, my husband and I have resumed travel and are planning in earnest for what's next after I "retire retire" in a few years. Life is good; blessings abound... but the struggle continues.

I do still wonder when the concept of equity will take root. Equity meaning that all candidates who show up for a particular opportunity have the same support, champions, strokes of luck, and other factors throughout their careers to help them get to that point.

I believe everything happens for a reason, and there's still something better waiting for me. Or not. I could stop pushing for more and be satisfied with my life and blessings, but I'm not quite ready for that yet. So, I keep moving forward.

Part of that moving forward is offering other women opportunities I have control over. Recently I was able to add two technology leaders to my team, which to that point was all men. Very smart, capable men I enjoy working with. But I intentionally sought diverse candidates. After several levels of interviews, being very aware of my own inherent biases, I selected two women. They are smart, experienced, and have the right kind of open mindset for the job. I feel I did my part in making a hiring decision that benefits the company, my team, and these women. I'm proud of that. Like my dad has said jokingly since we were kids, "I done good."

Caroline Belmont

Head of US Global Innovation and US Regulatory Affairs, Boehringer Ingelheim Animal Health, Inc.

I lead the US Global Innovation Team. We're responsible for discovering the latest and greatest new veterinary medicines and getting them onto the market to address unmet needs for our customers' pets and livestock.

Passion for Animals

I grew up in the Northeast of England with my younger brother. When I was about four-years old, we moved into an old Victorian terrace house that overlooked the sea. My primary school was around the corner.

I loved doing scientific things. I loved biology and developed a strong love for geography. I loved doing sports and different outdoor activities as well. As a family, we used to travel a little bit. We would go on holidays, camp overseas, drive to France, and visit other faraway places. I loved traveling. I had a passion for science and travel, which sort of steered me in the direction I am today.

We also had a cottage, a second home, out in the middle of nowhere in Northumberland. We would go there on weekends. It was very rural. I just loved being out in the country. We had a few farming connections, and one of our neighbors who had a horse would let me go horse riding occasionally. I really enjoyed that. My entire career has been involved with animals in some form or another. We had cats and a dog at home throughout my childhood. I've just had this passion for animals ever since I can remember, especially for horses. Personally, I was never able to have one, but every time I got the opportunity to go riding or pony trekking, I would take it. I was absolutely enamored with animals as a whole, but with horses in particular.

I got through high school and wanted to be a veterinarian.

In school, we had large classes, typically about thirty-five students. I quite enjoyed high school. I also did all kinds of musical things, like playing the piano and the flute. Back then, when you finished high school in the UK at around sixteen, you took a range of exams called 'O' Levels. That helps drive what you specialize in over the next two years.

After high school, I went to Sixth form college, which was basically the last two years of secondary education, when you did more advanced work in your specialized subjects. I think at that point, it was biology, chemistry, and geography for me. That's when you decided where you'd want to go to university and what sort of courses you'd like to study there.

I was aiming to be a veterinary surgeon but didn't entirely take the right courses to get there. I knew what to take, but I was just scared to death. If I wanted to go to veterinary school, I had to do four 'Advanced' Levels, one of which had to be physics or mathematics. I didn't like either of those very much. I even had nightmares for years afterward about taking exams in mathematics.

So, I thought, "Okay, let's be realistic."

It was extremely competitive to get into veterinary school. Back then, it was even more competitive than medical school in the UK. It felt like you had to be a genius, and I didn't think I was really on that level.

So, in the end, I didn't go to veterinary college and thought, "Okay, what else can I do that allows me to work with animals?"

Cow Dung

When I was around sixteen, I was looking into what to do if it wasn't going to be veterinary work. It was suggested that I join the 'Young Farmers' organization, a global organization centered around rural communities. There was one near me. It's basically a club for people aged from about fourteen to twenty-six. You get involved in all types of different activities, go on trips, and see different types of agricultural things. One or two farmers' sons and daughters were in the group, so I made a few connections there and learned a lot. That's how I thought, "Yes, this is what I need to do. I need to be in this game."

I studied agriculture and did a specialized degree in agricultural biochemistry and nutrition at Newcastle University in the UK.

At the end of the day, I made the right choice.

Newcastle was not far from my home. I could live at home, get on the train, and go up to the city to do my classes. I continued to socialize with my friends up in university and also with the Young Farmers, keeping that connection.

I also liked to work. I worked my way through university. I always had little jobs working in hotels or wine shops (liquor stores). I used to do all kinds of things that would help pay the fees. I was fortunate enough to come out of university with no debts, a small miracle these days.

In my second year, I got an opportunity to do a really interesting project over the summer. It involved working on a farm, doing a specific study for an animal health company working with cattle. We were looking at a dewormer for cattle.

The animal health company was looking for somebody in the university with some experience working with farm animals. Only nine or ten of us were in the course, and everybody else lived outside of the area except for me. They were looking for someone local because the project was local. I could drive to the university farm, which was quite close by.

It just all made sense.

I was offered the summer job, and of course, I jumped at the chance. This company sponsored the study I was involved in. They needed somebody to do all the basic sample collecting and just the general dog's body, to be honest. Yes, you are sampling cow dung, and you don't pick it up off the ground either. It can be a mucky business, collecting feces samples directly from cattle. But it was great! We did a lot of lab work, too, but I never enjoyed being in the lab as much as I enjoyed being outside.

It led to a very interesting thesis project for me, and it secured the fact that I really enjoyed working with animals.

That thesis would also get me my first job as soon as I graduated university.

Exactly the Right Thing

You might not realize what you're doing at the time, but when you look back on it later, you think, "Yep, I did exactly the right thing." 'Cause, you just followed what you really wanted to do.

When I was in my final year, I was ready to enter the workplace. I wanted to go out and do something. I was looking for jobs before I graduated. I felt like, "Okay, I'm ready to get going. What am I going to do next? But I've got to get my exams done." I didn't even wait for the results. Other people were traveling the world or having a summer off, but I just wanted to know what I would do next.

So, I started applying for jobs during my final year.

That's how I came across my first real career job. I saw an ad in a New Scientist publication that said they were looking for a junior scientific officer who would be doing some microbiology and diagnostic parasitology, which was essentially a little bit like what I had been doing for my thesis. I thought, "I've got some experience." So, I applied. The lady in charge who was interviewing me was very interested. She liked the experience that I had and the project that I had done. So, I was offered the job almost immediately out of university. I just had to pass my exams and get my bachelor's, which, fortunately, I did.

Then, I had to relocate.

I had been living in the Northeast, had a steady boyfriend, and everything was fine. But this job was in Milton Keynes, about fifty miles north of London. I had to leave home and move. So, I did. And my boyfriend came with me. He left his job and found a new one locally. We bought a little house right away.

I was working half in the lab and half outside. The company had animals on site. They had horses, cattle, and sheep. Occasionally they had turkeys and pigs. The animals would be part of different clinical studies, which would help develop new and different products, such as animal health vaccines and dewormers for different species.

I did a bit of everything. Sometimes I would work with some animals or help with clinical studies, take samples, and then process them. And then sometimes, we also ran studies with different owners, clients, and vets. So, we would get samples in the post, then we would process those samples, collect information, and write reports.

That's how I started out.

I didn't care for microbiology in the lab. But I liked the work outside and the diagnostic parasitology.

Coming Inside

But it wasn't busy enough.

I assume there were spending cuts or something similar. So, there were times when there wasn't enough to do. I didn't like that and didn't know what to do next. It was suggested that I should move roles; apparently, nobody wanted to lose me. They thought that if I moved into the regulatory affairs side of the business, I could help somebody else.

And that's exactly what happened.

After about a year, I switched roles and became a regulatory officer with the same company. I moved from being outside and doing lab work to doing paperwork in the office.

At that time, there was only one lady in the office who did all the regulatory work for products all around the world. And she was swamped. So, I helped her and learned an enormous amount about the information and data required on each product, following regulations, and how to license products in different parts of Europe. So, I was in the office, but it was so interesting to me. I was doing something different every single day.

There was always something new.

At first, I had no idea what a regulatory specialist did. I didn't even know the role existed. For the first three years, I wasn't even certain what I was doing. It took three years to really understand and appreciate what a regulatory job was all about. Even now, it can be quite difficult to describe—we take all kinds of data generated about a product, producing a dossier submitted to the government agency that regulates these products to gain their approval to license and sell the product on the market. There are always questions and answers to discuss and negotiations with the agencies, such as the FDA.

Finally, I saw the importance of the work, and I thought, "Oh, I'll enjoy this."

I like to do things. While others like to focus and go right into the details, I prefer to work on lots of different things, more variety. So, this job provided the perfect opportunity. It also opened up the rest of the world and allowed for interactions and working with different countries and cultures.

Regulatory affairs became the foundation of the rest of my career afterward.

I was not working directly with animals, but I was still contributing to animal products in development and seeing it to the end. It was getting the product on the market and then working with the marketing people to launch it, seeing it come to fruition and become available for customers and their pets and livestock. In regulatory, you're in the middle of a project almost all the time. So, you get a much broader picture of what's going on from start to finish. You also become involved in interesting negotiations with the government about the product, all the rules and regulations, and so forth.

I could work on the same products in different countries, too. Occasionally we would travel to headquarters, which was in Germany, or I would get to go overseas on a business trip. So, I got to travel, which certainly interested me, too.

Making Moves

I was with that company for about eight years and got a really good foundation. I was also getting a bit bored, and I thought maybe now was a good time to go and do something else. My boyfriend was still with me at this time, but we'd met very young, and we seemed to be coming to a natural end. We eventually split up. He went back to live in the Northeast. We're still in touch and friends, but ultimately it didn't work out.

Around this time, the housing market crashed in the UK.

We had bought our house in Milton Keynes when the interest rates were astronomical. We couldn't sell the house without losing a lot of money. We had negative equity. My now ex-boyfriend was happy to take his name off the paperwork. We were probably very naive when we went into that not being married, but luckily it all worked out. I was able to keep and ultimately rent out the house for some time.

Meanwhile, I was also wondering what type of job I would like to do next.

I loved the regulatory work and thought, "Okay, there are three areas I could work in. I could go to another company and do the same thing." Second, "I could work for the government and learn more about their side of the licensing process." Third, "I could consider a job as a consultant, working for a contract research organization."

And that's what I did.

I took a job with a contract research organization in Scotland that works for different pharmaceutical companies, crop science, animal health, and human health. They have experts consulting on various specialized areas to provide advice, train others, and conduct clinical studies. And that's the option I took. So, a job became available, and I stayed there for about a year.

I met my best friend while working for the same contract research firm, and we hung out and did all kinds of fun things, but I didn't enjoy that job so much. With the previous company, I could see all the different stakeholders and work with different people. I used to know what happened to the product. Take it all the way through the pipeline to the point where it would get launched onto the market. But in a consulting role, you usually only get to see a piece of a project. You work on part of a project and then hand it back to the sponsor; you don't know what happens next. I didn't care for that very much. Then, after about a year, one of our clients was looking for a regulatory specialist for their own company. They hired me for that role, and I moved south once again.

I went to work for that company only briefly. They were based in London. So, I moved again but could go back and live in my own house in Milton Keynes, which had been rented out while I was in Scotland.

I discovered very quickly that I didn't like the unethical way the company did business and the way they handled certain matters. I thought, "This is not for me," so I got out quickly. I wasn't prepared to work under those circumstances.

Once again, I looked for another regulatory role, found one, and immediately accepted the job.

It was west of London. Again, I could live in my house, though I had more of a commute. At this company, Boehringer Ingelheim, I was responsible for all their animal health registrations and product licensing for the UK and Ireland. I was there for three years. I worked a lot with the company headquarters, which was in Germany. And so, I again traveled occasionally, and that was great.

Ultimately though, I found the job quite simple and straightforward and not very challenging or with much room for growth. So, in the end, although they did try to find a way to get me to stay, I took a job with a different company.

I was still living in the UK but working with another animal health company doing a broader role—more European regulatory work, as well as the UK and Ireland, and I was working with a broader range of products. This company was also located in North London, so I could continue living in my home.

This role was very different. I had huge amounts of work to do. I thoroughly enjoyed the people I was working with. It was also very challenging. It was almost an all-male group of regulatory experts, which is quite unusual for this type of work. I actually found it quite fun.

I worked there for a couple of years.

The Call That Changed Everything

Then, I received a very interesting phone call, which changed everything.

The head of Regulatory at Boehringer Ingelheim (who I knew quite well from work) in the past called me and said, "Do you know anybody who would like to work in the United States in International regulatory?" I think he expected me to suggest a couple of names, but I said, "Yes, *I would*." I literally stuck my hand up and said, "Yes, me. I would like to go to the US." I don't think he expected me to be interested! In fact, it was a huge bonus because he already knew me. And because I had worked for the company already, I could also qualify for a better visa to get working permission in the US.

I enjoyed working for the company I was at in London, but the opportunity to go to the US was really attractive. My parents were supportive. I had a partner, and he was delighted as well. He really wanted to go to the US too. We ended up getting married just before we relocated, so it was possible for him to come too.

So, in 2003 we both relocated to the US. The job was fascinating, licensing products in many different countries and getting to know a whole new group of people and cultures.

My motivation, quite honestly, was partly the open spaces and traveling in a new and exciting country I knew little about. After some homework on where the location was going to be, in Missouri in the Midwest, I thought, "We can buy acreage. I can have my own horses." While I used to take riding lessons in the UK, and I would take any chance I could to help out at different stables, I had never owned my own horse in the UK.

Of course, we got a horse in Missouri!

The first horse was a shire draft horse called Commander. Then he became two, and then two became three. And then there was quite a herd after a little while. It was pretty much a small horse ranch. We bought acreage close to St. Joseph, Missouri. We lived there for a while, but we also wanted more land and could not buy any around our property. I was still working at Boehringer, but we decided to move to try and find a bigger acreage property. So, we moved to southern Iowa, where we could buy more land. We had a really nice property and lived up there for a number of years.

Before my partner moved to the US, he owned a successful fitness center business in the UK. When we married and moved, he left it in the hands of his management, which, unfortunately, after a couple of years, didn't work out so well. So, he cut ties and sold it. He didn't know what he wanted to do for a while. He was thinking about different part-time jobs. He enjoyed being outside and looking after the horses, but he needed his own income for his own peace of mind. Eventually, he joined the post office and became a mailman.

And he just loved it.

Meanwhile, business at Boehringer Ingelheim in Missouri was expanding. The site produced vaccines for different animals, particularly livestock and horses. I enjoyed doing all this regulatory licensing work and working with new agencies overseas. I started to work with the USDA, and I also got to work internationally. We were trying to get our products exported overseas, so I could travel to some exciting places in those first years—South Korea, Japan, and several times to China.

It was just fascinating.

So, my role developed. I was lucky to be offered different opportunities over time. I took on responsibilities over different areas for various groups throughout my career. Not because I asked for it, but because I seemed to get along well with people and got the work done—and it was recognized. I was promoted several times and was able to develop my career that way by working on different projects.

It was all fascinating. Every day was different, which I also liked and appreciated.

Missed Signals

In 2008, I was involved in a project that had me working a lot of extra hours. In addition, the company was looking at the acquisition of another business.

Around that time, my husband was just not very happy at all. I didn't really know why, and I was not there enough to notice the signs either. I just knew something was wrong, but he wouldn't talk to me about it. He didn't say anything. He was just kind of ignoring me, doing his own thing. We didn't tackle it. Then I came home one day, and he'd gone. He'd just left a note which said, "It's all your fault."

I just was floored, absolutely devastated.

I was so busy that I could at least immerse myself in work and keep going. My husband vanished for a while and wouldn't talk to me for quite a long time. I was able to keep going, and of course, I had to look after the horses, which was also a blessing and helped me through it. I also had friends in the area who helped me out. It turned out later that he had found a girlfriend during his post office work, apparently. At the time, I didn't know anything about this. I was told maybe a year or two after he'd gone. Friends who had known, but didn't want to say anything, broke the news.

We separated and divorced.

Yes, I clearly missed some signals and didn't deal with them. I had a gut feeling that something was not right, and I didn't act on it. I should have listened to myself! I still, to this day, don't really know why I didn't. Maybe I'd known that this might happen and that it might be the best thing for us in the long run.

I would say, "Make sure you have those conversations and communicate."

Sometimes it's more difficult to communicate with your spouse than with others—but I think work became too high a priority for me. I didn't pay enough attention to him. But I also think I couldn't have scaled back this project at that time. I was so engrossed and thinking, "This is going to be fantastic because we're going to become a bigger company, and there's so much more opportunity."

The company did nothing wrong at all. They didn't. And I didn't tell them what was going on at home. That's my fault. I know from another experience later that I could and should have told them, and they would have helped me out.

If such a situation happened now, I know the company would support me if I needed to put my personal life first. But this was back in 2008 and 2009. At that time, I didn't want to say anything. I didn't want to make a big fuss.

Today, I'm absolutely sure that there are ways to help employees get around issues like this. There was just not the level of flexibility and support compared to what is available today. And certainly, the COVID pandemic's impact has significantly increased flexibility. As a result, we've seen even more workplace flexibility and the importance of work-life balance.

It's absolutely fantastic the progress we've made. It's so different from what's on offer today. Of course, there's a lot more needed, but it's night and day compared to the relatively recent past.

Two-Country Arrangement

I enjoyed the two or three years living on my own in Iowa.

I had a great friend who would come in and help me with the horses. She kept her two horses with my herd. We used to ride together and had lots of fun. If I had to go to Germany or overseas elsewhere for a week during the year, she would come in and feed the horses and the cats and keep an eye on everything.

Everything was working great.

Except I started to get a bit lonely after a while. I had to get the divorce over with and wasn't really all that interested in dating for quite some time, but then at some point, I thought, "Yeah, it's kind of lonely," and started looking at dating again.

I found a guy who lived in Nebraska and worked at FedEx through an online dating site. He was a little bit different – very entertaining and charismatic. So, I would head over to Nebraska, then I'd come home, and we'd swap weekends and so forth.

He told me early on that he had chronic pain challenges and was on all kinds of medication for pain. I sympathized and did whatever I could to support him, but I didn't really appreciate well what that might mean in the long term. As time progressed, things were going quite well, and ultimately, I decided to move yet again. I bought a house in Nebraska to move closer to where he lived. This was around 2012. I purchased the acreage, and I moved all the horses.

I also started to discover that not only did he have ongoing chronic pain issues from former back surgery and neck surgery, but he was also quite . . . how do you put it? I suppose *unstable* would be the best word for it. He spent a lot of time at various doctors and was under various treatments. But he also had anxiety and major depression challenges. I suspect he was bipolar. He could be happy and excitable and a pleasure to be around for a week or two, then fall into a depression and struggle to get out of bed for a week. I wasn't as aware of what was happening here as I needed to be. This was all new territory for me, but I was learning a lot and doing as much as possible to support him. Anyway, it could be quite tough on occasion.

We got through it for a while.

Meanwhile, I started to travel more for my job. Then suddenly my boss left the company to take another job. So, the company asked me if I wanted his job. He was the global head of the regulatory team. The challenge for me was that this job was located in Germany. I fully intended to turn it down. I thought, "I can't support my partner, do all this traveling, and look after the horses from another country. What's going to happen?" My partner said,

"Don't worry about it. I can manage the horses. You should do it." At this time, he was already doing it. He was outside all the time and appeared to love all this work looking after everything on the acreage. He was doing other work for local farmers and driving semis during harvest.

He said, "It'll be fine. Talk to the company to see if they will regularly let you come back to the US." So, I did, and they agreed. So, the arrangement in 2013 was that I would spend two or three weeks in Germany, and then I would come back to the US for two or three weeks. I had their support.

The Unthinkable

I started a period of frequent traveling between Germany and the US. The jet lag was exhausting, but it was working well otherwise. I was doing what needed to be done. The company was happy. I enjoyed the strategic role that I had in Germany. I had a little apartment. It was peaceful and quiet. I could walk everywhere and get the train to different places. And then I could return to the US, and the horses would be there, and my partner would be there.

Two different worlds almost, but it seemed to be working.

But over many months, my partner had more problems than he cared to admit while I was gone. For whatever reason, things were not going well for him. He didn't like me gone, but then he didn't like me being home. I just didn't know what to do next. This wasn't a reaction like anything I had experienced before, and it wasn't very logical to me. . And he started doing stranger and stranger things. I was very worried about him and about the horses and the farm. I asked a friend of mine to come in and help him if he needed it. Sometimes he appreciated that, and sometimes he didn't.

It just started to become a real worry.

Sometimes he would answer the phone; sometimes, he wouldn't bother. I didn't really know what was going on. Looking back, I think he was spiraling into a really bad state of depression.

Then he committed suicide while I was in Germany.

It was completely unexpected.

Weeks ahead of that day, he was, again, argumentative over the slightest thing. Everything was my fault. This had been going on for a while. He could be very passive-aggressive and managed to turn anything into something that was my fault. I didn't know how to handle this at all. I was going to counseling, looking for advice to keep up my morale . . . no, not morale . . . I started to think everything *was* my fault. I had a fantastic counselor in Nebraska. I thought, "This is not sustainable." What do you do with somebody . . . how do you break up with somebody who is in this kind of frame of mind and refuses all help?

Then things were decided for me.

I had been in Germany and was due to come back to the US that weekend. I had not been able to contact him for several days. He wouldn't phone me. There was no response, no texts. We had just had . . . not a blazing row, but one of his rows, and I thought, "Okay, he's just sulking again. But I'm not sure." After four days of hearing nothing, I had to ask my friend to find out what was going on and if everything was all right at home.

She was the one who . . . who found him. I still feel appallingly bad that someone else had to deal with the immediate situation, but she was absolutely fantastic. He'd used a handgun. The house was a wreck, the dog and cats trapped inside. She was able to sort things out, call the right people, and take care of the animals.

I was able to get home within two days to try and pick up the pieces.

In terms of work and the company . . . everyone just bent over backward for me, for which I will be eternally grateful. Even though I was in a global leadership position, they said, "Take as long as you need. Come back when you're ready. We'll deal with it; don't worry." Boehringer even allowed me to move back to the US and continue my job in the US. I returned because there was no question that I could not stay in Germany with a house and all my horses and animals to manage.

So, nearly two years later, that was the end of my traveling back and forth to Germany.

Everyone I interacted with on a daily basis was just absolutely fantastic. I have a lot of loyalty to this company for how they supported me afterward. I was in an important role, yeah, but people jumped in—oh, how they did! People brought me food. They came up and visited me and helped with the horses—many people who knew me. So many people came to the funeral to support me, which was incredibly touching. It really blew me away.

When I look back, it was definitely not a good way out, terrible and sad, but it was a way out of a very difficult situation.

I moved to Nebraska in 2012, and it was September 2014 when everything changed. I thought, "You get to my age, and you can't expect everybody to be perfect," but discovering how difficult it is for people to live with mental illness really opened my eyes. I had never come across this before and not since, either.

I learned a huge amount.

From Projects to People

Before, to me, work was all about projects and getting things done.

Then, all of a sudden, it was like a switch flipped.

After my partner's death, it's been all about people and relationships. My role was to get things done, deliver on deadlines, and so forth. The critical piece, though, is the people who do it. I changed my approach. I spent even more time with the people in the teams, getting to know people one-on-one, supporting them, and trying to learn, "What do we need to do to make life better for you working for us? How can we help you?"

I became a much more dedicated servant leader overnight. It was a wake-up call, for sure!

When you focus more on the people, the projects work better. The projects themselves become better.

I still see some colleagues who don't focus enough on people. But I strongly believe that if the people working for you are happy, they'll bend over backward to do anything for you and the company. If they understand where we're all headed in the vision, they're happy, and you can help address their individual needs, they will reward you and get everything done that needs to be done.

And so, I moved from a very project-oriented approach to this people-focused one.

I was managing lots of different teams and different people. As a result, I spent a lot more time than I had before getting to know team members and occasionally being able to help solve someone's specific challenges too.

I also found that after that extremely emotional period, work still gets done. A lot of people reached out and were extremely kind. After this switch flipped, I just thought, "All this work has been done, and they didn't even need me there. I need to repay people for that and help them out when they have difficult circumstances."

The company had enabled and supported me, and it was certainly time overdue for me to give it back and pay it forward.

And interestingly, the benefit to the company is how the work gets done. The rewards afterward can be enormous. Just by going out and talking more to individuals about what they needed, I was able to fix a lot of things or make a difference to a person, which then made the project better or something else move faster, which ultimately benefited everyone.

Final Stop, Kansas

My partner's death was a significant shock and wake-up call.

I had some adaptation time, not just with dealing with everything at home but also after spending a lot of time in Germany and then returning to the US. It was a bit of a culture shock. I had to react and readapt to life in the US again. It's expected that things move on and that you're expected to do the same. Business moves on. I just guess I got by. Everybody was extremely kind and accommodating. I returned to the office in Missouri and carried on where I had left off. I managed to keep my head above water.

It was a period of change, certainly.

Later that next year, I met my husband.

It was just very unexpected. Honestly, I didn't know whether I ever wanted to date anybody again. But he was very persistent and very considerate! Over the course of the next couple of years, I was going slow. But we just got on famously, and now we're married.

So, I moved again. I hope for the last time!

I'm in Kansas now. I left the house in Nebraska and sold it. I was okay with living there for a while, but it wasn't. . . well, I didn't want to live there anymore.

And then I married my husband!

That was at the end of 2016, and happily ever after in this case! We live on a 'real' farm. He's a farmer born and bred, with his own business working at home on the farm. He has all the huge machinery and quite a bit of land. He's out planting and then later harvesting wheat, soybeans, and corn, looking after the cattle, etc.

I don't have any children. But now I have a stepdaughter who's twelve. So, I'm constantly learning. The horses are all in Kansas with us. Currently, I have nineteen horses, which is more than enough! Some of them are very elderly. I've had them for a very long time. They're my pets.

My husband is an angel. He even enjoys the horses! But he also looks after me. Number one, he looks after me. It doesn't get much better than that. So, someone's now looking after me and challenging me on some of my independences.

I've also learned that I'm resilient. I bounced back. I remarried. I moved to Kansas, and that's it. I'm done. There will be no more moves.

Organizational Changes

Regulatory is still one of my top interests.

I worked in my global regulatory role from the US, and at the beginning of 2017, the company decided to acquire another animal health organization. So, there was a big merger between the two companies.

We went into significant organizational changes. From 2017 onwards, my role changed. About six months into the merger, I was offered the opportunity to lead the whole of the new global regulatory organization. I was part of the R&D leadership team. The scope of what we were doing, the number of products, and so forth, had more than doubled. It was a much larger endeavor, role, and responsibility.

I worked on the integration activities and all that it takes to bring two organizations together. But, again, I focused on people, trying to provide clarity for others in their roles as we all went through more changes. Where do they sit in the organization? What are they going to be doing? That took up a very significant amount of my time.

At the beginning of 2019, my boss, the head of R&D, retired. A new leader was appointed. He asked me to return to Germany. I said, "Nope, it's not going to happen. I've been there before. I made that decision already. I'm not leaving the US." So, the decision was made to find someone else to take over the current role. I can understand that. He offered me an alternative leadership role working in his organization, but from the US.

Now I oversee the US regulatory team as well as the whole of the US R&D organization. It's US-focused. I lead a team of six hundred plus R&D scientists and regulatory people in the US in animal health.

I wasn't very happy about the way this all transpired, to be perfectly honest.

However, after I took on this new role, I appreciated that this was exactly the right thing for me. It allows me to focus more on people once again. I have a broader scope of people that I look after and assist. And that means I have more influence on how we can do things right the first time and build up the best US organization.

So, for me it's a good fit.

We work on projects that bring new animal health or new veterinary medicines to the market. It could be new vaccines to help prevent disease in cattle, swine, or chickens. It could be important innovations for pets that help with chronic diseases, cancers, and help prolong life. Anything like that; that's what we do. We research new innovative solutions to prevent disease and also to treat disease in different species. Then we develop those products. A good idea with sound research, good market potential, and that fits with the company's strategic direction, is a really valuable product for our animal health customers.

I now also know the end-to-end process from a slightly different perspective. I'm not just thinking about, "How do we get this product licensed with the government?" but also how to actually get it through the development process, including all the lab's challenges. What equipment do they need? Do we need new facilities? The *challenges* are slightly different, with the same goal in mind but with a much broader scope.

I've been in this role for over two years, and I'm constantly learning. We've gone through another reorganization and multiple changes. For me, once again, it's about people, about the impact on people. People appreciate the opportunity to be heard when they know that they will be affected by changes if you genuinely listen to their story, even if you can't give them the answer they are hoping to hear. That's been particularly important.

Listening to people goes a long way to building trust, even when you give people news they don't always want to hear.

That's where I am today.

I work for a great company and with some interesting people. I'm always curious how other types of organizations work and whether I've just been fortunate to be hired by good companies. Sometimes it might take a while to find the right employer, but it's worth sticking around when you find a good one.

Caroline's Reflections

On Seeing What's Really Important

One of the biggest challenges and most common problems for people is prioritizing. People always have too much work to do. They get swamped and have pressure coming from all angles – home and work. Often it can be sitting down with an individual or a team leader to say, "Look, what have you got on your plate? Let's see if we can prioritize it. Let's see what's actually important to the business and see if that helps.

Where does this fit into the big picture?"

I recommend people not get engrossed in their work to the exclusion of all else like I have done in the past. Instead, try to always consider the balance they have between their home life and work life. I thought I had a good balance earlier in my career. I did many other things outside of work, but over time, particularly moving up into leadership positions, it gets easier and easier to get swallowed up by overworking. I think it's really important to try to discover the cutoff point for you and what makes the most sense to have a good balance across all aspects of your life.

I've overdone it on the work side on a number of occasions, and there's been a heavy cost to that. Unexpected things always happen, but it's easy to get too excited by work and prospects and maybe not consider the other part of your life. I think it's easy to feel, "Oh, I've been promoted, so I'm important, and now I need to do even more. That's what's going to be expected of me." When actually, and this depends on your organization and how it operates, it's really about *enabling* people that work for you to do the actual work and for you to set a really good example so that *they* don't overwork.

If you overwork, then people around you think they're expected to overwork, and a negative ripple goes through your teams as well. The sense of pride that comes with a promotion makes you feel that you need to work twice as hard, but that doesn't mean you are more effective. How you tackle that promotion opportunity and how you operate afterward is more important because your team can and will continue to do much of the work.

You shouldn't feel the need to take it all on yourself individually. That's not what's expected.

It also allows you to develop others and secure the next generation of talented people in your teams.

On Asking for Help

I hope that my story helps just one person understand that reaching out to people for help is often the best way to go. I think they'll also find that they will receive that help. I've had nothing but positive experiences in that respect, even though it was difficult to ask for help. Ultimately, it helped me stay in the workplace, learn from my mistakes, and move forward.

I would hope that if anyone finds themself in a situation that just isn't working for them and is considering leaving, they can find someone within their company they trust to talk to and bounce some ideas and options off before they make any decision. Reach out to people who will listen, then present your challenge and possible solutions. Ask some challenging questions and maybe get their advice or find out what the company can offer. I hate to see people decide to leave a workplace when they haven't talked to anybody about it first because there are often flexible options available now that didn't used to exist.

Building those trustworthy relationships within the company is fantastic. If you don't ask, you will never know the answer, so asking is always worth a try, even if you ultimately don't like the answer.

Flexibility in the workforce is absolutely crucial for the success of companies in the future. COVID has only emphasized that fact.

At the end of the day, most companies don't want to lose talented people. So if they can find a way to make something work, they will likely try to do that. I think it's critical to find that degree of flexibility and agility to allow staff to contribute at their best and be innovative. In the end, you will be rewarded with loyalty and the benefits that it brings to the business.

I don't think there's any other alternative anymore.

On the Value of Trust

I've gained a lot of trust in others over time. I will talk to anybody and everybody now! I know so much more about individuals in the teams, and I am much more willing to share my stories with others. Previously, I just didn't find the time and learned the hard way how important relationships are both at home and in the workplace.

Building trust and providing an environment for people to say what they think leads to all sorts of good things in due course.

People must be able to provide feedback and express opinions without fear (psychological safety). Listening and being heard are important to building trust, even if you disagree. For people to have a voice and to be able to share their concerns is a huge value. Carving out the time to listen and pay attention goes a long way.

People become engaged. They raise issues and find solutions. Developing those relationships has made an enormous difference.

I know that now.

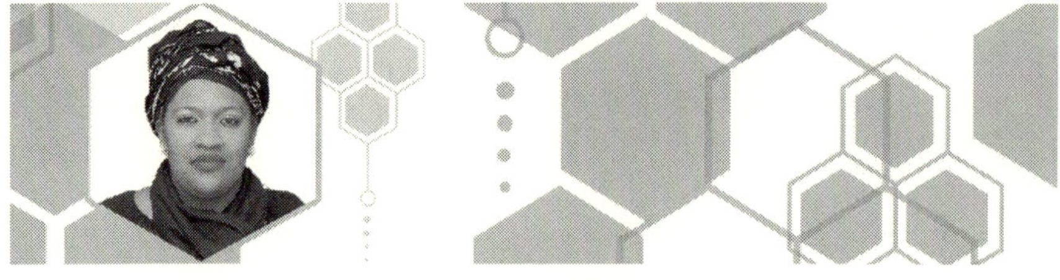

Lorraine Sefolo

**VP Gartner Executive Programs Africa,
former CIO South Africa Broadcasting Company**

I lead a team of mostly former Chief Information Officers (CIOs) who provide advisory services to other CIOs across Africa in a wide variety of industries.

Soweto's Little MacGyver

I grew up in South Africa in a province called Gauteng in Soweto. This is the same neighborhood where Mandela grew up. At the time, we only had about three TV channels, which were segmented according to language. The English one had a lot of American-type series. I liked dreaming about things I'd never seen before and watching sci-fi movies like Back to the Future. MacGyver was one of my favorites because MacGyver broke things up and built something else out of them.

As a little girl, I was very much an introvert. I liked to spend a lot of time by myself. I recently saw a LinkedIn post that said, "I like thinking." That just hit the nail on the head for me. As an only child, I loved thinking about and wondering how things worked. My cousins, who lived in the same neighborhood, were the only ones in my immediate friend group. So, I would spend time alone learning how to break things apart, experimenting with them, and then putting them back together. I would get into a lot of trouble for it, and often thought, "If I break this, am I going to die?" because my mother was super strict, and I thought she would kill me if I couldn't put it back together again.

I remember one time when I was about eleven, there was a voice recorder that I used for studying. I was fascinated by the mechanics of how various things worked. I didn't know what was inside this recorder and wanted to open it up. I was able to pull it apart very successfully, but, of course, I couldn't put it back together very successfully. It looked tampered with. My mother questioned me, "Why doesn't this recorder work?!" I had to admit the truth. I said, "It was working. I just wanted to know how it works, so I took it apart." She was very frustrated with me. This was not the kind of thing kids my age—especially the girls, were doing. I continued to break things up, electronic stuff more than anything else, even though I would get into trouble. I didn't know it then, but this curiosity about breaking things and electronics would later serve me well.

Another side of me became fascinated with fashion design. When my mother was learning how to do dressmaking, I'd read her books and look through the images. It just made sense to me. I would put the book down and start fiddling around, teaching myself how to design a garment. I would watch my mother carefully at the sewing machine, then in my mind, I would start piecing together all the steps, "Oh, first you thread in this sequence, then you place the fabric and hold it to keep a straight line, etc." – the rest is history.

In this introverted world of mine, I could observe what happened around me, learn from it and try to do it. I wouldn't ask, "Please teach me how to do this." I would just keep quiet and watch. If something didn't make sense, I'd maybe ask, "Why do you do that?" And then whoever I was watching might explain it, which helped me put together my portfolio of steps on how to do it. I still watch and learn today. Watching is how I learn.

"Go and Lean on that Wall"

My mom is a very quick learner and taught herself a lot of skills. She was a factory worker before losing her job when I was in grade eight. Immediately she thought, "I'll go into business for myself." She's always been very entrepreneurial. Even though she had been a nine-to-fiver during her time as a factory worker, she would also sell things on the side, like socks. She was very frugal with money. She didn't like wastage. She still owns a washing machine from back in 1987. I learned from her that when you buy something, you should look after it and not be wasteful with money. It's all about taking the little that you have and growing it.

She was also very strict with me. As a little girl growing up in a township, she was very clear that she wanted me to study. She would say, "Look, I didn't go very far from an education perspective, but I want you to go as far as you need to go, and you must be anything you want to be." I didn't grow up with a parent who said, "You need to be this. You need to be that." My parents gave me the freedom to be whatever I wanted to be as long as it got me out of trouble. I think my mom was always very conscious of the possibility that if I were idle, I would get into trouble, do the wrong things, and mess up my future. She was all about "Stay away from boys. Stay away from trouble. Don't get in with the wrong crowd. Stay at home and study and do the best you can—and then the sky's the limit for you." Early on in my childhood, she instilled in me a sense of discipline and the ability to do things on my own.

During one particular conversation, I remember she actually said, "Go and lean on that wall. Put all your weight onto that wall." And I'm like, "Ma, I don't know why I'm doing this, but okay." She said, "Imagine if that wall were to just suddenly crumble; what do you think will happen to you?" And I'm like, "Obviously, I'll probably fall," because I was leaning on it so hard. And she said, "Okay. So, I don't want you to lean on me," meaning herself. I was still in primary school, probably about eight or nine years old, when she had this conversation with me. She said, "Everything I'm teaching you is so that you can lean less and less on me and learn to stand on your own." And I'm like, "But Mommy, I'm a child, and I'm an only child." And she said, "No, I want to make sure in life that you are able to do things on your own, that you don't rely too much on someone outside of yourself. Because when you're relying on someone, they will not always come through for you."

She continued, "Specifically when you get married one day, don't be expecting that your husband will buy you a car or buy you a house. You need to be in that relationship as a partner, not one who's dependent on them," which was the worldview at the time. In South Africa at the time, it was the cultural norm for women not to have their individual voice. But already, at that young age, she was shaping a different belief in me that there is a marriage institution where you partner with someone equally. You both plan your future together. And you both are able to contribute to that future.

But more than anything, she taught me to be aware that there isn't a human being born into this world who is obliged to cater to my every whim. This was her message to me; that was how she raised me. If you want things, you have got to be the one who will work at it to achieve them. I was an only child, but I was not a spoiled brat. Instead, I became somebody who learned how to do a lot of things very early on and on my own and was accountable for my actions. The independent, entrepreneurial spirit my mom inspired in me has guided decisions throughout my life.

My dad, who has now passed, was a very quiet man. He never imposed his opinions on me. He kept to himself and didn't engage much with me or anybody else for that matter, to the point where I thought, "My dad doesn't really love me. He doesn't like me." Our relationship improved in adulthood, but it was a very difficult relationship and caused me quite a bit of pain and problems, as you will come to see.

It was my mother who shaped me and inspired me to dream big, as big as I could dream. My mom is the definition of fearless. Not only in her business ventures but also venturing to be different from the era in which she grew up, in what you were supposed to be as a woman in South Africa then. So, I learned that from her too.

Growing up in Apartheid

When I was in primary school in the eighties, South Africa was completely segregated to a point where there were black people buses and white people buses; they were actually written on that way. There were certain parts of the city we couldn't go into being black. They were public spaces as well that were not free.

There was a lot of unrest.

One day a large military vehicle came into our primary school. Not a police car, a military vehicle. We used to call them "mellow yellow." They were yellow with a dark blue stripe army vehicle. The way the dynamics worked in the country at the time, cops were not people you ran to for safety and security; cops were people you ran away from as they were a threat to your life.

So, this truck came into our school while we were playing outside during one of our break times. We were children playing. They came towards us, and we started spreading, but not yet running, just spreading away towards the classrooms. Then they pulled out the tear-gas guns and shot tear gas at us. After that shot went off, I was not sure whether I was shot or not. As I was inhaling this gas, my thoughts were, "what is this thing that I'm inhaling right now. My goodness, what is this? Is this going to kill me?" It was such a frightening experience. Now we are all running away, but also, we're thinking, at least I was thinking, "What did we do wrong? Did we do something wrong?" "Is it because I didn't do my homework?" It's foolish when you think about it. But even as an eight-year-old, you think this cannot be happening for no reason.

I ran home. I ran all the way home. When I got there, I told my parents what had happened. They were like, "We're just glad you are alive." Nothing ever happens about it. This had become a normal way of life in the township. You don't report it to anyone. You just hope tomorrow it doesn't happen again. The second time they shot tear gas at us, at least then, I knew it doesn't kill you. It just makes you very uncomfortable. But you do get to survive it. That's how primary school was.

These incidents were happening all over Soweto. We didn't know what was going on with the ANC (African National Congress); we didn't know about Mandela. It was a very taboo subject. You never spoke about Mandela openly, even with your parents. I remember asking my dad directly, "Who is Mandela, and who's the ANC?" He said, "Don't talk about that guy. Don't talk about him. And don't say anything to anybody about that guy," meaning Mandela. One could get into trouble by just mentioning Mandela or the

ANC.

Standard Grade

Fast forward to my first year in high school, 1989. We were moving toward the release of Mandela and starting to open up the country. Some white schools had started accepting Black pupils. I got my opportunity to go to a Catholic school about fifty kilometers away from my house. To get there, parents in the township organized a minibus taxi, not a taxi like the ones in America but a minibus, what we call a combi. This became a thriving business to take children from the township to the white schools in the suburbs. We would all board this vehicle in the morning and get ferried to the schools, then come back home very late in the evening.

It was my first time closely engaging with white students, and I didn't quite understand the way teaching happened at my new school. I remember in my first week, the teacher said, "You need to enlarge your vocabulary." I didn't even know the meaning of the word, vocabulary. So, I just nodded and thought, "I'll go to my dictionary and learn what this word means." There was a vast difference between the teaching happening in these schools versus where I had come from – the township public school system. Because my husband went to these schools earlier than I did, he got a little bit more of the foundational stages that I didn't get; for example, he did things like phonics, where they train you to pronounce words. I didn't have that in my school, and I sometimes mispronounced things, and the other kids in the class thought, "Do you even speak English?" You know how kids can be. So, I worked extremely hard, doing my watching again. How do the other kids behave? What do they do so I can fit in as quickly as possible? But I was not thriving at all. I was struggling in all elements. I was struggling with language. We were obliged to take both English and Afrikaans, Afrikaans closely linked to what they speak in the Netherlands. You cannot take any other languages; you can't even take your own native language.

I very quickly started getting into trouble over my opinions and views of the world. Remember, I was raised by a woman who taught me from as young as I could remember that there was nothing I couldn't do or be. But now her teaching had started to clash with this new world that I was in. I was beginning to be told what I couldn't do. I was being told I was not smart enough.

At the time, in South Africa, there were higher grade classes, standard grade classes, and lower grade classes in the same school at the same time. The kids who excelled in their subjects would go into a higher grade. And by virtue of being in a higher grade, by default, it guaranteed you entry into university. All your subjects would be in higher grade, which was a prerequisite for university. Then they had standard grade. You would go through grade twelve but would not be eligible to get into university. You would only be able to get into what they called Technikon, where you learned specific technical skills. However, when you entered the workplace, you'd not be on par with a university graduate.

I got put into a standard grade class. I started wondering about my future. I had this wonderful future that I'd created in my mind–I was going to become a mechanical engineer. I wanted to design the ultimate BMW engine, the best one ever, and it was going to be engineered by a woman—because she could. I told you; I was a dreamer. But now I have come into this environment, and all these limitations were being imposed on me. These imitations would shape all of our future careers, which would also shape mine.

One day, a list of names was read out to us, including mine. "You're going to meet with somebody from Kelly Green Oaks to talk about your career," the teacher said. I raised my hand inappropriately because asking questions is not the norm. "How did I get on that list?" I was told, "You're not doing well in your subjects. So we want to help you to become a secretary." And I was like, "I don't want to be a secretary. I want to design the ultimate BMW engine, so being a secretary is not going to work for me."

So, I went to the principal. He really heard me and said, "I will help you. I won't help you with the studying—that you've got to do yourself—but I'm going to help give you more exposure in school so you can be perceived a little differently." So, first, he registered me to take part in the Toastmasters community that the school was affiliated with to help me with public speaking and that sort of thing. Then he enrolled me in a two-week program called Edutrain that the country was trying to get our generation to be more reconciled in how we socialized with each other across various racial groups in the country. They took thirty students of all races and brought them to live together on a train that traveled nationally throughout the country.

Our school had never gotten into this program before. Every applicant would have to go through a hectic interview process. The principal said, "If you can get chosen out of all of the kids in the country and become one of the thirty, I will support you in whatever way you need." I asked him what I needed to do. He said, "I need you to read the newspaper, understand current affairs, and more than anything, think about how you would solve some of the big problems in the country. That's what's going to set you apart." I'm like, "Wow, someone is allowing me free thinking!" So, of course, I took that opportunity. I went through a three-layered interview process that narrowed us down to thirty.

And I got in.

I was the first student in our school to ever go on this monumental trip. The principal even got the local newspaper to interview me. I was still not very highly regarded because I was in the standard grade class, but suddenly, my confidence grew. I thought, "Even here, Lorraine, you can thrive." My math started improving. Then I pestered my teachers, "Give me extra work." I didn't even mind staying back after school every day to be given extra work. I needed this chance to go to university. I needed this education to change the trajectory of my family.

I didn't manage to get good enough marks to graduate into the higher-grade class, but I was doing pretty well in the standard-grade class. So, I said, "Okay, this is what I've been dealt with. Let me pursue my dream of building the ultimate BMW Engine and go to Technikon to become an engineer. Then maybe after I start working, I'll be able to go further." And I did just that, except the first year of Technikon didn't go very well.

I flunked horribly, to the point where they kicked me out of the faculty. So next, I entered the Industrial Engineering faculty, the only faculty that would take me at the time. Industrial engineering is essentially the study of how people work. This is where work study, process engineering, Six Sigma, and stuff like that comes from. Going down the route of information technology hadn't connected with me yet because I was still holding on to this dream of becoming an engineer. But at this point, I had an unnatural fear of failing because I knew that failure went together with getting kicked out of the faculty. And if I couldn't study, then I would have to sit at home. And if I was sitting at home, then the chances were that all my dreams would not be possible anymore.

So, I just worked hard. I worked like you cannot believe. I started learning about process reengineering. I did extremely well in the new faculty and got distinctions all over the place.

My Dad's Problem Becomes My Problem

I went to Wits Technikon, the major Technikon in the country at the time. I was still living at home, and my dad was paying my tuition. A little bit of an uncomfortable situation began unfolding. My dad had started drinking quite a bit. He became very abusive at home to my mom and me. My dad worked for an insurance company and got paid monthly. The drinking became such a problem that after he had given me money for school, he would come back late at night and demand the money back.

This happened for the first two years I was at the Technikon. That was my life. I remember one particular weekend when my mom had gone to a funeral out of town. I was left alone with my dad. I had just gotten my driver's license and could drive my mom's car. My mom said, "What you must do is take the money to your aunt's house on Friday when he comes and gives you the tuition money. Then when he gives you grocery money, first thing in the morning on Saturday, go and shop with every cent of that money. Then, bring the groceries back home, park the car, and go on foot to stay with your aunt until I come back." So, I did exactly that. Then he came looking for me. He wanted his money back. I'm laughing now, but it wasn't a funny thing at the time. I hid in the bedroom as my aunt told him, "She's not here." I hid until Sunday when my mother returned, and then I could go back home.

The Solution to My Problems

Around this time, I bumped into a high school friend at the grocery store. She told me she was into computer programming. I said, "Oh, wow. What's that?" She had a grocery receipt in her hand and explained it to me, "There's a program someone wrote that produced this receipt. The program can identify the product, the cost of the product, and the money I've given them. And it works out the change that the cashier has to give me. This is what programmers do. I'm learning how to program using COBOL." And I was like, "Oh my goodness, I'm sure that's expensive. How much do your parents have to pay for this schooling?" She answered, "We don't pay anything. I'm sponsored by a company because they're trying to bring these skills into the country. They want to attract a lot more Black kids into this industry. You just do an aptitude test, get accepted into the school, and then get an organization to sponsor your studies. They give you a bit of a monthly stipend, and after you pass the program, you get to work for them." I said, "So where do I go?" and she gave me the phone number.

At home, I told my mom, "Ma, I think I found a solution to all our problems." She was highly suspicious. "You promise me this is a proper school? Are you going to get a proper job after that? You're not going to be walking the streets?" I was like, "No, I think this is the real thing." So I took the aptitude test and was accepted. And that's how I got into COBOL programming.

I didn't have any prior experience with computers, so this was all new to me. In South Africa, unemployment in the community I lived in was very high, even for people who went to university to study. So this whole information technology thing was pretty new. The first time I worked on a computer was not in high school but at the tertiary level when I was doing engineering. Fresh out of high school in 1993, I was probably working on the DOS program, which I didn't understand. I didn't even know human beings did that sort of thing. It was a very foreign profession in my world. I had never even met anyone who worked with computers before and couldn't ask anyone for career guidance.

For me, the decision boiled down to not having to struggle to get a job. The question I was facing was if I persisted in engineering at the Technikon, would I find it easy to get a job? Because it was already difficult to get a job, even for those who had gone through a lot of training. The biggest pull for me to go down the IT route was that they would pay for my fees so that I wouldn't have to depend on my dad, and then they would give me an opportunity to be offered an internship position and if I worked hard, maybe stay on longer with them. For me, there were too many pluses. So, I went for it even though I didn't fully understand what I was getting myself into.

Against the Cultural Grain

Growing up, I was very dependent on my dad financially. So, I didn't like this thing hanging over my head where my dad, or anyone, would be able to decide what happened with my future.

My mom raised me to not have ideas of "I'll get married, and someone will take care of me." She always said, "Yes, I'd love you to get married, but you must get married for the right reasons. I'd love you to have kids, but you must do that for the right reasons. It must never be about another human being having to put food on the table for you. You do that for yourself, and you do that for your kids."

As the strong woman she was, my mom's entrepreneurial perspective went a little bit against the cultural grain. There were increasingly more women who wanted to be independent, but it was unusual to be so at that point. Women like that were labeled undesirable as marriage material, too independent to be married to a man. I know that some of the strife in my parents' marriage was because of how independent my mom was. They were married "in community of property," meaning that all her financial decisions had to be supported by my dad. For example, a friend of my mom's husband would not allow her to buy curtains until she got his approval.

My mom was a cash woman. She was against going to the bank to ask for any kind of money. For all her businesses, she would save up. She would set a target for herself and work toward it—and I'd watch her do this. She bought her first car with cash, and she built her own house with cash without any bank loans. She was very opposed to any system that was going to require that she first get permission from my dad to be able to do it.

This was the model I grew up with. I saw this with my aunts as well and how independent they were. So, in my mind, it was a normal thing. I think the reason I'm married to my husband versus any other guy was probably because of the fact that I was always very clear about my ambitions. I didn't see anything wrong with my aspirations. My husband is my biggest supporter.

Equal Partners

Knowing that I wanted to become an equal partner in a marital relationship, I didn't subscribe to the culture around me of "these are household roles—boys do this, and girls do that." I was attracted to my husband because he was different. My husband's family consists of only boys. His mom is another very strong, independent woman. She raised her boys to be, I won't say, "domesticated," but they can cook and clean. They are very comfortable around strong and independent women.

It was very easy for me to connect with my husband because we grew up in the same neighborhood. We'd known each other since we were kids in high school. He also didn't treat the notion that "this is a woman's job, and this is a woman's place." He treated me like an equal from when we were kids up until today. I remember a very fancy Christmas lunch he once cooked for me. I was like, "You cook; you're a guy," and he was like, "Yes, I cook. And if you marry me, you'll discover everything." And I thought, "Okay, hang on. I grew up in the same neighborhood as you, but you don't seem shaped by the neighborhood culture that said guys did this and women did that. You are fluid and confident." So, I was fortunate enough to meet a man who, from my own perspective, was created for me, and I for him. We're partners in love, life, and all things fun.

Back in the day, when I was still in primary school, there was a program on local TV, I can't remember the name, but it meant "a light." It was about women's empowerment, and every week it would feature different women in different industries, trying to show both the rise of women in corporate settings, as well as women being moms, wives, and those other roles women play. There was a time in my life when I thought that if I wanted to rise in my career, I would have to forfeit being a mom and a wife. I didn't like that because I knew I wanted to marry and have kids. I didn't want to have to choose.

I looked at my mom and thought, "Okay, she did it." But she didn't rise in her career in the way society sees it. So, this program was my view into other women's lives. One particular woman said, "I have the most supportive husband in the world. I would not have been able to get to this level in my career if it hadn't been for him." And I thought, "Wow." I was still a kid at that point, but, as you know, if I could see it, I knew it was possible even for me to be it. So, I think that program shaped the way a lot of girls thought. They knew they could "have your cake and eat it too."

So, all my life, I carried this in my spirit, which said, "I need to be with a guy who will allow me to be a mom, to be a wife, and to rise in my career. To be equal partners." That was my standard every time I met a guy; I measured them to see whether this would be a lasting thing or not.

Community of Property

Before we started dating, my husband got an opportunity to study in the

United States. When he was there, I started admitting my feelings for him. I thought, "I think I feel for this guy much more than I'd feel for just a friend." And then, 9/11 happened.

I remember praying to God to save him. We had lost communication with each other. He wasn't even in New York City then, but a small county called Sullivan, which I didn't know exactly where it was – he was nonetheless in America, and to me, that meant he could have been in that same building for all I knew. Eventually, he called me about a week later when he could get back on email and phone. When I was praying, I made a promise to God that I was going to tell him how I felt about him. We'd been friends since we were kids, but we weren't really dating at the time.

I was willing to join him in the States to stop my life here in South Africa and move to the US. I was even starting to look for a job and things like that. But he didn't believe that I would actually uproot myself from the country of my birth to come to the States because of love. He was like, "No, I had a plan B. If you were not going to come, I was not going to give you up. I was going to make sure I married you as quickly as possible." Sometimes when women hear that kind of passion, they worry that marriage signifies the end of their lives. For me, it was the opposite—it was actually the beginning of my journey of courage.

In our cultural system, a guy who wants to marry a woman pays a bride price called "lobola." First, he has to speak to his parents, and then his parents will write a letter to the bride's parents and talk to them on his behalf to say he would like to marry their daughter. But there need to be negotiations between the elders that exclude him and me. This is a very traditional thing. Only after this process has been settled in full would we be allowed to be formally engaged and then be able to get married.

Traditionally in some cultures even today, men feel that once this has happened, they now own the woman as a commodity of some sort. My husband had been raised with a very different mindset. He doesn't like people controlling other human beings, including women, and he feels strongly about my independence. He was actually the one who introduced me to the concept of having a different type of marriage contract compared to the standard arrangement, which is called being married in "community of property," which is what my parents had. Instead, we got married "out of community of property" because he wanted me to still maintain my independence and be able to make financial decisions on my own.

So, we got married "out of community of property," and we have an anti-nuptial agreement that says whatever we've come into the marriage with, we keep separate. Knowing that my husband would not think of me as his commodity, I was also comfortable with going ahead with the tradition of "lobola" because it gave our parents the ability to bless our union and support us in getting married. We were married by my minister, whom I was very close to from when I was a little girl, Archbishop Thabo Makgoba, who was also Madiba's (Nelson Mandela) minister in his final years and who delivered his homily.

My Journey of Courage Begins

I've been blessed with being married to a man who has helped me have the courage to stand up for myself in the work environment and pursue my studies further. On our wedding anniversary every year, my husband takes me away, just the two of us. I remember one time we were in Cape Town, and he sat me down and said, "Girl, what are your plans this year?" I was like, "What do you mean? We are on our anniversary to get away; let's go shopping." And he gave me this talking to. He said, "I really believe that women are about to be needed by the world. There are specific problems that only women will be able to handle. I think the era of women is starting, and I don't want you to be left behind." I was like, "But I've got a job, and I'm okay with my job. Why can't we just go to the beach?" This was before I became a CIO. He replied, "We'll go to the beach, but first, let's make our plans." He was almost drilling it into me. "Love, you've got to make the best use of what God has given you. You are a smart girl. You can do this...," and he would pump me up.

He continued, "Remember when you told me you were praying for my safety during 9/11 and promising God that you would tell me that you loved me more than just friends? I've prayed all my life ever since I met you that if God gave me the ability to marry you, I would support you in every way I could. I would protect you and help you be the best that He created you to be." I think we were married about five years when this conversation came up. I was like, "Oh, that's so sweet." And he said, "But I'm dead serious. You've got a purpose, and you've got to fulfill that purpose. And I need to make sure that I don't stand in the way of that purpose." And I thought, "Oh my goodness. Okay. I need to get my act together."

At programming school, I became friends with a girl who would later become the wife of the governor of Gauteng. Before her husband became governor, she was a Chief Information Officer (CIO) and was trying to help me to become a CIO too. The problem was that only a few women of color could be found in CIO positions about fifteen years ago. And the few opportunities that were viable or accessible to me as a woman of color existed outside where I lived, in other, more rural provinces. So, when her husband rose the ranks in politics, it came to a point where she no longer worked and was preparing to join him in Joburg. So, she called me up, "Listen, I want to coach you for this position. Would you be interested if I were to help you and open some roads for you so that you can get hired as a CIO?" At the time, I was residing in Gauteng, the place of gold, the powerhouse of South Africa, and the province where Johannesburg is located. And I said to her straight up, "No, because that would mean I've got to leave my husband and son." My son was around five years old at that time.

My husband decided to make the biggest sacrifice. He said, "I know very well that you will not take this opportunity if I don't come with you. I am willing to put my money where my mouth is and leave my job to come and support you and our family. I'll get into business, and then you will be able to have the freedom to take this job." He actually chauffeured me out of town to that interview. I got the CIO position, and we moved. It wasn't an easy ride, but it exposed me to so much. Sometimes I attended board meetings until late in the day, and my husband would be at home with our five-year-old son. Because we were from out of town, it wasn't very easy for him to get into business the right way, so at this point, I was carrying the household on my own. I was not very happy with this dynamic because I felt guilty, internally, to be very honest. I felt like his parents would look at it in terms of, "Why is he giving up his career to support her?" But he always says, "This is the best thing that ever happened." He has always been a big support structure for me.

I've been really blessed because of my husband's support; I can sit in a board meeting and not be worried about the dynamics at home. I know that many women experience these kinds of challenges. For example, a female executive I worked with would have to excuse herself midway through the board meetings, saying, "This is getting too late. I've got to go home and look after my kids because no one else is going to do it." But I had that freedom to stay. My journey of courage was around making steps in my education and career that I had not made before. I know very few people who have had this level of support from their husbands to make these kinds of steps.

Building Roads And Networks

The first time I was appointed CIO was in 2009 in Limpopo. My IT portfolio also included looking after building management in a company called RAL (Road Agency of Limpopo) – I was also seconded to the parent department called Limpopo Department of Roads & Transport. We were responsible for the road network of the entire province. So it was like an agency of the government, a private company to fast-track the building of roads and bridges.

As the CIO, I was the only female at the table from a technology perspective. My colleagues were mostly engineers and very well-matured gentlemen who were very traditional concerning the place of a woman. Though they were my colleagues, I had to call them Mr. So-and-So. My boss, the CEO at the time, was younger and appreciated my position a lot more. I would call him by his first name.

It was a very interesting time. I learned a lot about being an executive. One time, golf clubs were delivered to my office, and I was told, "By the way, you need to start your lessons now." I'm like, "Lessons for what?" They said, "For golf. All the executives need to be able to play golf." The company had a program that provided training for executives and learning how to play golf was part of it. They would also buy you a set of golf clubs if you didn't know how to play golf or have the equipment. I also had to go for defensive driving training to learn how to control a car that goes out of control. Sometimes we had to travel with an important member of the local government and follow their vehicles. The company didn't want the executives to get into accidents unnecessarily because they were always driving at high speeds. I also needed gun training, but I was pregnant with our second boy at the time, so I couldn't take the course. They would also even get you a gun. The role exposed me to a lot of country politics. I found myself going into parliamentary meetings with very senior people in government and engaging at those levels. It helped elevate my profile and made it easier to open doors later in my career.

Throughout this journey, the governor's wife would coach me in areas I wasn't very confident in. I could call and say, "I'm struggling here and there," with regards to the job, and she would be there to say, "Okay, do this and do that." She provided that level of coaching along the way, which was very important for me. A lot of the steps I was taking were scary simply because I had never taken them before. My husband was there to reassure me, but I was like, "You're not a CIO. I'm stepping into this unknown territory by myself." Having her in my network gave me courage and a role model for my career.

My White BMW

My portfolio was not just IT but also included building management. Because I worked with a lot of civil engineers, I was also learning the nuts and bolts of building large brick structures, mainly traffic center facilities for the province.

At the time, I had a white BMW convertible. I remember one particular instance when I had to go out onsite. I was a high-ranking executive at this point, and I was driving a BMW convertible in a rural town where my car stood out wherever I went. So, my BMW was coming into this building construction site driveway where everyone else was driving up in SUVs. Plus, in a rural province like Limpopo, there were still a lot of traditional views of women.

My role as a woman could now receive more respect than usual because I'm the one who signs the checks and approves progress payments for the entire construction project. So even the guy who owns the construction company is there to put on his best foot forward. The power dynamics shifted simply because I was approving their payment. I found myself getting a lot of respect. I was the big boss, and the way that I rocked up to the site just set the tone. So, I got treated very differently than the other women who were onsite as part of the building crew. I remember some of the women who saw me were like, "Wow! Hi." I gave them special attention and went to wherever they were working to speak to them. Just to acknowledge them and their work in the male-dominated environment that they found themselves in.

We encountered a huge challenge when we built a traffic station on someone's property. This gentleman wrote my office demanding that the traffic station be demolished or that he be compensated for his land. South Africa at the time had left-wing and right-wing parties and white parties that were pro-apartheid. The letterhead this man used had one of the names of those pro-apartheid parties. As a black South African, I had to get protection to attend that meeting. I drove with an armed officer in my white BMW; another officer followed us. When we entered the room, having such an entourage was a new experience for me; I was being exposed to a certain way that people would treat me based on my rank, not on my being a woman or the color of my skin. The dynamics had radically changed in this situation. I learned that the one who controlled the money got the respect. I'm glad my upbringing was such that I could still be humble and not let my rank get to my head. I still went home and did the usual mommy and wife stuff.

That white BMW was the first and the last one I would ever have in my life.

I was very involved in church activities as a youth minister at the time and was going to attend a church meeting. I had just arrived when two guys walked in. I thought they were coming to church. I was like, "Wow, this is wonderful. The more, the merrier." But they were there to take my car. I was very naive. My childhood and the violence of the era I used to live in had become very distant memories. I wasn't suspicious or fearful of people anymore.

I still see this scene playing out in slow motion in my mind. I was quite afraid for the people who were in the church. The one guy had a gun. I remember touching this gun and wondering if it was real or not – as if I knew the difference at the time. Once it passed my "it's real" test, I persuaded him to lower it by dangling my BMW key in his eyes. My worry was if they had to use the gun, they could shoot someone, so I tried to hurry them to take what they wanted and to leave quickly. As was his normal practice, one of my kids in the youth group came over to meet me at the car to carry my bags into the church. As he walked toward me, I gave him this very straight look that said,

"Go back into the church now!" One of the guys barked, "Who's in the car with you?!" I'm like, "No. No one is. Here are the keys – take them and go!!!"

They drove off, and no one got shot or hurt in any way. I say this lightly now, but it was very traumatic for me for a long time. I couldn't drive at night by myself, and I could never drive a BMW again. So that was my very short stint in my very nice car.

A National Scandal

A few years later, we decided as a family that we needed to return to the place of our birth, Gauteng. My husband is the kind of person who always looks for opportunities for me. I came home one day, and he had printed out a copy of an advert for the CIO position at the national broadcaster. He said, "You'd be good at this. This is your job." I wasn't sure if I'd be interested or good at the job. He gave me one of his pep talks, and I applied. I reluctantly went to the interview. I was not expecting to get the job, to be honest. But I got it. We moved back to Joburg, and he was also able to start working again since it's a metropolitan area with more opportunities.

In South Africa, many commissions are set up to investigate wrongdoing in government and corruption. When you are not corrupt and stand up for what is right and do what's right—for example, awarding tender contracts to people because they deserve it and not because you're getting kickbacks—you will not have a warm welcome in those corrupt organizations.

The public broadcaster I was working for, the South African Broadcasting Corporation (SABC), became notorious for being one of those. There are a lot of horrendous stories that have come out now.

Because I was the CIO, I was responsible for all technology procurement. I was in charge of a hell of a lot of money. I always got executive committee (ExCo) approval for the budget and tendered the contracts on the open market. I followed the proper process. But I was under a lot of pressure to stop going out to the open market. I said, "Up until you explain this to me through a proper ExCo meeting, chaired by the CEO, I am going to proceed."

And I did.

This was how the horror show to get rid of me as an executive began.

An active and very hostile environment started manifesting in the organization. The company had practices of getting people on suspension—there would be a bogus charge against somebody. They couldn't quite find anything on me to be able to do something like that.

The corruption got so severe that the South African government opened an inquiry at the end of 2016. The scandal was making news. South Africa finally got to hear what this gentleman was doing at the SABC. The COO was running the show as if he were the CEO. He gave himself salary increases, removed broadcasters' rights, and changed the editorial policies. SABC is a public broadcaster. He was interfering with how and what viewers were getting from the media. Everybody was afraid of him. He could control the news.

All this happened while I was pregnant with my third child and studying for my MBA. That is why I say, "My testimony here is that I'm still alive. I survived; I made it. I'm not dead. I found a way."

A Dream Come True

When I joined the SABC, the previous CIO had gotten a Gartner membership for the CIO position. Gartner is a research and advisory service that supports CIOs and other senior technology leaders and is very well respected and admired worldwide. So I felt very privileged to have inherited a membership to the service.

My Gartner Executive Partner at the time helped me through the challenges I was facing. I was able to have these monthly calls with her and to analyze engagements that would help me maneuver myself in the organization in terms of the politics that were unfolding. I would find myself coming out of my Gartner sessions with her not only feeling empowered but also understanding the politics and how to remain safe throughout these things as they unfolded. It also helped to give me a point of peace. When you know that someone has heard you and can empathize with you. I ended these calls feeling, "I'm going to be okay."

At the same time, Gartner was helping me to fast-track and move forward my agenda in my role in IT as the CIO. I was actually overdelivering. I was exceeding their expectations and not getting involved or caught up in the trauma of what was happening. I was forging ahead. Studying had stretched me so much that I couldn't really go back to what I had done before; I was now operating at a higher pace and level. I became increasingly impressed with Gartner as an organization. I wrote in my journal all the qualities of my ideal role, and I concluded, "Gartner fits a lot of this list with what I desire."

In 2017, Gartner contacted me and offered me a job as an Executive Partner. It was my absolute dream come true. But at the core of me was also my faith. Throughout the whole ordeal, there had to be something else that I could hold on to besides the things that were manifesting themselves in the physical realm, and I had to be very prayerful to get through the trauma. So, fast forward to this moment, and I prayed about it to ask, "Is this the right move?" Everything in my being wanted to say yes to this job, but I was cautious of making moves in my career based on pure emotion. I had gotten to a point where I needed to be rational about stuff while also being prayerful about it.

Ultimately, I didn't get the job in 2017. I was gutted. I was like, "Lord, you know how passionate I am about what Gartner does. It's a dream come true. Look at these points. This is a prayer answered for me." I didn't understand that maybe I still needed more time at SABC to learn more about leading people. I stayed at SABC and managed to get involved with bigger projects within the broadcasting world. I learned more about managing diverse people, such as TV people and journalists. Then, my five-year work contract at SABC didn't get renewed. Even though it appeared that the dust had settled, the workplace culture was that of - if you didn't want someone, you got rid of them. So I started doing my own thing as an executive consultant, helping people with data governance, IT governance, and that sort of thing.

In early 2019, out of the blue, my former Gartner Account Executive reached out and said, "They're looking for a team manager in Africa." I thought, "Oh, this is the answer I am looking for." But I still had some apprehension. I had been too attached to the outcome in 2017, and my heart had been broken. I didn't want to go through that again.

I interviewed for the job, and I got it. I would be looking after Gartner's CIO members through my team of Executive Partners who were former CIOs like me. I soon saw that my extra time at SABC was good preparation for my people development and leadership capabilities. This is why I say, "There's a path that we are all on." I look back on the things my mom taught me, my husband's pep talks, and the journey I have been on. It all fits. And I knew that somehow my path would connect with Gartner's in some way. I told Gartner during the interviews that the Gartner membership had helped shape how I delivered IT services and elevated my game as a CIO. I wanted to join the company that had helped me so that I could do the same for other CIOs in Africa.

For me, it's a little bit deeper than being just a job. People say, "I am called to minister," or "This is my calling in life." I feel I'm here to help professionals, whether they're the same color as me or not. I help them through periods of drought and being in the wilderness. Like I said to a CIO earlier today, "Don't worry about it. We got you. We'll get you the support you need to get through this." She came off the phone feeling very much in a place of hope.

Being able to do this for people is my dream come true.

Lorraine's Reflections

On Who Can Be the Girl

My husband has really supported me in advancing my career, studies, and being a mom. Wanting to advance your career or wanting to be a mom shouldn't be one-sided.

We've got two boys and one daughter who is four. In our household, they aren't boys' or girls' duties. Everybody is going to be able to do everything. We are also allowing everyone to be "the girl." For example, one day, we were sitting on our couch, and my daughter said, "This is the couch for girls. The boys sit over there. This is just for girls." But I told her, "In our house, everyone has the freedom to be everywhere...whether you're a girl or a boy."

We, as women, have the power to liberate the guys as well. Sometimes there are dynamics in relationships where women don't want to have the guy there, "You can be daddy over the weekend, everything in between that's my place as the woman."

I also think that as moms, we need to shape our little boys' world, just like the daddy shapes their world. To tell them it's okay to also be sensitive. My kids sometimes talk about when they will be dads and moms. And I say to my boys, "It's going to be okay for you to change a nappy. You are going to do it not because your wife has gotten sick and tired of doing it, you are going to do it because that is what your baby needs. A baby needs to be changed, not by a woman or a guy but by an adult." So, it becomes a norm for them. We're trying to raise them similarly to how my parents-in-law raised my husband and his brother. So, they can be members of the community that understand that women have equal rights as any other human being to have dreams, aspire towards them, and balance home and work.

Women have just as much right to dream.

On Coming into This World to Be Answers

I'm a firm believer that we've come as a woman or a man into this world to become answers to certain problems.

Just because I'm wearing a coat of a woman or someone else is wearing a coat of a man doesn't mean there isn't a purpose for us. There is. Humankind would be foolish to look at solutions in terms of being either from a woman or a man. Those solutions will come through the varied and diverse human beings born into this world at any given time in history.

On Doing It All

I challenge the idea that a woman cannot possibly do it all. The messaging has been all around us: You got kids. You got your responsibilities at home in making dinner, cleaning the house, and that sort of stuff. You've got your work stuff. You couldn't possibly cope with all of that.

Messaging like this has made some women doubt whether they have the capacity to do it all. But we have to go back and remember that we were in those traditional roles as children too. Many of us can recall having to do all these responsibilities at home when we were little girls, while our brothers didn't have to tidy up or get supper ready. Meanwhile, we still had our homework to do and still had to excel at school. We have developed enough of that muscle to do that, too, in the workplace and at home as adults.

Women are probably naturally hard workers because we've been socialized that way.

It has become our norm, whether that's wrong or right—and that's another topic altogether. I really want to challenge the thinking that a woman is weaker. How can that be when we've got all this going on—kids, a home life, and a career? It's just not true.

When I was doing my master's degree, the day I finally submitted my dissertation, I took a picture of my two-month-old daughter. She was on the bed with her nappies next to her. My work laptop was on one side, and the laptop I used to do my dissertation was on the other. I was like, "I made it; I survived. Tough as it was, I did it!"

It's very difficult for me to think, "I can't do something." Unless I've tried it and failed, I can't allow that thinking into my subconscious. These negative statements become the very disabling thing that stops people from going after what it is they need to go after.

I get emotional whenever I look at this photo of my daughter. It had been a tough road for me to get here. I self-funded my degree, and I remember my boss telling me at that time, "You need to choose between studying and working because it cannot be both." I hated that another human being thought they had the power to decide what answers I was able to provide in this world. Of course, I cannot answer all the questions in this world, but I firmly believe I can answer some. And my education was helping me to create a path toward those answers. So I thought, "I'm going to take what I'm hearing from this guy and throw it out. I'm going to carry on."

And I did. I finished my masters in July 2016.

I remember two years before that, in 2014, I was traveling with my boss for work. We were at Heathrow airport. I had my laptop in my hand, and he said, "Why do you have your laptop with you all the time?" I said, "It's for school." I was doing remote studying at a university in the UK at that time. He said, "So you didn't listen to me when I said you had to choose between your job and studying. You still carried on?" This boss was a very traditional guy. He had a stay-at-home wife and a way about him of treating women. But I was very clear that I wouldn't submit to people who wanted to write my life journey without my permission. So, I had a choice. I could keep quiet and fearful and listen to what he said, or I could go ahead and continue with my studies because I was not doing anything illegal, and I was not asking anyone to pay for my master's degree. I replied, "With all due respect, you're talking about my life. And my life will be done by me. Not by you. You pay me a salary, and I do that job to the best of my ability. If my work is suffering, you have every right to say so, but until this point, you didn't even realize that I was still studying because you didn't see a drop in my performance."

When I completed my master's, he wasn't even my boss anymore. Imagine if I had gone along with his idea of what my life was supposed to be and given up on my dream.

I recognize that we're doing this to pave the way for the girls coming after us. We're not doing this just for ourselves. We are carrying a load now, but let's not lose sight of why we are doing it—so that maybe someday my daughter or granddaughter might have a better-paved way to walk on. And so, I continue with the reverence and understanding that I am carrying people on my shoulders. And then they'll carry others, and so on and so forth.

My boss didn't understand that this was what was driving me.

On These Scars We Carry

It's essential to talk about the difficult parts of life and equally important to show that light at the end of the tunnel. Let's take one of the icons in the world, Jackie Kennedy Onassis. She was fashionable. She was beautiful. She was regal. But her pain and her trauma were publicized for the world to see. In South Africa, we saw the public event of President Kennedy being killed. We saw the documentaries play that scene over and over with her climbing onto the back of the vehicle after the shot. And we saw how glamorous Jackie Onassis was even after. We saw how well put together she was all her life. But if it hadn't been for that very public trauma earlier in her life, we wouldn't have known what it took for Jackie to get to that point.

Society expects us to show up in our lipstick with our hair done; they don't know that there are all these scars we carry.

I saw this meme on social media of a woman with the scar of her Cesarian section very visible, not hidden by anything, with the baby sitting on the mommy's tummy. The mommy was saying, "I'm happy to show the scar because out of this scar came you." We have to start changing the way that we view our pain. Floyd Mayweather is my husband's and my ultimate favorite boxer. My husband always says, "Not anyone can fight with Floyd Mayweather. As a boxer, you've got to earn your way there to enter the ring with him."

The processes that shaped us, some of it has been violence, some of it has been extreme trauma through a very tragic loss of somebody close, but out of all that, we've still survived. We've made it. That's the message. We must remind everyone to get out of looking at themselves as "I've been so hurt." But guess what? You made it. The fact that you're breathing right now is a testament to the fact that this thing couldn't take you out. You get to be here another day to make a difference, to be that answer to the world that I spoke about.

To be honest with you, it took a whole lot of therapy and all kinds of stuff to get to that point where I now view my circumstances in that way. My archbishop here in South Africa has been my friend and counselor for many years. And he would say, "Despite everything that's been thrown at you, you are still here. That stuff didn't kill you. It killed others, but it didn't kill you. And you need to celebrate the fact that you are still here. And because of that, I think there is meaning to why you're still here." So it's important that you hear the positive side of the story too. Everyone tells their story of pain, but the light at the end of the tunnel is also important to tell so that it gives someone who's about to throw in the towel hope.

Pain will always come, but pain also gets easier as a burden to carry over the years. It doesn't hurt with the fresh sting of it forever. You get to learn how to carry it and live with it. We've got to be concerned about other lasting things in this life. For example, how did we impact someone else? How did I make the path easier, even if it's just for one other little girl?

On Seeing Past Fear

There is always a continuous passage of events. Whether those events are good or bad, things do pass. But sometimes, the terror of a situation creates the opportunity for us to make bad decisions.

For example, when I was young, I made the silly decision to stop studying because someone broke up with me–as if nothing was on the other side of that breakup. I tell my children that there's always something on the other side of this bad thing; it doesn't last forever. It is going to shift, and something new will come up. That something new may be something that challenges you in another way. But again, that also is going to shift. There's constant shifting. It's like a window in a car. This window has got a little bit of a small peak through. It's a window through time as it passes. If you are terrified that this thing will swallow you up whole and you are not going to make it, you might make one type of decision at that moment as opposed to if you were able to see that three months down the line, you were going to be okay. If you could see that, you would probably make a different decision in that moment.

When you make decisions based on fear, they're very, very different from decisions you make in the absence of fear.

Sometimes we close ourselves in based on what we only know at a certain point in time. These situations tend to limit us. We get locked up in ourselves, and we're not open enough to hear that there is another perspective. But there will be a day when you wake up and are okay. And guess what? Later on, you might give advice to somebody else in the same shoes as you were. You will be able to do it in such an authentic way. We all want someone to understand us, to really empathize with us.

Imagine if I could give that kind of hope to any reader of this book. The beat of my heart would be to give the reader, not just a woman but anybody who might say, "There's no hope," some inspiration. I connect with people who've gone through pain because pain softens you in a way where you can be a lot more vulnerable. You can say to them, from the point of experience and empathy, "There is hope. There are answers. There's that next moment that comes."

Epilog

A little over a year and a half has passed, and as I read some of the sections, I realize that telling this story brought further peace and healing that I wasn't aware I needed. This pandemic has set in motion some good and some not-so-good. In July 2021, South Africa had massive riots that opened up wounds I thought had been healed when the "mellow yellow" stormed my primary school. The pain was unreal to almost witness a regression of a country happening, a country that fought so many years to uphold itself as a democracy. In a few days, we witnessed a mini-war zone. That period has passed, and with its passing, there was an offer of choice regarding how this memory will settle in the safe we call history.

During this time, I learned new skills, a hobby that has helped me slow down the pace of my life and soak in the now – I am grateful for what seems so small.

I am intentionally looking for the beauty in me, around me, and in others.

Critical Questions

To seek truth requires one to ask the right questions.
– Suzy Kassem

Within these stories' plot twists and life lessons lie shades of meaning and important questions about being a woman in a male-dominated world. Their lives and thoughts can be used as neutral ground to question assumptions, think critically, foster empathy, and facilitate problem-solving.

Below is a starter set of questions for self-reflection and engaging in critical conversations at home, school, and work.

Two or three questions alone could fill a book club discussion or Employee Resource Group meeting. Or select the ones most relevant to you and use them for journaling, goal setting, or with your coach or mentor.

The important thing is to start thinking, talking, and making change happen.

Building Strong Women

- Why was Title IX, which prohibited sex-based discrimination in education and opened up opportunities for girls to participate in sports, such a positive development for Renee and other girls?
- Daphne and Renee enjoyed the challenge of high-end math and science courses but not the loneliness. What tactics can educators and parents employ to mitigate the "lonely-only" syndrome in STEM courses and in the workplace?
- Melanie sat happily at her father's feet as a child, playing with motherboards. Frani escaped her childhood through video games, which she credits with developing her critical thinking skills. Lorraine had an insatiable desire to break things apart despite knowing she'd get in trouble. Meghan found her passion in reading, music, art, and computers – the very things that were

taken away as punishment for not performing well in school. How do perceptions of acceptable play shape children's views of themselves? Why is curiosity a critical skill for the technology industry?

- Why was it important to Meg to learn about and share her son's interests? What are the key differences between sharing and directing your child's interests?
- Parents and educators often direct children toward careers they are most familiar with. But the jobs of the future didn't exist when they were growing up. How do we strike the right balance between encouraging children to believe in their future without dictating it?
- Melynda had caring and supporting teachers who actively encouraged her to be anything she wanted. Andi's private school education taught her to be an independent thinker and confident leader. Was there a teacher or person in your life who influenced your career path or made you feel you were talented in some way?
- Being the smart kid gave Melynda a language to communicate and lifelong friendships. How are smart people typically portrayed in the media compared to those in entertainment and sports? How might social cues influence a child's sense of self and career choices?
- Mor̩ẹnik̩ẹ wants readers, especially African girls, to know that "it is not conforming, not fitting in, and not belonging that will attract your calling, purpose, and tribe." And that the "things that are now celebrated about me were not the things that made me feel like I fit in or belonged anywhere." What awkwardness did you feel as a child or young woman that you now see as your strength or superpower? What would you tell your younger self?
- Meghan recalls her interest in STEM spawned from the Madeleine L'Engle series, the Time Quintet – A Swiftly Tilting Planet, A Wrinkle in Time, etc. As a young girl, Melynda carried around a grown-up anatomy book and credited Dr. Carson as her roadmap for becoming a doctor. Which book or movie character resonates most for you and why?
- Melynda's teachers recognized how hard it is to enter a field where you don't know anyone who's done it before. They encouraged her to "Find the roadmap" and "Find people who've done it before." Who provided the roadmap for your career? How can you be that for others interested in your field, especially for young people who struggle to see a future for themselves in

STEM?

- When Janet told people she wanted to be an astronaut, they laughed or listed all the reasons why she couldn't. She dug deep and listened to her father's voice in those times. Morẹ́nikẹ́ felt she couldn't say her grandiose dream of curing HIV out loud, but her lollapalooza childhood gave her the confidence and skills to take on such an egregious health inequity problem. Talk about a time someone discouraged you from dreaming big. What would you tell your younger self at that moment? What purpose or mission drives your work today? What gets in the way of your dreams?
- Juliana recalls the young female Marine who heard her voice over the radio and said, "I've never heard a female pilot's voice before. I never knew I could do that, too." Melynda talks about the "special connection I could make with patients as a person of color. It was unexpected to them." Discuss why having role models and representation across industries, roles, and levels are crucial for girls and women of all ages. How do businesses benefit when teams are not monolithic? What happens when we are not represented in the decision-making rooms?
- Lorraine highlights the strength and beauty that can come from going through difficult periods in your life. Andi says her challenges strengthened her and gave her greater purpose. What scars do you carry, and in what ways have they produced something positive in your life?
- Why is raising boys to be empathetic so important to women, men, and society? Do you think women are more empathetic leaders? Why or why not? How might organizations cultivate emotional intelligence, and why is it essential for innovation, production, and growth?

Building Healthy Lives and Relationships

- Caroline cautions that "over time, particularly moving up into leadership positions, it gets easier and easier to get swallowed up by overworking." Share how you make time to prioritize self-care and treasure the small moments in life. How do you decide where to spend your time and strike balance in your life?
- Morẹ́nikẹ́ and her husband have monthly "red flag" conversations to address risks in their relationship so that they can grow together and celebrate each other while keeping outside expectations at bay. If you have a partner, how do you manage to grow together?

- How did growing up in the company of strong women influence Lorraine's choice of husband as well as shape her husband's view of marriage? What cultural norms shaped your perception of gender roles and marriage? In what ways are they the same or different now? What does being a partner in a marriage mean to you?
- Of the married women in the book, forty percent had stay-at-home spouses, and another twenty percent were the primary breadwinner in the relationship. According to Chief, "Of men in the top 1% of earners, 70% have a stay-at-home spouse, but only 22% of women at the top can say the same." What are the advantages of having a stay-at-home spouse, and is that secret to getting (and keeping) a seat at the table?
- On the other hand, Janet and her husband were able to balance family life with two intense careers that required significant travel (astronaut and pilot). And Morẹ́nikẹ́ describes her husband as the most feminist man who wants her to reach her full potential. Why is it easier to succeed in male-dominated fields when your spouse actively supports your career? What sacrifices have you and/or your partner made for each other?
- When Melanie and Daphne were preparing to return to work after maternity leave, they felt a push/pull for the baby they loved and the careers they loved, plus the sheer logistics of how to make it all work. If you have children, what was your maternity or paternity leave and return like? What worked well, what didn't, and what could be improved?
- What does equality at home really look like? How does the idea of men taking on traditionally female roles at home, like changing diapers or being a stay-at-home-husband, make you feel? Would others see this as liberating or emasculating, and why?
- Do you feel the management of your household and caregiving is equally shared, including the planning and follow-up; why or why not? What areas of control in the home are you, or women in general, reluctant to let go of and why?
- Meghan says, "Society isn't set up to support male primary caregivers." What pressures or stigma do men feel when they take paternity leave, attend their child's open house, or make a move to support their wife's career?

Building Great Careers and Workforces

- Forty-six percent of Black women with STEM degrees came from HBCUs!! (Despite vast funding disparities!) In what ways will you encourage your organization to tap into and support this incredible talent pool?

- Daphne's managers at Lockheed Martin were proactive, empathetic collaborators throughout her career. How does that help Lockheed hire and retain top talent?
- Andi and Renee talk about the importance of exploring different roles early in a career. On the other hand, everything Janet did in her life was to prepare her to be an astronaut. Was your career path intentional, linear, more serendipitous, or in-between? What advice would you give your younger self about early career choices?
- Renee learned to lean into her network to advance her career. Why are sponsors and advocates so crucial to women's careers? How are they different from mentors or a personal board of advisors? Why do women need both?
- Melanie created a framework to help her decide which career opportunity to pursue. How do you make career decisions? When discussing your current role, would your spouse or friends say your energy level rises or falls?
- At In-N-Out Burger, Frani found it "very gratifying to see that as long as I was able to prove that I could do these things, I could get promoted." Describe the promotion criteria in your organization. Is it clear, concise, unbiased, and visible? Is it possible to have a meritocracy in organizations with murky promotion criteria? Why or why not?
- Juliana didn't consider applying to the Naval Academy because she looked at the criteria and decided she wasn't qualified. Her counselor disagreed, convinced her to try, and she got in. Talk about a time when you counted yourself out. What would you do differently?
- Lorraine talks about the difference between making decisions based on fear or in the absence of fear. Melynda says, "Everything you want is usually on the other side of fear?" What fears might be holding you back from the things you want?
- Discuss a time when an unexpected difficulty changed the course of your life or career in a positive way.

Building Skills and Leadership

- Meghan experienced firsthand the disruptive transition from physical art to digital art. What disruptive technology forces are bubbling up right now, and how are you preparing for them?

Why is digital literacy economically and socially vital for individuals, communities, and societies?

- Why are college degree requirements becoming increasingly optional for some high-tech jobs? Discuss the pros and cons of various alternative educational resources, such as bootcamps, certification, online training, etc.?
- At one point, Lorraine's and Frani's bosses pressured them to deprioritize their education, but neither gave in. Is your boss more of a partner or an adversary in your career advancement, and why do you think they play that role? Which type do you think is in the best interest of the company?
- Meghan distinguished between learning to code and making stuff that has code in it. Why is this distinction important to encouraging more girls and women in STEM at all levels, including leadership?
- Renee, Frani, and others had roles translating customer and business needs into technical requirements at some point in their careers. What role do empathy and EQ (emotional intelligence) play in product, mission, and business success?
- Why do you think the "putting the player first" model in game design works better than the top-down "genius vision" model? How can you apply game development principles of "finding the fun" and "putting the player first to engage your customers or employees?
- Morẹ́nikẹ́ believes if you lead well and trust people, you are more profitable than if you track and treat human beings as units of productivity, "Teal Organization evolve towards self-management, wholeness, and a deeper sense of purpose." Caroline flipped from focusing on projects to focusing on people after her partner's suicide and discovered that people were not only happier, but the projects were also better. How does a people-first approach affect employee well-being and engagement? What do you think is the impact on customer satisfaction and company profitability?
- When Renee was competing for the CIO role at NASA, she told her future boss she wasn't technical, but if he wanted someone who could "build a strong team, have them deliver results together and play well together, then I'm happy to compete for the job." He replied, "Renee, this job's not technical. It's all about people." Why would NASA want a people-first leader in such a highly technical role? As a leader, how do you gain the trust and respect of extraordinary talent who may be smarter than you?

Conversely, how do you lose their trust and respect?

- Pick two women and discuss how luck, tragedy, opportunity, circumstances, and environments shaped their lives, careers, and perspectives on leadership and life.
- Reflecting on the women's career trajectories, what do you think made them different? What do you believe was their secret to success? Which skills and traits contributed to their rise? What surprised you the most? What will you do differently after reading their stories?

Building Better Environments

- How did the tiered structure of Lorraine's new post-Apartheid school impose limitations on the future she dreamt of for herself? In what ways did her mother's life lessons, her principal's belief in her, and her own desire to "figure it out" change that imposed career trajectory?
- As a child in Nigeria, Morẹ́nikẹ́ was taught western art, causing her to choose the sciences path instead of the art path. Discuss the challenges and emotions you would undergo as a child being taught art history, or any subject, where the content and people were all foreign and had no context to your life. Did the textbooks in your school or your children's school fairly represent your community or all people?
- The disconnect between Meg's passions and her environment at home created deep unhappiness to the point where she left home and school, "You can't deny who you are." Discuss parallels with being your authentic self at work.
- At first, "being one of the guys" at work made Meg feel special. But over time, she felt dehumanized and devalued. In what explicit and subtle ways do bro cultures inhibit women's career advancement?
- As noted above, 70% of men in the top 1% of earners have a stay-at-home spouse. But disturbingly, studies also show that men with stay-at-home wives view women in the workforce unfavorably and are more likely to make decisions that prevent their advancement. Discuss the negative consequences of this bias on women and organizations. What can organizations do to identify and prevent this behavior? What role can male allies play in changing this paradigm, and how can we enlist them to take action?
- After Frani was taken hostage at GameStop, her manager was more concerned about damage to his store than harm to Frani or

his customers. Why do people focus on the broken window, not the person in our workplaces? How do callous cultures negatively impact an organization's profitability and future potential?

- What are the economic costs of toxic people and hostile environments on women, organizations, and society?
- Why did Frani wait to tell her new boss she was pregnant until after she was hired? What would you do in her shoes; what would you do in her boss's shoes?
- When Leah was ill, Frani's career was deprioritized. Once Leah passed away, Frani threw herself back into her work and her career. But her relationship with her manager and with the organization had changed. She questioned, "Is there really a place for me here?" How does the motherhood effect impact women?
- We often hear that women lack confidence and suffer from imposter syndrome. Give examples of how women's internal negative self-talk is influenced by external factors in our homes, schools, societies, and workplaces.
- People can be confident in their abilities to do the job but doubt their success due to external factors, such as bias and favoritism. Why is labeling this doubt imposter syndrome harmful?
- You stand out as an "only" on a Naval ship or in business. Discuss how this extra scrutiny and the weight of carrying your gender and/or your entire race on your back might affect your confidence, risk-taking, and communications.
- Morẹ́nikẹ́ experienced multiple layers of suffering when her white employees left her pharmacy. Why does she say the second layer of not knowing if it was racism was almost worse than if they just said it to her face? What does being a good ally and advocate mean to you?
- If you could wave a magic wand to make the biggest blockers to your career or happiness disappear, what would those be?

The last question I asked in my interviews was, "What question would you want to ask other women in the book?" Below are their responses.

- My mantra is always, "If not me, then who?" It reminds me of my training and how that hard work built grit and empathy. What do other women say to themselves as their mantra or soul song when tackling tough problems?
- How do you see your purpose with different clarity with each year passing? I think of it as refocusing a camera lens. How are

you responding today to that "refocus"?

- When did you realize what you were doing was really important and impacted bigger issues you were fighting for?
- What do you think is the most significant barrier to female leadership?
- It is so important to create an environment where everyone has access to those in power and is given a chance. How can all of us, women and allies, intentionally be part of that change? How will you seek to understand and manage your biases to create a constructive team environment, whether at work, school, community, or home?
- I suffer from imposter syndrome. I don't know if I'll ever get rid of that feeling. How do you know that you're doing a good job? At what point do you know you're doing well and feel totally confident in your decisions? How do you know you've made it?
- How do other women decide to return to the workplace after having kids or figure out a work-life balance? I'm trying to figure it out now, but I'm determined to make it work.
- We often talk about female issues (I don't downplay these) and male issues. But I think we have fundamental human issues regarding how well and unwell we treat each other with little or no empathy. What is your perspective on this?
- If you are in a position of power – a manager, coach, politician, or whatever that may be – what are two-three practical actions you will take to build a diverse community around yourself that includes men and women of different races, ethnicities, and abilities?
- What are ways women can build strong communities and become more supportive of each other at home and in the workplace so that all of us will thrive in whatever we do?
- What do you think is your personal superpower, and how can you use that in very practical terms to advance and encourage women to join and stay in STEM fields?
- When did you know it was enough; that you were satisfied? Did you get to a point and say, "Yes, this is it?"

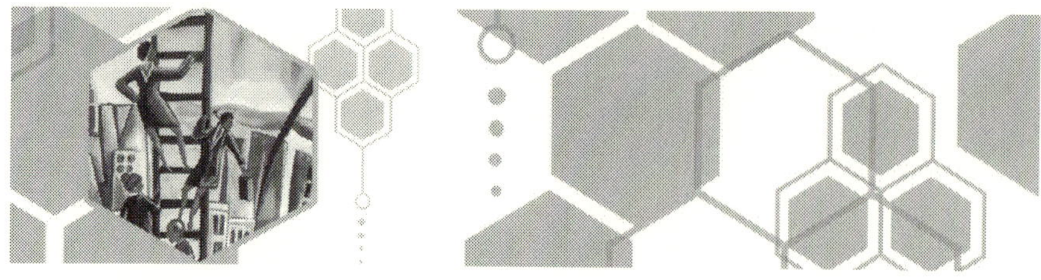

What's their Secret?

A champion is defined not by their wins but by how many times they recover when they fail. – Serena Williams

I hope you enjoyed hearing these stories and picked up a bunch of tips you're putting into practice in your life.

I know I did!

Janet's mantra to "Never Give Up" and Melynda's, "If not me, then who?" play in my head now too. I love how Renee turned mentors into advocates and used her one-liner to prime the promotion pump, "What do I need to do to be competitive for this position?" I've used Melanie's job decision matrix to negotiate a career decision and taken her husband's advice to notice which choice increased my energy and which didn't.

Lorraine's metaphor of time passing by like scenery through a car window reminds me there's life on the other side of fear and pain. Morẹ́nikẹ́'s story about the dual suffering of racialized people helps me see the hidden trauma so many Back women experience in the workplace. Caroline's unthinkable tragedy shifted her focus from projects to people proving that empathetic leadership not only feels good, it's also more productive and profitable.

So many nuggets of gold. Their mini-lessons guide my path forward.

Even so, I still haven't answered the questions I posed in the introduction, "What was their secret?" and "Why were they different?"

There were two things I noticed as I analyzed their stories. Initially, I was less than thrilled with my findings. To be honest, I was pissed! The first finding was about their home life. That's a taboo topic, right. Why do we ask women about their home life and we don't ask men about theirs? And the other, resilience, sounds cliché. Besides, telling someone, "You need to be more resilient," can be misused to dismiss that person's suffering.

I wasn't happy.

But the more I sat with the findings and the more research I did, the more

I realized these two findings provided significant potential for dialogue and lasting change!

Home Life

The first secret is that the women figured out how to solve a math problem.

1 + 1 = 3

Nope, that's not a typo. Unfortunately, that's the life of a couple today. Seventy years ago, the equation was 1 + 1 = 2. But now, it totals three.

In 1950s America, the marriage rate for women was ninety percent. In those marriages, the dominant cultural norm was for the husband to enter the paid labor market and for the wife to take care of the home and family. The same was true for many cultures around the globe. In 1940, only fourteen percent of married US women were in the labor force.

One spouse was in the unpaid workforce and the other in the paid workforce. Two people, two jobs.

And because the paid labor force was generally made up of men, the rules of work were defined by and for men with the idea that the man would go home to a perfectly quaffed house where his wife had taken care of all his non-work and family needs (only 4% of households were single men). Of course, there were always exceptions, but this was the norm. Our work, education, and home institutions were based on those norms.

Things started to change in the 1960s. For example, the first birth control pill was introduced, as were home technologies like microwaves and self-cleaning ovens. Betty Friedan's book, The Feminine Mystique, ushered in the second wave of feminism. Congress passed the Equal Pay Act and the Civil Rights Act. And women went to work in droves. According to a special report on the 1970's census, women accounted for two-thirds of the increase in total employment in the 1960s.

While women were on the move entering college and the workforce, stereotypes and institutional norms were slow to catch up, as were their husbands. (I am intentionally speaking about heterosexual couples here.)

So, now we have two people in the paid labor force, and we still have one full-time job taking care of the house.

Two people now equal three jobs. 1 + 1 = 3

What does this have to do with the women in the book? Like same-sex couples, they figured out how to make the math work. Of the married women in the book, forty percent had stay-at-home spouses, and another twenty percent were the primary breadwinner in the relationship. Seventy percent of men in the top one percent of earners today have a stay-at-home spouse. In the book, sixty percent of the women had swapped traditional gender roles at home, allowing them to focus on their careers like those male executives with stay-at-home wives. Meanwhile, the women with dual-career families figured out how to effectively and fairly divvy up or outsource the household management and equitably share in any caregiving responsibilities.

Together, as a couple, they solved for the third job.

In the US, working moms are more than twice as likely as working dads to do housework on the same days they do their paid jobs. Working moms spend significantly more time doing housework and caregiving than their male partners. For single moms, add an additional 10% of time spent. By bearing the bulk of this "second shift" work, women free up time for their male partners to focus on other things like career and leisure time. This disproportionate distribution of who does the dishes and the diapers impedes a wife's career advancement opportunities and economic power.

So, when life gets hard around mid-career, especially when child or elder care is involved, the decision to step back from a career often lands on the woman. Why? Because she earns less, works more (at work and home), and can't see a path forward in her career. Frustration and sheer economics make the choice simple. The wife steps out. Of course, single moms aren't afforded this choice, nor are lower-income wage families.

The way forward toward a more equitable home life is fourfold.

- Crucial conversations with partners.
- Breaking down stereotype backlash against women at work and men at home. Celebrating being a good husband and father.
- Benefits and initiatives that support balanced lives for all.
- Raising the next generation to see and treat women as equal partners at work and home.

Resilience

The second pattern I observed is that these women were extraordinarily resilient and adaptable. They've been through some shit and came out stronger. Although, to be honest, I was kind of angry when I did the analysis and research. I mean, who wants to be told suffering is good for you!

So let me explain what I mean by resilience and why it really was crucial to their success.

We all will face tragedy and difficulty in our lives. Resilience is adapting well in the face of adverse events or circumstances. It's making an active decision to view misfortune as an opportunity to learn, grow, and move toward a better place. It's bouncing back and not succumbing to negative thoughts and effects. It's focusing on what comes after, not what was lost.

It's preparedness, sustained well-being, and the courage to stand up and belong. It's a continuum in differing degrees across various aspects of your life. It's hope for the future and a belief that, yes, you can figure it out.

Yet, resilience seemed so broad and ambiguous to me. You can't prepare to be resilient, can you?

I needed to dig deeper. So, I spent months analyzing the stories and researching resilience. And here's what I discovered.

The women carried curiosity, intentionality, hard work ethic, and a sense of belonging in their resilience toolbox. They cultivated these four characteristics throughout their lives, beginning in childhood. Each in their own measure in their own way. And when faced with a decision, a period of difficulty, or a tragedy, they had tools they could use to get them through to the other side.

So, let's explore these four pillars of resiliency.

Curiosity

Curiosity is the desire to acquire knowledge or skill. It's your motivation to learn. It's that "what is it?" reflex when you see something new. That craving to go check it out. Curiosity is that intellectual itch you gotta scratch that often leads to your purpose. It's the insatiable desire for knowledge and wisdom. It's intellectual humility. It's playfulness, purpose, and problem-solving.

It's why TikTok exists.

Melanie advises us on how curiosity builds resilience, "Life throws you curveballs and surprises. Things don't necessarily work out the way you plan them. Be open-minded about that. Be curious; lean into it."

Frani credits playing video games for her problem-solving skills, "I think that persistence, 'I'm going to solve this,' definitely played into my personality in general. I'm one of those people who stick with stuff for hours until I figure it out; I actually prefer it."

Despite getting into trouble with her mother, Lorraine was an insatiably curious little girl, "I continued to break things up, electronic stuff more than anything else, even though I would get into trouble. I didn't know it at the time, but this curiosity about breaking things and electronics would later serve me well."

Facing the heartbreaking reality of health inequity in Africa, Mọ̀rẹ́nikẹ́ used curiosity to turn the unacceptable into purpose, "I was very curious about that. Why is that an acceptable situation in Africa, and why is that the case? Her healthtech startup was born from leaning into that curiosity.

As children, Melynda and Meghan whet their curiosity appetite through books. And through books, found their purpose. Meg recalls, "Books were a huge part of our lives. I read a lot of science fiction. My initial interest in STEM spawned from the Madeleine L'Engle series, the Time Quintet – A Swiftly Tilting Planet, A Wrinkle in Time, and stuff." Before age ten, Melynda read Ben Carson's Think Big and Gifted Hands. "In a sense, Dr. Carson became my roadmap. He overcame challenges in school and being from a lower socioeconomic status to become a neurosurgeon at Johns Hopkins. I didn't have difficulties in school, but I found inspiration in his ability to achieve his dreams when others told him his dreams were impossible."

Meg created an interactive software company rooted in curiosity expressed through play, purpose, and problem-solving. "We wanted our job to feel like we were hanging out with our friends every day and solving problems together, enjoying our time together, and feeling a sense of accomplishment from doing things together."

Curiosity is a mix of playfulness, purpose, and problem-solving.

Playfulness kicks in after curiosity begs, "hey, check it out." It's that shift from exploration to play. It's finding fun, humor, and amusement in situations. It's not taking ourselves, or others, too seriously. Playfulness is spontaneous, energetic, adventurous, cheerful, silly, sociable. It's finding amusement in the mundane. It's the internal engine that keeps us motivated. It's nature's way of ensuring we acquire the skills to survive.

It's happiness and well-being.

Purpose gives meaning to life. It's the beacon of hope that propels you forward, even in your darkest moments. It's when your passions, values, and what's important to you align with your pursuits. It's individualistic yet collective. Altruistic yet personal. It's the spring in your step and why you get out of bed in the morning. It's fulfillment, motivation, bliss. It's your reason for being. It's Ikigai.

It's crafting a life well-lived.

Problem-solving is discovering, analyzing, and finding solutions to challenges and conundrums. It's overcoming hurdles and outsized obstacles. It's dealing with the glitches, hitches, and snags you encounter on the way to your goals. It's your search for answers. It's dealing with the things you'd rather ignore so that you can make progress on that other thing that's so important to you. It's how you cope with what life throws at you.

It's figuring it out.

Yes, you can improve your curiosity. Good news, you've already taken a step by listening to these women's stories!

- Set aside dedicated time for wandering and exploration, whether physically or mentally. Pay attention to what you see, hear, smell, taste, and feel. Read different genres, cultures, and people.

- Step out of your comfort zone. Learn a new skill, try new foods, visit new places, regularly apply for a new job, and read about topics that challenge your assumptions.
- Keep a curiosity journal or sketchbook to document your thoughts, observations, and ideas.
- Talk to people with different backgrounds and perspectives to learn about their experiences and gain new perspectives. Go to diverse networking events. Follow a variety of people on social media.
- Be open-minded. Embrace ambiguity and be willing to be surprised. Don't be afraid to make mistakes or take risks.

Intentionality

Intentionality is consciously living life purposefully versus allowing things to just happen to you. It's taking control.

It's defining your values, beliefs, and desires. Setting goals and then making them happen. It's a mental process that places value on one thing over another, like truth, justice, beauty, and purpose. It's how you understand yourself and others. It's how you decide and prioritize. It's reflection, ownership, and courage.

It's acting on what matters.

Renee posits that "All careers are intentional" and counsels women to have the courage to own their careers. "Invite your boss and others into a board of career advisors. People you talk to, trust, and can ask, "What do I need to do to be better?" It's not only what someone can do for you. It's also being intentional about what you are striving for."

Being a child actress taught Melanie "how to express myself, take on different roles and characters, and reflect on who I am and how I can become a certain role." She used this skill of intentional self-reflection throughout her life and career.

Andi's child-centered Montessori education taught her to be self-motivated and intentional about her time. These skills helped her to become the CFO of a billion-dollar company at twenty-six. She advises women to "own your role and own your value. To advocate for what you're good at, be transparent about what you're not, and trust that you'll figure it out." Owning it also means getting "comfortable with taking risks and being open to failing."

Lorraine credits her mother for teaching her to dream big, be fearless, and never lean on anyone else. Her mother knew Lorraine would need those skills because just showing up to elementary school in South Africa during Apartheid was an act of courage. To realize her dreams of becoming an engineer and independent woman, Lorraine faced down institutionalized racial segregation, cultural norms within her community, and corruption. Still, she rose to become the CIO of SABC, the BBC equivalent in South Africa. Now she works for Gartner, using the skills her mother taught her and her IT experience to coach other CIOs on how to succeed in their roles and initiatives.

Wanting to have a good life and a successful career should not be an act of courage. Yet for too many women, just getting out of bed knowing what the day might bring becomes an act of bravery – from white staff walking out on you to needing armed guards to go to a meeting or to shouldering the daily burden of being a visible "only." Even the most privileged among us don't escape misogynistic tendencies in the workplace, like being overlooked for a well-earned promotion, treated like a workhorse carrying a load someone else will take credit for, or being asked to get coffee, call a cab, or take notes from a male peer or subordinate – even when you wear that C-Suite title!

We must recognize this reality and work together with each other and our allies to create a better reality. Every day. Every interaction. Full stop.

Intentionality takes reflection, ownership, and courage.

Reflection is honestly evaluating your past so that you can adapt and go forward with greater understanding and purpose. It's reframing challenges as opportunities and failures as learning. It's insight and personal growth gained through overcoming traumatic experiences. It's seeking wisdom and questioning your beliefs. It's being fully present, open to new ideas, and pivoting as circumstances change or information comes to light. It's thinking on your feet.

It's "know thyself."

Ownership of self is being clear about what you want and what's important to you. It's investing your attention, time, and effort on what matters, including self-care. It's walking the talk. Ownership of self is taking responsibility for your thoughts, actions, successes, and mistakes. It's the wisdom to know what you can control and letting go of what you cannot. It's seeing the good and the bad as transient steps on your journey of growth and well-being. It's choosing optimism, forgiveness, and gratitude. It's owning who you are, who you want to be, and the discipline to become it.

It's showing up. Authentically.

Courage is the strength to persevere in the face of pain, grief, or fear. It's the thoughtful, purpose-driven middle-ground between cowardice and recklessness. It's rising to the occasion. It's taking calculated action in the face of fear for a worthy cause or purpose. It's remaining faithful to yourself and your values while choosing to act or standing firm despite the personal risks. It's grace under pressure.

Courage is intentional.

Take these steps to become more intentional day by day.

- **Set SMART goals** (Specific, Measurable, Achievable, Relevant, and Time-Bound) for yourself and make a plan to achieve them. Take ownership of your actions, decisions, and outcomes.
- **Practice visualization** by picturing yourself achieving your goals and living the life you want.
- **Take time for reflection** regularly. Reflect on your actions, decisions, and progress toward your goals. Adjust accordingly.
- **Practice failure**, be brave in some small thing every day, and take strategic risks.
- **Surround yourself with people who encourage you** to grow, hold you accountable, and will be there to lift you up when you need it.

Hard Work Ethic

Hard Work Ethic is the idea that effort is intrinsically virtuous and rewarding. It's building the self-confidence to put aside doubt, push yourself to new limits, and make the tough sacrifices needed to focus on reaching your goals.

It's the grit and grind to go above and beyond to reach your objectives even when the work stops being exciting or fun. It's staring up at space, taking a deep breath, and pushing yourself toward the stars.

It's never giving up.

Hard work ethic marries focus, grit, and self-confidence with sweat equity.

Looking back on the extraordinary demands of medical residency, Melynda says that the "grueling nature of the training was on purpose because it needed to be difficult to build resiliency." She shows how "training and hard work built grit and empathy" and explains that it is "difficult, but it has a purpose. To build grit. You need that in order to mature."

From elementary school, Melynda focused on becoming a doctor. Caroline on animal health. Morẹ́nikẹ́ on solving for HIV Aids. Frani on becoming an animator. Their career aspirations shifted along their journeys, but they adjusted their focus with each shift. And they let go of activities and principles that no longer served their new direction. When Frani was vacillating between video production and her lifelong dream of becoming an animator, a colleague pulled her aside and cautioned, "You need to decide soon whether you want to go to art or focus on production because they're very different skills. And if you don't focus on one or the other, you won't get really good at either one."

Meghan sums it up this way, "Embracing what you're passionate about now will lead you to what you're going to be passionate about in the future. For example, the thing that I was really passionate about as a kid was drawing and making stuff, and that led to learning how to use computers and create technology that other people can use." This philosophy carried over to her management style, where her team is intentionally allowed to focus on their passion projects, leading to product innovations.

Grit got Janet through a rigorous, condensed college schedule. "Over my desk, I put in big block letters, underlined with exclamation marks, the Winston Churchill quote, "NEVER GIVE UP!!" And I had a picture of an astronaut floating in space underneath those words. I knew that if I gave up and was tempted to go to sleep at two in the morning, I would fail that physics class, and everything would go down the drain. I just could not quit."

To become a combat-ready leader, the Navy taught Juliana grit – from demanding physical training to practicing engine failure to exposure to tear gas. And Mọ̀rẹ́níkẹ́ noted, "If I decide I'm going to do something, I will die on that hill doing that thing." Grit.

When Morenike was going through one of the most intense years of her life, she took strength and confidence from her childhood, "where nothing, just nothing, seemed impossible. Nothing felt like it was too much to ask. Nothing seemed like you couldn't figure it out."

Andi echoes that sentiment, "confidence comes down to believing you can learn anything. And once you acknowledge that, you realize you can do anything." She never compares herself to others, "I don't want to have the exact pedigree of someone else, as impressive as they may be. If I did, I wouldn't be me." Those aren't just empty words; she proved it by taking risk after risk early in her career, "I now know that it'll be okay if I don't fit the mold. If I think I can do it, then I'll be able to do it." And she wants you to know, "if you know you can do it, you'll be able to do it too. You have to believe in yourself."

The building blocks of hard work are focus, grit, and self-confidence.

Focus is the act of adjusting your vision towards a central point with increasing clarity, concentration of effort, and direction. It's establishing discipline, setting boundaries, removing distractions, and making tough sacrifices to reach your goals. It's saying, "no," or as Renee puts it, "yes and...." It's chunking your long-term goals into today's action items and not letting anyone tell you, "You can't," not even your inner critic. It's the wisdom to know what to prioritize and when.

And the explicit act of letting go.

Grit marries effort and passion and wraps them in an armor of perseverance as they journey toward long-term mutual goals. It's that scrappy "can do" spirit that doesn't know impossible. It's getting knocked down, gritting your teeth, and willing yourself to stand up one more time, again and again. It's the discipline to push through the daily grind, despite pain or monotony. It's mission-driven. Making your own luck.

It's being unstoppable.

Self-Confidence is simply the belief in oneself. It's trusting in your skills, knowledge, and judgment. It's feeling good about yourself and your capability to do something, despite imperfections. It's tuning out the doubters, quieting your inner critic, never underestimating yourself, and igniting the spark to act. It's measuring progress against yourself, not others. It's finding strength, motivation, and happiness from within.

It's believing, "Yes, I can."

Strengthen your hard work muscles with the following exercises.

- Create **Atomic Habits** to nudge you toward your objectives.
- Use mindfulness to focus on the present moment and fully engage in your actions.
- Accept conflict as a normal part of life. Reframe minor annoyances and negative thoughts.
- Find your mantra to stay positive and push through when you feel like quitting.
- Accept personal flaws and mistakes as opportunities to learn.
- Practice self-compassion and self-care. Schedule time to rest, recharge, and celebrate small wins.
- Keep a victory journal. Track your achievements. Include numbers whenever possible. Use it for career conversations, resume updates, and to keep your confidence high.
- Have a bias for action.

Belonging.

Belonging is feeling accepted and valued for who you are when your pretenses are down. It's a culture of shared purpose and practice. It's believing that others see you, want you to succeed, and have your back. It's social inclusion, mutual trust, and "no-questions-asked" support. It's feeling like an insider. It's relationships, culture, and in-group confidence.

It's having a best friend at work.

Being Nigerian and Canadian, Christian and Muslim, Introvert and Extrovert, Morenike jokes about being interstitial, not quite being one thing. "I think I have a home everywhere that I identify with. It's more in the feeling of belonging that's home for me."

As a Tuskegee University student, Daphne practiced the art of belonging by tutoring other female students in STEM. "I realized I wanted to help them stay and knew they needed somebody else. It's good to see somebody who looks like you or somebody you can relate to. 'Oh, she did it. She looks like me.' or 'She's in this field with all the guys and holding her own. I wanted to help make them comfortable and make sure they had what they needed to stay."

Lockheed's proactive culture of caring and Daphne's managers mirrored her kindness, especially when her brother was murdered. "Having a good support system within my company was one of the reasons I really fell in love with them. They made sure I had what I needed. And it was their thoughtfulness too." When Daphne became a manager, she saw there were business benefits of belonging, too, "what you get when you have so much diversity and people who can bring in so many new perspectives is that it can help change the culture, make the product more innovative, or help come up with better ways to do things more efficiently and effectively."

After her partner's suicide, Caroline shifted from focusing on projects to developing relationships. Then the projects got better too! "Listening and being heard is important to building trust. For people to have a voice and to be able to share their concerns is of huge value. Carving out the time to listen and pay attention goes a long way. People become engaged. They raise issues and find solutions. I know that now."

Gallup's employee engagement survey backs up their sentiments. For example, it has repeatedly been shown that having best friends at work is critical to employee engagement and job success. In addition, Gartner says that all employees want to feel that they belong in the workplace and that being seen as a person, not just an employee is important to eighty-two percent of employees.

Organizations with a culture of belonging also acquire and keep the best talent.

Melynda chose Mount Sinai for medical school because they not only talked about diversity, they were "actually doing many wonderful things in their very diverse community. Medical school is hard enough. I'd never done anything like it before, and I didn't know anyone who'd gone to medical school. So, a program that was really looking to support people like me was the best place for me."

Not wanting to be a "lonely only" kept Renee from studying engineering. But, on the other hand, seeing role models and feeling part of a "strong community of women was one part of why I stayed in the federal government for my glorious thirty years."

When you feel like others have your back, it gives you wings. Andi points out that "believing that others believe in you and support you enables you to take risks. "Because people thought I could do X, Y, or Z, it paved the way for me to believe it too." But she cautions that "Unfortunately, as a woman, there will be times when people will not believe in you. But guess what? They are not the only people in this world with a voice or an opinion. So find a way to believe in yourself more than you believe the people around you."

That's good advice because we don't always enter a school or workplace that greets us with open arms.

For a young Lorraine, the end of Apartheid tested her confidence as she struggled to fit in at her new school. "I sometimes mispronounced things, and the other kids in the class thought, "Do you even speak English?" You know how kids can be. So, I worked extremely hard. How do the other kids behave? What do they do so that I can fit in as quickly as I can? But I was not thriving at all. I was struggling in all elements." Luckily, the belief in herself, so well cultivated by her mother, gave Lorraine the courage to stand up and claim a different future than others had laid out for her.

Later when she rocked up to construction sites as the big boss, she learned the potency of power to shift relationship dynamics. Even staunch pro-Apartheid men now had to take her authority seriously. "To attend that meeting. I drove with an armed officer in my white BMW; another officer followed us. When we entered the room, I was exposed to a certain way that people would treat me based on my rank, not on my being a woman or the color of my skin. The dynamics had radically changed in this situation. I learned that the one who controlled the money got the respect."

On her amphibious assault ship, Juliana had guys telling her she didn't belong. "Their words were spoken and unspoken but very, very clear. Of course, not everybody said this; But there were some assholes using really bad language. Telling me I didn't belong in their Navy. I didn't belong on their ship."

Unlike the other three pillars, much of the work of belonging in STEM is out of our control, particularly for non-white women. I won't sugarcoat that. Nor will I pretend that working on ourselves will solve bias and discrimination in the spaces we find ourselves.

It's not about fixing women. We are not broken.

But it is about building our collective bench strength. And acquiring tools to step into our power, whether that's owning the space where we work today or creating new, better spaces elsewhere.

It's about becoming the heroines in our own stories.

Take Future Club, for example, Frani's co-op game development studio, which makes games for people who feel "there isn't a place for them in the gaming industry because it's always been so white male-dominated." As the CEO, she also created a healthy, positive culture within her new organization in direct response to the abusive behavior at her previous company.

In Morenike's pharmacies, her foundation, and her HealthTech startup, she intentionally adopted a "Teal Organization, where organizations evolve towards self-management, wholeness, and a deeper sense of purpose."

Before returning from maternity leave, Melanie spoke to her CEO about creating a program for people returning to the office from leave. Her CEO responded by giving her the team and the authority to change things. "You can run the People Operations team." After she helped that company through its acquisition, she found her way to another startup, "a media company focused on empowering women and uplifting the voices of marginalized communities through content and experiences."

After a Yale Hospital board meeting, Melynda was excited about the difference she was making and thought, "how can I do this on a larger scale? How can I improve how healthcare is delivered and optimize that experience for more than just the Yale community." That thinking led her to Ro, where she's helping "build a new way of delivering affordable healthcare that meets our patients where they are."

These women lift as they rise!

They intentionally create relationships, processes, and organizations that engender a sense of belonging, purpose, teamwork, and mutual success. As a result, they are changing the game.

Belonging is the result of your relationships, culture, and in-group confidence.

Relationships are the connections between people. They're the dynamic processes of give-and-take, compromise, and negotiation that enable us to coexist in a complex and ever-changing world. They're the social fabric of our lives and how we shape our sense of self and our behavior. They're the building blocks of community and belonging. Relationships are the social capital we invest in others that yields reward but carries risk and uncertainty. It's our intimate partners, close friends, acquaintances, and the people we know.

It's our relationship with self and others.

Culture is the shared beliefs, values, customs, and behaviors that shape how a group lives. It's the lens through which we view the world, ourselves, and our experiences. It's our shared history, traditions, and practices. It's the glue that binds us together. Culture is how we communicate ideas, establish social hierarchies, and hold onto power.

It's the vehicle through which social change and progress can be made.

In-Group Confidence is the self-assurance you experience when you're recognized and accepted as a group or community member. It's being treated with dignity and empathy by others in the group. It's a sense of security, safety, and belonging in a social setting. In-group confidence is a state of mind that can be cultivated through positive social interactions. It promotes teamwork, mental health, and well-being. In addition, it leads to greater success and achievement for the individual and the group.

It's an antidote to imposter syndrome and self-doubt.

Belonging is a shared social endeavor, so some things are out of our control. That said, we are not powerless. There are things we can do to cultivate belonging at work and in life while also standing up for ourselves and others.

- **Connect with others.** Build healthy relationships with friends, family, and colleagues. Seek mentors and allies to join your personal board of advisors. Find people who will advocate for you when you are not in the room. Be an advocate and ally for others. Network regularly with industry peers and other women in STEM. Find opportunities for 1:1 time in-person or virtually.
- **Build community.** Participate in shared activities, company events, and team-building exercises. Create an inclusive and welcoming environment. Recognize and appreciate the contributions of your colleagues. For example, send a personal note thanking a colleague for their contribution. Be thoughtful and specific, and cc their boss.
- **Speak up.** Seek advice from your personal board of advisors about how and when to communicate your needs and experiences to your manager or Human Resources. This includes negotiating increases, flexibility, and promotions, asking for high visibility work, or if you are experiencing bias, harassment, or discrimination.
- **Don't normalize offensive behavior**. Learn how to call out bias as unhelpful to a productive work environment and how to be a supportive ally (not a white knight).
- **Be prepared.** It's always good to keep your resume up-to-date, and your interview skills sharp by regularly applying for new positions. Be ready for new opportunities or to leave people and places that don't value you.
- **Prioritize self-care.** Take mental and physical breaks when needed, do stuff you enjoy, and prioritize time for yourself. Don't

hesitate to seek professional help.

Final thoughts

Through these stories, I hope you've realized that success is rarely a straight path and comes in many forms. And that whatever your background, education, or experience, you can find a place in STEM where you can be valued and belong.

I won't minimize the burden of being undervalued at work, overwhelmed at home, or dealing with egregious bias. Unfortunately, working in male-dominated fields may take its toll, especially around mid-career or where racism and bias reign.

That said, there are things we all can do to build our resilience and fortify our souls. We don't have to stay stuck and unhappy. We don't have to quit our careers. Instead, these remarkable women showed us the way. We can build our resiliency toolbox using curiosity, intentionality, hard work, and belonging.

We, too, can break through and flourish.

For inspirational quotes and resources to help you build your resiliency toolbox visit www.stayinstem.com.

www.stayinSTEM.com

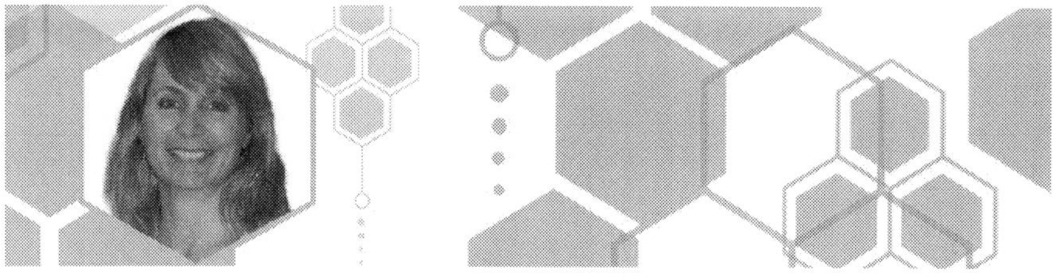

About the Author

Lori Rodriguez is a mother of five with over twenty-five years in the tech industry.

She is the Chief Digital Advisor and US Chapter President for the global non-profit Women in Tech. Ms. Rodriguez writes and speaks regularly on women in STEM, leadership, and digital transformation. She's appeared on Economist Innovation@work, Gartner Evanta, Accenture, and HubBerlin.

In her prior role as VP, Strategy, Innovation, and Operations at Gartner Inc., Ms. Rodriguez built products and services that helped C-Suite Technology Leaders grow in their role, achieve breakthrough results for their organizations, and use technology to move the world forward. She has personally interviewed over a thousand CIOs and Senior-most technology leaders.

An experiential learner, Ms. Rodriguez dropped out of college and bought twenty acres in Vermont to live off grid. When reality set in, she became a graphic designer during the dawn of the desktop publishing revolution. Rapidly promoted, Ms. Rodriguez was soon the head of IT and digital production for the number three marketing promotions agency.

Hooked on the power of technology, she pivoted her career toward digitally transforming every industry, networked her way into Gartner, and stayed there for nearly twenty years before shifting her career again to focus on increasing the number of women in STEM and ensuring a more equitable future for all.

Made in the USA
Las Vegas, NV
03 March 2023